The Inner Word
and the
Outer World

Renaissance and Baroque Studies and Texts

Eckhard Bernstein
General Editor
Vol. 7

PETER LANG
New York • Washington, D.C./Baltimore • San Francisco
Bern • Frankfurt am Main • Berlin • Vienna • Paris

Patrick Hayden-Roy

The Inner Word
and the
Outer World

A Biography of Sebastian Franck

PETER LANG
New York • Washington, D.C./Baltimore • San Francisco
Bern • Frankfurt am Main • Berlin • Vienna • Paris

Library of Congress Cataloging-in-Publication Data

Hayden-Roy, Patrick Marshall.
    The inner word and the outer world: a biography of Sebastian Franck /
Patrick Hayden-Roy.
       p.   cm. — (Renaissance and Baroque: studies and texts; vol. 7)
    Includes bibliographical references and index.
     1. Franck, Sebastian, 1499–1542. 2. Reformation—Germany—
Biography. I. Title. II. Series.
BR360.F73H39   1994   230′.092—dc20   [B]   93-382
ISBN 0-8204-2083-2   CIP
ISSN 0897-7836

Die Deutsche Bibliothek-CIP-Einheitsaufnahme

Hayden-Roy, Patrick:
The inner word and the outer world: a biography of Sebastian Franck /
Patrick Hayden-Roy. - New York; Bern; Berlin; Frankfurt/M.; Paris; Wien:
Lang, 1994
   (Renaissance and baroque: Studies and texts; Vol. 7)
   ISBN 0-8204-2083-2
NE: GT

Cover design by James F. Brisson.

The paper in this book meets the guidelines for permanence and durability of
the Committee on Production Guidelines for Book Longevity of the
Council on Library Resources.

TABLE OF CONTENTS

INTRODUCTION

The memory of Sebastian Franck has turned about in the course of time. Reviled even before his death, he was condemned afterwards as a dangerous heretic by the magisterial reformers. What recognition he did find was either muted or forced into silence by the disapproval of the authorities. Gradually he became an obscure figure, remembered mostly only in the histories of heresy written by orthodox theologians. In the nineteenth century, though, he received a full pardon, in fact was elevated to the status of saint, the first promoter of modern values in an age marked by dogma and intolerance. While the modern literature on Franck has in general extolled his exemplary character, it has not considered him from a single vantage point. There is the Franck of the philosophers, of the mystics, of the folklorists, and the like. In writing on Franck one must come to terms with this shifting memory and perspective.

The perspective of this study will involve viewing Franck over the course of his life, and with close attention to the environment within which he lived. While writings on Franck are abundant, they have frequently had only a marginal relationship to the larger historiographical world. Often Franck has been portrayed as not really participating in the sixteenth-century world, as a man out of time who anticipated the shape of the modern world. This study will portray Franck as very much a part of the world of the early Reformation in Germany, a person whose life reveals better than most the new intellectual possibilities of this age, and the shifting relationship between structures of power and religion.

In and of itself Franck's life is representative of the experiences of a few lonely figures who wandered the cities of southern Germany, finding only temporary haven, people such as Caspar Schwenckfeld, Hans Denck, Hans Bünderlin, Michel Servetus, and others. Even among this group Franck was an anomalous figure. He started no movement, nor had he any following during his life, which was as he wished. Though he had his encounters with the authorities he suffered relatively minor punishment for his unorthodox ideas and writings. He was no martyr, nor did he desire to be. In fact during most of his life as a lone prophet of the inner Word of God he was able to find a provisional place for himself in the cities of the southern Holy Roman Empire. Though he eventually was viewed as an unwelcome guest in Straßburg and Ulm, these tangles with the structures of power reveal the parameters of tolerance and control which existed in these cities.

Franck's biography is not *terra incognita*. Though much written about him has been published in out of the way places, there is still a wealth of material to draw from in investigating his life. There are three main arguments for the existence of this study. First, I would argue, there are no full length biographies of Franck which are not either antiquated or marred by serious flaws[1]. Second, the interpretive focus of this study will concentrate on how Franck fit into his world, from where he drew his ideas, and what modulated the response to these ideas by his contemporaries, and seek to correct the picture of Franck as a man out of time. Last, the study will add significant research on the context of Franck's life in the city of Ulm, and the struggle over his presence in that city. Taken together these elements set Franck's life into a context not previously drawn, and in turn throw into relief features of the society which surrounded him.

This study began as a dissertation at Stanford University under the direction of Prof. Lewis W. Spitz. I have valued his teaching and aid in my scholarly pursuits. In addition the work benefitted from the critical scrutiny of Profs. Judith Brown and Paul Seaver. Research for this work was facilitated by a year's stipend from the Friedrich Ebert Stiftung, as well as a DAAD summer fellowship. Much of the writing was done with the support of a Charlotte Newcombe fellowship. The preparation of the manuscript for publication was supported by Nebraska Wesleyan University through an E.C. Ames Fellowship. Finally I would like to thank my wife Priscilla, who originally suggested Franck as a subject of study, with whom I have discussed most aspects of it, and who has read and commented on the entirety.

---

[1] There are two main biographies of Franck published in the twentieth century, Will-Erich Peuckert, *Sebastian Franck. Ein deutscher Sucher* (Munich, 1943), and Eberhard Teufel, *"Landräumig": Sebastian Franck, ein Wanderer am Donau, Neckar und Rhein* (Neustadt a.d. Aisch, 1954). Both are marked by interpretive structures which do not adequately relate Franck to the world around him. I will argue in the body of the study that in Peuckert's case his analytical perspective is too idiosyncratic, in Teufel's case it is too narrow.

CHAPTER ONE: FRANCK'S LIFE TO 1531

The early life of Sebastian Franck is only very sparsely documented. In discussions of Franck's life this has often led biographers to speculate freely about his formative experiences. There are a few well-established facts concerning his early life. He was born in the Imperial city of Donauwörth, then known as Werd or Wörd, in the year 1499. Franck wrote in a letter dated May 22, 1539 that he "has now forty years laid on me,"[1] and barring any rounding off by Franck, the year 1499 saw his entrance into the world. The exact date is nowhere recorded. Will-Erich Peuckert proposes January 20th as the likely date, since it is St. Sebastian's Day, it being a common practice to name children after the saint's day on which they were born and baptized.[2] Unfortunately the patron saint of Donauwörth was St. Sebastian, and thus Peuckert's conjecture loses a good deal of its plausibility; it was equally common to name children after the patron saint of a locale. Peuckert and others have also suggested that Franck's parents may have been weavers, judging by Franck's use and knowledge of certain terms particular to weaving.[3] Maria Zelzer, in her history of Donauwörth, goes so far as to pick a certain Sixt Franck, a weaver, as Franck's father.[4] This is pure conjecture, although Franck did come from somewhat impoverished circumstances.

He was brought up in an Imperial city of the Holy Roman Empire, an important fact for understanding the shape of Franck's career. Throughout his life Franck would gravitate toward the Imperial cities of south Germany, the only environment in which he felt at home. Donauwörth itself was a relatively small Imperial city, which saw its high-point in the late fifteenth and sixteenth centuries. Speculation has also centered on whether Franck received his early schooling in Donauwörth, or in nearby Nördlingen. Franck had an uncle in

---

[1] Franck to the "Seckelschreiber zu Bern." Bern Staatsarchiv: Epistolae varii thematis et miscellanea ecclesiastica, B III, 31, pp. 55-58; p. 57. Printed by Franz Weinkauff, "Zwei Briefe Seb. Francks," *Alemannia* 4 (1877), pp. 27-30; p. 29.

[2] Will-Erich Peuckert, *Sebastian Franck*, p. 14.

[3] Peuckert, *Sebastian Franck*, p. 13.

[4] Maria Zelzer, *Geschichte der Stadt Donauwörth von den Anfängen bis 1618, vol 1* (Donauwörth, 1958), p. 154.

Nördlingen who ran a guest house,[5] and since Nördlingen had a Latin school, it is possible Franck would have received his early training there. Peuckert suggests that Franck received his training in Donauwörth from the Abbot Bartholomäus, head of the Benedictine monastery, who was trying to build up the cloister by sponsoring the training of promising young students. It was the Abbot, according to Peuckert, who subsequently sponsored Franck in Ingolstadt, as he did also for the future head of the cloister Nikolaus Hayder.[6] There is no hard evidence to substantiate either scenario.

One way or another, Franck received schooling which prepared him to enroll in the University of Ingolstadt on March 26, 1515, for which he paid the poor students' fee of one *groschen*.[7] Here he studied for almost three years and received his *Baccalaureus* on December 13, 1517.[8] Little is known about Franck's studies in Ingolstadt. According to Franck himself he was educated before the revival of letters in Germany.[9] But this was part of an apology for any mistakes in a translation to Latin, and was twenty-five years after the fact. In fact, Ingolstadt in 1515 could boast as strong a humanist influence as any university in the empire. Jacob Locher had followed Conrad Celtis as the salaried poet of the University, and during Franck's stay Johannes Aventinus was in

---

[5] Franck, in his translation of Philip Beroaldus' *Declamatio ebriosi, scortatoris et aleatoris*, titled *Ein künstlich/ höflich Deklamation* (Nuremberg, Friedrich Peypus, 1531), dedicated the work "seinem liebsten vettern Michael Francken Burgern zu Nördling" (p. A-v). Franck went on to talk about his uncle's work as an innkeeper, exhibiting some knowledge of its problems, which might persuade one that Franck had spent time in this environment, perhaps while living with his uncle and attending the Latin school.

[6] Peuckert, *Sebastian Franck*, p. 15-16.

[7] G. von Pölnitz, ed. *Die Matrikel der Ludwig-Maximilians-Universität Ingolstadt*, vol. I (Munich, 1937), p. 378.

[8] Franz Weinkauff, "Sebastian Franck von Donauwerd," *Alemannia* 7 (1879), pp. 1-66; p. 65.

[9] "Nam Germanus natus et in seculo barbaro a teneris inter amusos educatus fateor me iuvenem ante festa, hoc est ante ortas literas et redivivas postliminio linguas." Alfred Hegler, *Sebastian Francks lateinische Paraphrase der Deutschen Theologie und seine Holländisch erhaltenen Traktate* (Tübingen, 1901), p. 21.

residence as ducal tutor, during which time he formed a short-lived sodality.[10] Urbanus Rhegius, the future reformer, tutored on poetry and rhetoric. In 1515, the first movement toward curriculum revision began at the University, under the leadership of Leonhard Eck, the ducal counselor, although changes in the statutes were not approved until 1518 or 1519.[11] It is plausible Franck's interest in humanism and historical study first stemmed from his time in Ingolstadt, for Franck spoke highly of Aventinus[12] and evinced a strong interest in humanism throughout his life. But Franck's humanist education, like Ingolstadt's reforms, remained incomplete. Later in life Franck would apologize for his lack of erudition, and there was some basis for this besides modesty. As Franz Weinkauff has shown, Franck's knowledge of Greek was limited, his knowledge of Hebrew practically nonexistent.[13] His knowledge of Latin was functional, although he composed very little in it. One could speculate that his short stay at Ingolstadt was not enough to ground him in the humanistic disciplines. In contrast to a figure such as Aventinus, he did not have the money to absorb his education at a leisurely pace. On reception of his *Baccalaureus* Franck left Ingolstadt and in early 1518 he appeared in Heidelberg as a student at the Dominican college.[14]

The Dominican college was incorporated in the University, although students were not automatically a part of both institutions.[15] Franck was en-

---

[10] Gerald Strauss, *Historian in an Age of Crisis; the life and works of Johannes Aventinus, 1477-1534* (Cambridge, Mass., 1963), p. 67.

[11] Arno Seifert, *Statuten- und Verfassungsgeschichte der Universität Ingolstadt (1472-1586)* (Berlin, 1971), pp. 89-93.

[12] Franck states in his *Chronica*, "wie ich dann hoff/ dz vil/ sonderlich Jo. Auentinus/ mein fäl redlich erstatten sol/ das ich auch von hertzen hoff vnd beger." *Chronica Zeitbuch vnnd Geschichtbibell* (Ulm: Hans Varnier d. Ä., 1536) p. aiii.

[13] Franz Weinkauff, *Alemannia* 7, p. 64.

[14] Martin Frecht in letter to Martin Bucer dated October 30, 1533 stated "Quod postea intellexi ex Franco, quem, ut olim Heidelbergae in Jacobitarum collegio notum sodalem mensae duntaxat adhibueram." Strasbourg City Archive, Th. A. 156, #339, fol. 819. Quoted in Horst Weigelt, *Sebastian Franck und die Lutherische Reformation* (Gütersloh, 1971), p. 13, footnote 15.

[15] For a short sketch of the Dominican college see Johann Friedrich Hautz, *Geschichte der Universität Heidelberg*, vol. I (Mannheim, 1862), pp. 207-210.

rolled only in the college; his name appears nowhere on the matriculation lists of the University. The Dominicans held fast to scholasticism, but this did not prevent the winds of change which were gathering force in the Church from blowing through the cloister. On April 26, 1518 the Heidelberg disputation took place, the theses for disputation being presented by the Augustinian brother Martin Luther.

Franck's fellow students and future evangelical opponents Martin Bucer and Martin Frecht were present at the disputation. Bucer's imagination was fired by what he heard,[16] and thirty-eight years after the fact Martin Frecht would write to an acquaintance of his, a former secretary of the historian Johannes Sleidan, questioning the exclusion of the disputation from Sleidan's *Commentarii de statu religionis et rei publicae Carolo V*, an event, Frecht said, which had made such an impression on Bucer, Johannes Brenz, and himself.[17] Luther noted that he had made an impression on the youth in his audience, telling Spalatin in a letter (dated May 18, 1518) that his great hope now was to transfer this true theology to the young.[18] Whether Franck had any personal contact with Luther, as Bucer did,[19] is nowhere reported, but it seems reasonable to picture Franck, himself a future evangelical pastor, as an interested observer of these events, and to date his interest in the new theology from this point.

Certainly the theses Luther handed to the Augustinians for debate were a very pithy and pointed presentation of his theology as regarded free will, works, and the theology of the cross, as well as a critique of Aristotelianism. In

---

[16] Bucer's letter to Beatus Rhenanus dated May 1, 1518 speaks enthusiastically of Luther's positions, particularly of his attack on Aristotle. For the impact of the Heidelberg disputation see the analysis of Karl Heinz zur Mühlen, "Die Heidelberger Disputation Martin Luthers vom 26. April 1518: Programm und Wirkung," *Semper Apertus: Sechshundert Jahre Ruprecht-Karls-Universität 1386-1986*, vol. I, *Mittelalter und frühe Neuzeit*, ed. Wilhelm Doerr (Berlin, 1986), pp. 186-212, esp. pp. 201-205. The letter is printed in *Luthers Werke* 9, pp. 160-169; and *Correspondance de Martin Bucer*, vol. I, ed. Jean Rott (Leiden, 1979), pp. 58-72.

[17] The letter is printed in W. Friedensburg, "Ein Brief Martin Frechts an Mathäus Nägelin von Straßburg, vom 22. Juni 1556," *Zeitschrift für die Geschichte des Oberrheins* 86 [N.F. 47] (1934), 387-392.

[18] See *Luthers Werke: Briefwechsel* 1, p. 174.

[19] According to zur Mühlen, "Die Heidelberger Disputation," p. 201, Bucer had spoken to Luther during a pause for the midday meal.

particular Luther's theology of the cross, as stated in theses nineteen through twenty-one, exhibits a way of thinking about the world which would stamp Franck's later thought:

> 19. That person does not deserve to be called a theologian who looks upon the invisible things of God as though they were clearly perceptible in those things which have actually happened.

> 20. He deserves to be called a theologian, however, who comprehends the visible and manifest things of God seen through suffering and the cross.

> 21. A theology of glory calls evil good and good evil. A theology of the cross calls the thing what it actually is.[20]

It is hard to know how Franck heard and responded to this theology. His own later theology comes to its juxtaposition of the perceived meaning and the actual meaning of things in a much different manner than Luther's. In his later writings Franck exhibits little understanding of the nuances of Luther's theology. Perhaps what was later superseded was also discounted and forgotten. The fact is that Franck left the Roman Church, and, for a time, joined the evangelical camp, as many of his fellow students also did. And while Franck was to reject the movement, the influence of Luther on his thought is perceptible in much of his writings. In Franck's case the Heidelberg disputation planted seeds which bore a fruit very different than the sower's intent.

Taken as a whole Franck's formal education provides a few clues to his future thought. Whatever of the humanistic discipline was conveyed to him at Ingolstadt stayed with him for life in his interest in history and his intense admiration for Erasmus. His training as a Dominican monk is perceptible not only in Franck's fervid hatred of monkery and the Roman church, but perhaps also in the influence the famous Dominican mystic Johannes Tauler exercised on his thought. His encounter with Luther's theology marks the beginning of his road away from the established church. For the most part, though, Franck's real education lay ahead of him, in the world, just as Franck would have desired.

The next ten years of Franck's life are documented only very sketchily.

---

[20] "19. Non ille digne Theologus dicitur, qui invisibilia Dei per ea, quae facta sunt, intellecta conspicit.

20. Sed qui visibilia et posteriora Dei per Passiones et crucem conspecta intelligit.

21. Theologus gloriae dicit malum bonum et bonum malum. Theologus crusis dicit id quod res est." *Luthers Werke* 1, p. 354. English translation is from *Luther's Works*, vol. 31, ed. Harold Grimm (Philadelphia, 1957), p. 40.

It is known that in the first half of the 1520's he was a priest in the bishopric of Augsburg.[21] Other than this fact nothing is known of this time. Sometime before early 1525 he had taken up the teachings of the reform, and was called to be a pastor in the small village of Büchenbach.[22] This was done by the city council of Nuremberg, where he was tested and then sent to the village.[23] There Franck lived through the Peasants' War, which he neither participated in nor sympathized with.[24] Franck lived very nearly the life of a pauper. His position was not an established pastorate. He was paid from the local church funds 3/4 of a gulden, so long as the local people desired his sermons.[25] That we know these details about Franck's life stems from a letter Franck wrote

---

[21] In the conclusion to the report to the Ulm city council concerning Franck written sometime between August 13 and September 23, 1538, one reads, "Basti Franck, etwan ein päbstischer priester im bistumb Augspurg geweihet..." Hegler, *Beiträge*, p. 205. See also Horst Weigelt, *Sebastian Franck*, p. 14, footnote 18, where he suggests that Franck could have been a priest in Benzenzimmern near Nördlingen.

[22] A letter from the Nuremberg city council, dated October 26, 1527, which verified that Franck had conducted himself honorably during the Peasant's War, also states, "Das gegenwertiger priester Sebastian Franck von Thunaw Werd biss in drey jar in unserem dorff Büchenbach by Rot gelegen," putting Franck's move to Büchenbach sometime in late 1524 or early 1525. Document published in Christoph Dejung, *Wahrheit und Häresie* (Zurich, 1979), p. 277.

[23] Franck states in a letter dated April 3, 1526, "Weil schier der mertail nurnbergisch ist [referring to the village] so haben si doch mich darzw beruft aus rat der von Nurnberg, da ich dan verhort bin worden vnd in zugeaignet bin, zu verkunden das wort gotz..." The letter is published by K. Schornbaum, "Beiträge zur brandenburgischen Kirchengeschichte IV. Seb. Franck, Frühmesser in Büchenbach bei Schwabach," *Beiträge zur bayerischen Kirchengeschichte* 10 (1904), p. 40-42; p. 42.

[24] Franck comments in his *Chronica* (Ulm, 1536): "die pauren wurden ye langer ye freydiger/ verwenger und döllen/ keins gleichen wolten sy eingehen/ was man jm anbot/ alle vernunfft/ rhät vnd fürschläg verachteten sy/ vnd je mer man sy bat/ vnd nachgab/ oder flohe je böser sy wurden..." p. Yiiii-v.

[25] Franck writes, "darvon si mir raichen vnd geben all wochen drei ort eins guldins, so si haben aufzuheben von dem gotzhaus daselb, so lang si wellen vnd vermegen. ist kain gestiftet pfrend oder pfar." Further down Franck states, "doch mit dem gedingt, so lang si es vermogen, vnd ich in gefall, von ainer wochen zw der ander wie ein ander tagloner vnd caplon." K. Schornbaum, "Seb. Franck, Frühmesser," p. 42.

seeking relief from the tax assessed by Margrave Kasimir of Brandenburg-Ansbach.[26] It is not recorded if Franck's plea was successful, but with or without the tax Franck's existence was tenuous.

Franck's future attitude toward political authority may have been shaped by what he experienced in Brandenburg-Ansbach under Kasimir. His behavior during the Peasants' War reveals a ruler of marked viciousness. While the Peasants' War was avenged brutally by most of the authorities and nobility, Kasimir outdid his brethren in his brutality. With the defeat of the uprising the city of Kitzingen, which had sided with the peasants, sent messengers to Kasimir, begging pardon. Kasimir, assuring the safety of the town dwellers, came to the town to settle the score. After collecting the town's weapons, he named over a hundred citizens who were to be incarcerated in the basement of the town hall. The rest of the citizens were sent home. The next day he named the prisoners' punishment to the town: they were to be punished "in the face", that is, have their eyes gouged out. This was then done to sixty of the prisoners. Entreated to show mercy by members of the City Council, Kasimir replied:

> His princely grace could not retract any of the determined punishment. For the seditious citizens had let it be known that they would not look upon (*ansehen*) his princely grace and recognize him as Lord: thus they should not also see (*sehen*) him any longer.[27]

When the punishment was complete Kasimir called for the confiscation of the victims belongings, and directed that they, with their wives and children, should be expelled from his territory the next day. When twelve of the victims died the next day, he instructed that their wives and children still be expelled. The same day five peasants were brought to the marketplace and beheaded by sword in front of the populace, the bodies left to lie in the street the remainder of the day. The next day three more were executed. After assessing a heavy monetary penalty on the city Kasimir took his leave. This story circulated widely in the area, and Franck includes the story in one of his later writings. Kasimir ruled

---

[26] Büchenbach was in the Margraveship of Brandenburg-Ansbach ruled by Kasimir and his brother George.

[27] "Laß sein f. Gn. von dieser festgesetzten Strafe nichts ablassen könnte. Denn die aufrührerischen Bürger hätten sich zuvor vernehmen lassen, daß sie sein f. Gn. nicht ansehen und als Herrn nicht anerkennen wollten; so sollten sie ihn denn auch nicht mehr sehen." *Der deutschen Bauernkrieg in zeitgenössischen Quellenzeugnissen*, vol. 2, ed. Hermann Barge (Leipzig, s.a.), p. 187. This document stems from the hand of the city scribe, and reports the events recounted here.

until 1527. Franck's own later strident judgements on the nobility come into better focus if the actions of Margrave Kasimir are kept in mind.

Less than two years after Franck wrote his letter to the Margrave he changed residence. From Büchenbach he moved to the tiny village of Gustenfelden, just west of Büchenbach, to take up the position of *Frühmesser*. It is possible that this also marked an improvement in living conditions, since such positions were normally endowed. Probably the larger change in Franck's life was his marriage to Ottilia Beham on March 17, 1528.[28] Franck never spoke about his marriage in any of his works. His few comments concerning women in general are negative.[29] Little is known about Ottilia, though it is possible she is the sister of the famous brothers, Barthel and Sebald Beham,[30] two of the so-called "three godless painters of Nuremberg." These were the three students of Dürer's who, along with Hans Denck, were brought before the Council of Nuremberg for their unorthodox religious ideas. It was the painters' testimo-

---

[28] The entry in the marriage book reads "Seb. Franck Ottilia Behamin. 17 März 1528. S. Lienhard." Published in K. Schornbaum, "Aus dem 1. Ehebuch der Pfarrei St. Sebald zu Nürnberg," *Beiträge zu bayerischen Kirchengeschichte* 10 (1904), pp. 82-86; p. 84.

[29] "Niemandt ist groß oder Edel/ er sei dann mit gold behengt/ Gleich als sei diser der beste/ der am meisten goldt trag/ also möcht man wol ein bloch oder Esel zu Ritter schlahen/ vnd Edel machen. Zu dem stuck seind furnemlich die frawen uppig und bawfellig/ Dann es gar ein hofertin thier darumb ist/ das viel von jm selber helt/..." *Von dem grewlichen laster der Trunckenheit* (Frankfurt a.M.: Cyriacus Jacob, 1550), pp. niii to niii-v or 284 to 284-v. (First edition, Augsburg: Heinrich Steiner, 1528)

Franck comments in his *Chronica...der Türkey* (Nuremberg: Friedrich Peypus, 1530), "Ich glaub das kaum ein landt sey da vngehorsamer weyber inne seyen dann in Teutschen landen. vnd seind warlich schier recht Amazones..." P. kiii.

In Franck's last published work, his *Sprichwörter* (Frankfurt A.M.: Christian Egenolff, 1541) there were listed under "Weiber" this saying: "Lesch das leicht auß/ so sindt die weiber all gleich." P. fiiii-v or 24-v. There are a number of other like sayings between pp. 24-v and 25-v. Franck's comments should not be interpreted, as they were by some of his contemporaries, as derogatory of marriage. Rather they show he participated in that common view of the period that women were controlled by their passions, and thus more prone toward vice.

[30] It is widely asserted that Ottilia is the sister of the famous artists, though nowhere is firm evidence shown. There is a certain plausibility to the connection judging from her reputation and Franck's later career.

ny that implicated Denck. Their answers to the various questions concerning Christ, the sacraments, and authority were highly unorthodox, to the point of denying the divinity of Christ and the inspiration of the Scriptures.[31] The painters radical protest against authority reflects the unorthodox views circulating in the city to which Franck undoubtedly was exposed. Any influence the brothers Beham exerted on Franck's thought was marginal, but it may be through Sebald or Ottilia that Franck was introduced to the writings of Hans Denck.[32] Ottilia herself appears to have sympathized with the teachings of the Anabaptists, and was known in their circles, at least later in her life.[33]

Franck's marriage corresponds to a period in which his views began to evolve. In 1528 and 1529 he would gravitate towards ideas that would cause him to leave his village and all forms of religious community. In 1528 Franck's name first graced the title page of a book. A translation of Andreas Althamer's *Dialloge*, this was one of Franck's few works that gave little cause for alarm on

---

[31] Theodore Kolde, "Hans Denck und die gottlosen Maler von Nürnberg," *Beiträge zur bayerischen Kirchengeschichte* 8 (1902), pp. 49-72; p. 65. The text of the trial is published by Kolde, "Zum Prozeß des Johannes Denck und die drei gottlosen Maler von Nürnberg," *Kirchengeschichtliche Studien, Hermann Reuter... gewidmet* (Leipzig, 1888), p. 243 and following; see the corrections to the text given in *Quellen zur Nürnberger Reformationsgeschichte,* ed. Gerhard Pfeiffer (Nuremberg, 1968), p. 324.

[32] Barthel left Nuremberg in 1527 for the court of Ludwig in Munich. Sebald fled the city in August 1528 because of controversy with the city council, but returned sometime after February 6, 1529. Clearly Franck's contacts with them must have been somewhat limited. On Barthel see Herbert Zschelletzschky, *Die 'drei gottlosen Maler' von Nürnberg* (Leipzig, 1975), p. 94; on Sebald see p. 78 and following.

[33] A section of Luther's Table Talk from 1538 refers to the praises of an Anabaptist, George Karg, for Franck's wife. Melanchthon relates his words; "Quomodo fuerit apud Sebastianum Franck, cuius uxorum maximis et coelestibus evehebat laudibus a forma ab eloquentia et spiritu, et ita sibi cum ipsa convenisse, das sein geist und ir geist sich so hoch verpunden hetten, als sie beide ein mensch weren, quomodo ipse cum summa delectatione 17 hebdomadas commoratus sit, postremo se ab illa discessisse sicut Helias ab Heliseo." *Luthers Werke: Tischreden* 3, #3699, pp. 543-544. Luther apparently remembered this, for two years later it is reported that he referred to Ottilia Franck as "plena des geistchs." By this time Ottilia was dead. *Luthers Werke: Tischreden* 4, #5121, p. 671.

the part of the orthodox.[34] In 1527 Althamer was pastor in Elterndorf just north of Nuremberg, then later in Ansbach, in which capacity he participated in the visitations which were held in Margraveship Brandenburg-Ansbach in 1528-1529. Somehow Althamer came into contact with Franck, whom he recruited to translate his work of 1527.[35] Though later opponents of Franck would accuse him of having to give up his pastorate because of his dealings with the Anabaptists, or suspicions thereof,[36] it is clear that, if true, these connections must have developed very late in his pastorate. Althamer surely would not have invited a known Anabaptist sympathizer to translate a tract aimed against the so-called *Schwärmer*.

Although he ostensibly intended to battle the errors of the *Schwärmer* by showing that Scripture spoke unambiguously, that any contradictions are only an appearance, Althamer's particular target was a certain tract by Hans Denck, *Wer die warhait/ warlich lieb hat*.[37] Denck brought together forty pairs of quotations from Scripture, each of which was supposed to demonstrate the contradictory appearance of Scripture. By doing this Denck hoped to demonstrate the difficulty, even the impossibility of understanding Scripture without being first enlightened by the Spirit. This was not a theme which was specific to Denck. He learned it most likely from Karlstadt and/or Müntzer. Tauler, too, had spoken of the seeming contradictions of Scripture. Althamer saw Denck's tract as a direct attack on the evangelicals' emphasis on the word rightly preached and proclaimed. Although the evangelicals recognized the role of the Spirit in opening the ears of the hearer to receiving the proclaimed word, the emphasis, especially in Luther, was on the clarity of Scripture. This was the ordained means through which God had revealed himself. Thus Althamer set himself the task of showing that the Scriptures are in reality univocal, and that God's unitary

---

[34] *Diallage* (Without cite or publisher, 1556); (First edition, Nuremberg: Friedrich Peypus, 1528). The 1556 edition is identical to the original.

[35] Andreas Althamer, *Dialloge, hoc est conciliatio locorum scripturae* (Nuremberg: Friedrich Peypus, 1527).

[36] The report from the "Schulpfleger" in Ulm (1538) charged "da er margrafschaft Brandenburg und Nürnberg der teufer halb hat miessen weichen." Hegler, *Beiträge*, p. 203.

[37] Hans Denck, *Wer die warhait/ warlich lieb hat* (Augsburg: Philip Ulhart, 1526). The piece is published in Hans Denck, *Schriften*. Part 2: *Religiöse schriften*, ed. Walter Fellmann (Gütersloh, 1956), pp. 67-74. See also Alfred Hegler, *Geist und Schrift bei Sebastian Franck* (Tübingen, 1892), p. 30.

truth is expressed there.[38] To do this Althamer took Denck's forty contradictory quotes and added sixty more, then showed the contradictions to be mere appearance which could be solved in a number of ways. It is highly ironic that Althamer chose Franck as his translator, and indicative of the distance Franck still had to travel, for he later would take up the very position that was attacked here, and promote it much more vociferously and on a much larger scale. A study of Franck's translation shows, though, that while Franck was still consciously an ally of the magisterial reformers, there are clues to his future thought and vocation.

The tract contains not only the translation of Althamer's original Latin, but a foreword by Franck himself. He starts by explaining why he accepted the offer to translate the tract. He hopes it will help many good-hearted people,

> for the holy Scripture suffers much violence in our times, and is stretched, interpreted, and pulled by many peculiar minds—even more than in the papacy—so that everyone thinks that Scripture is full of what is agreeable to him.[39]

Franck continues, apologizing in advance for any errors of translation and explaining why he may have deviated from the text. He seems somewhat defensive about what he has accomplished.

> I became master in a foreign book, and added my efforts to its accomplishment and increased it: if I have not improved it, I have at least not harmed it...: If he does not like it, why did he call me: he can leave me undisturbed next time, and translate his book himself. But I know it is the case that I have brought or set into his book no foreign meanings nor new errors or enthusiasms.[40]

These comments might lead one to expect that Franck has made major

---

[38] States Althamer in his introduction, "Dann der einig vnnd derselb unwandelbar will Gotes in der heiligen Schrift/ ist außgedruckt/ der mit jm selbs nit fichtet noch uneins ist." *Diallage*, p. aiiii.

[39] "Dann die hailig Schrifft/ zu vnsern zeyten/ von vilen gewalt leydet/ vnd wirdt auff manchen seltzamen kopff gedönt/ deütet vnd zogen/ schier mehr denn in dem Bapstum/ das ain yeder maynet/ was jm anmüttig sey/ deß sey die Schrifft vol/..." *Diallage*, p. biiii-v

[40] "...[ich] bin maister inn ainem frembden büch worden/ vnd mein fleyß zu seinem darthun etwa hinzu gesetzt vnd gemehret: Hab ich nicht gebessert/ so hab ich doch nicht gebössert...: gefellt es jm nicht/ warumb hat er mich gehayssen/ Laß mich zum nechsten vnuerworren/ vnd teutsche sein büch selber. Doch wais ich für war/ dz ich jm kain frembden synn noch newen irrthumb vnd schwermerey in sein büch hab tragen/ noch hynein gesäet." *Diallage*, p. bv-v.

revisions in Althamer's text. One might expect to find the same excursive approach to translation in this work as was to distinguish his later work.[41]   Indeed Franck seems to bring up many of the themes that will recur in his later writings.   For example, he states in his foreword:

> Ask God...that he awake his Word in us, and make it living and spirit, that we are not only taught, but also become sanctified. For in our time almost everybody seeks only artifice and sensuality in the Scripture... After that no one thinks how he becomes sanctified; and how he captures and brings the Word into the heart, and accordingly lives; only a lot of chatting and talk, although the kingdom of God consists not in words but in the act.[42]

The emphasis here on setting the word into yourself and its bringing forth good acts foreshadows Franck's future polemic about the futility of learning and the primacy of God's inward revelation.   Franck goes on to emphasize how faith always brings forth good fruits, and that the lack of these fruits is a sure sign that there is no faith.[43]   He emphasizes the reception of the spirit[44] and the example which Christ gave to humans.[45]   "For it was for this reason that he [Christ] has come, that he gives us through faith his spirit, writes the law in our heart."[46]   Accordingly "those born out of God do no sin, indeed can do no

---

[41] The most extreme case of Franck's "translation" technique is a work which was never published, the translation of the *Theologia Deutsch* into Latin. The translation is three times longer than the original, the result of Franck's elaborations and digressions.   Alfred Hegler referred to it as a "paraphrase" rather than a translation.   Albert Hegler, *Sebastian Francks lateinische Paraphrase...*, esp. p. 45.

[42] "...bitt Gott.../ das er sein wort in uns erweckte/ vnd leben vnd gaist mache/ dz wir nit allain gelert/ sonder auch Gotselig werden: dann zu vnseren zeyten fast yederman nur kunst vnd fürwitz in der schrifft suchet...nyemand dencket darnach/ wie Gotselig ir werde/ vnd wie er das wort ins hertz fasse vnd bringe/ darnach lebe/ Nur vil plauderens vnd schwetzens/ so doch das reich Gottes nit in worten/ sonder in der that stehet." *Diallage*, p. bvii.

[43] *Diallage*, p. bvii-v.

[44] *Diallage*, p. bviii.

[45] *Diallage*, p.bviii-v

[46] "Dann darumb ist er kommen/ das er vns durch den glauben seinen gaist gebe/ vnd das Gesetz in vnser hertz schreyb..." *Diallage*, p. c.

sin."[47] They have a new heart, mind and courage, for the spirit of God teaches and goads them.[48] Franck sets up a division then between flesh and spirit; the flesh comes from Adam, and is sinful, but the Christian is out of God and the two are far from one another. Adam denotes the will of the flesh, which is foreign to the Spirit, and stands in battle with the flesh.[49] Those who have the law written in their heart not only confess the sin in their flesh, but do penance daily.[50] Franck emphasizes here the works of faith which the Christian will do, the battle between the physical flesh and the Word of God set in the Christian's heart, and the need to do penance. None of these themes is explicitly a deviation from Luther's teaching, but the accents are distinctive, and show a direction in Franck's thought that could lead to a reevaluation of what he received from Luther, and a consequent return to the medieval mystics who had been such an influence on Luther.

Even where Franck sounds most like Luther, when he speaks of preaching the Gospel to those who despair, and the law to those who are unrepentant and have not despaired of themselves, he adds a typically Franckian touch, saying "only [keep] the Gospel far from the shameless, loose, unbroken minds, that one does not throw the treasure to the hounds."[51]

One controlling idea keeps Franck within the evangelical fold, and that is the physical written word of Scripture as the means through which God conveys his saving message. Scripture is still for Franck the primary source of revelation, even though one must come with a humble heart, desiring to be taught and not be master, conscious that when one comes with unwashed feet, according to the flesh, then the Scriptures appear to be against one another. He reminds his readers how everyone draws out of Scripture what he brings to it: "a thing is as one values it...thus he calls them righteous, as the world names them, although

-----

[47] "Wer auß Got geboren ist/ der thut kain sünd/ ja er kan nit sündigen." *Diallage*, p. cii-v.

[48] *Diallage*, p. ciii.

[49] *Diallage*, p. cv.

[50] *Diallage*, p. cv-v.

[51] "Nur weyt mit dem Evangelio von den frechen/ losen/ unerbrochenen köpffen/ das man nicht das haylthumb den hunden fürwerff." *Diallage*, p. cvi.

really in the eyes of God they are sinners."[52] This is the key to understanding the Scripture: that sometimes a contradiction is only the difference between how God views something and how man views it. The Bible speaks with both voices, and only he who has had his eyes opened by God will recognize this.[53] Those who have these eyes will see, although to the uninitiated it will be nothing but a chance to construct errors. Franck states this with one of his favorite examples—"The flower is good for the bee, bad for the spider"—which he uses repeatedly in his later writings.[54] Unlike in his later writings, Franck claims here that it is the *Schwärmer* who come to the Scripture with closed eyes, read it as it is not intended, and make it "sing their song."[55] Franck ends his foreword saying: "Thus is Scripture its own master and interpreter, for God has not forgotten nor held back...to him be honor and glory forever."[56] Franck expresses these views in order to explain how to see through the seeming contradictions of Scripture—its opacity to the unenlightened, the nature of flesh to read Scripture for its own purposes, the dual voices of Scripture. All this is used here to explain the errors of the "enthusiasts," but will later be turned against all of organized Christendom and against Scripture itself. Though all of what Franck says in this foreword may not have offended the eyes of an orthodox churchman such as Althamer, if he had looked on this writing after Franck's turn to the church of the Spirit, Althamer might have wondered if the work he gave Franck did not give him the opportunity to formulate and clarify ideas which were his eventual downfall.

We have no report on how Althamer reacted to Franck's work. Alfred Hegler has compared the original text with Franck's translation, and he judged

---

[52] "Ein ding ist wie man es achtet...Da haißt er sy gerecht/ wie sy die wellt nennt.../ so sy doch inn den augen Gottes warlich sünder seind..." *Diallage*, p. d-v.

[53] *Diallage*, p. diii-v.

[54] "Die blüm ist der byhnen güt/ der spinnen böß." *Diallage*, p. dii-v. The understanding was that bees make honey out of flowers, spiders poison. Carlstadt uses the same example to make the same point. See also *Diallage*, p. Hi-v for another use of this saying.

[55] *Diallage*, p. dvi-v to dvii.

[56] "Also ist die Schrifft ir selbs maister/ außleger/ darumb hat Gott nicht vergessen noch gespart/ das ainem frommen Schulmaister zustehet: dem sey lob vnd eer in ewigkait. AMEN." *Diallage*, p. dviii-v.

that the *Diallage* is "for the most part...a literal translation of the original."[57] The idea that the Spirit must lead in the understanding of Scripture is the continual message of Althamer, and was also Franck's main point in the introduction. Franck adds only a little to the text. As with the foreword, these additions show the elements of Franck's later thought, yet are still contained and directed by the principle of Scripture's primacy. The greatest influence on Franck's additions to Althamer was Luther himself.[58] In a few places Franck expresses himself as he will in later writings, but these passages are rare.[59]

It might seem to the modern observer that Franck had a very little distance to travel to reach his mature position. Really the controversy between Althamer and Denck was one of accents: Denck pointed up the contradictions in Scripture not to deny its inspiration, but to direct people toward the Spirit, to take away the outward stumbling block of the Scripture. After being taught by God inwardly, one could then return to the Scripture and, not being bound by the letter, find confirmation of what God had written in the heart. Althamer, too, points to the Spirit as the true guide to the Scripture. It is only that the Spirit teaches more immediately through the Scripture, in fact can be bound to the Scripture, be in the physical word itself as read and preached, just as the Word of God can be bound to the water in baptism. So Luther too understood it. All Franck had to do accentuate a bit more the role of God's spirit in the understanding of his Word, and Word would come loose from the physical word of the Bible and settle directly in people's hearts. When this happened a whole new perspective opened for Franck. Before that happened Franck wrote his first original work, which gives us a look at his experience of being a pastor, and his intense moralism.

The subject of Franck's work was drunkenness. By most accounts the Germans were unequaled in their love of alcohol. Luther, who was only the most prominent of those who preached on the problem, stated that it was not without reason the Germans were judged guilty of drunkenness and gluttony.[60] He charges the Germans with living like pigs. While it is rather hard to judge just what the general clamor over drunkenness signified—whether a general increase in drinking, or increased sensitivity—it loomed in the minds of many as

---

[57] Hegler, *Geist und Schrift*, p. 34.

[58] *Diallage*, p. 38. See Hegler, *Geist und Schrift*, pp. 29-49.

[59] Hegler, *Geist und Schrift*, p. 45 and following.

[60] *Luthers Werke* 47, p. 757.

the greatest social problem of the sixteenth century.[61] It is a good indicator of Franck's temperament that his first work deals with a question of human conduct. Throughout his later writings his voice achieves its most intense stridency when discussing humans and their behavior. It is possible that this is connected with Franck's reception of reform ideas. The reformers put aside a certain type of moral theology that marked late medieval nominalism, that is, the idea that through a series of congruencies people could increasingly bring their will into accordance with the divine will. While of course one never achieved divine perfection, to those who do what is in them God does not deny grace.[62] This was one of the supports for monastic life, which provided the environment in which the dedication to God's will was promoted. Luther's experience of the monastery, in part, had led him to the rejection of this theology and to develop his teaching of justification by grace alone. It seems his experience indicated that the best that was in one was not very good. What came with the Reformation was an emphasis on the word of Scripture read and preached as the avenue of moral regeneration, as people who trusted in God's free gift of grace turned in glad thanksgiving to doing works of love which are the fruits of Christian faith. The initial success of the reform teaching had led Luther to state in 1522 "I have only put God's Word in motion through preaching and writing, the Word has done everything and carried everything before it." Yet as time went by it became apparent to some that the reforms had not brought with them a transformation of human behavior. This was a theme exploited by Catholic polemicists. It weighed on the mind of Franck. As he said in his introduction

---

[61] Adolf Hauffen, "Die Trinkliteratur in Deutschland bis zum Ausgang des sechszehnten Jahrhunderts," *Vierteljahrschrift für Literaturgeschichte* 2 (1889), pp. 481-516, gives an overview of both the celebrations and bewailings of drink in German literature. Fritz Blanke, "Reformation und Alkoholismus," *Zwingliana* 9 (1949), pp. 75-89, gives a rather impressionistic report on the state of sobriety in Germany, drawing mostly on Franck and Luther, and thus painting a fairly bleak picture. There is no reliable account on this subject. Gregory A. Austin, *Alcohol in Western Society from Antiquity to 1800* (Santa Barbara, 1985), has sections on Germany, but these are based on secondary literature, some of questionable accuracy. There is a small section on Franck, pp. 154-155, which contains errors, mostly because it repeats the errors in the article by E.M. Jellinek, "Classics in Alcohol Literature," *Quarterly Journal of Studies on Alcohol* 2 (1941), pp. 391-395.

[62] "facere quod in se est deus non denegat gratiam" is the familiar formula. See the discussion of Steven Ozment, *The Age of Reform 1250-1550* (New Haven, 1980), pp. 233-236.

to Althamer "there is no faith, which is not followed by good works."[63]
Franck's high expectations were beginning to be disappointed by his experience
in the village. Given Franck's idealistic moralism such disappointment was only
a matter of time.[64]

Von dem grewlichen laster der Trunckenheit[65] (On the horrible vice of
drunkenness) has the air of desperation, a last attempt to bring about change in
the moral tenor of the times. Franck here is seeking the outward reform of
morals, which he sees as having been seriously damaged by the drunkenness of
the Germans. To this end he dedicates his book to Wolf von Heßberg, local
magistrate in Colmburg, whom Franck hopes to stir to enthusiasm for God's
Word. In his appeal Franck uses the vocabulary of German mysticism, speaking
of the *funklein* (spark) and *gluend kol* (glowing ember) which he hopes to stir in
von Heßberg's soul.[66] In contrast to later writings Franck still retains hope of
fanning this spark into a fire with his own writings, that is, through outward
means. Franck emphasizes here the process of sanctification; "[God] who verily
did lay the first stone within you will not cease to build until it grows into a holy
temple of God."[67] Franck ends his dedication with a comment which points
up the impossibility of his demands for sanctification and holiness, at least in
the physical world. "What is noble before the world is an abomination before
God."[68] Franck's penchant for contrasts between the world and God is already present, and set here as it is in an exhortation to an office holder to solve
the problem of drinking, it indicates the expectations and demands Franck has
for the efficacy of his message and of moral action. Franck demands that the
world be changed in accordance to the divine standard, and yet knows and
states that what is noble or wise to the world is an abomination before God. If
even an appeal to the noblest and wisest sentiments in world can only result in

---

[63] *Diallage*, p. bvii-v.

[64] See Steven Ozment's comments on this point, *Mysticism and Dissent* (New
Haven, 1973), p. 138.

[65] See footnote 29 for the edition used.

[66] *Truckenheit*, p. gii.

[67] "Also der gerecht des einfluß Gottes/ der den ersten steyn in euch warlich hat gelegt/ wirt nit nachlassen zu bawen/ biß er wachst zum heyligen
tempel Gottes." *Trunckenheit*, p. gii-v.

[68] "Was vor der welt Edel/ ist eyn greuwel vor Gott." *Trunckenheit* p. giii.

an abomination, how is anyone to go about changing the world? Franck's call is, by its own definition, to fall on deaf ears.

As yet Franck had not entirely lost hope, as is shown by the very exercise he had undertaken. Franck's voice is that of a prophet, calling as John the Baptist did, "Bear fruits that befit repentance."[69] The first task taken up in the main text is to show just how desolate the situation is in Germany. Drunkenness has led to the damage of men's souls, leading to sins and all types of vices.[70] Following their own reason men run much more happily into the wine house than the house of repentance, even though, states Franck, they are told by Christ that those who mourn are blessed.[71] Here lies the problem for Franck; adding alcohol to a person's already impaired reason is, as he says, "like pouring oil on a fire."[72] The only way to ameliorate the situation is to chastise the flesh. The Christian life on earth is an eternal battle. "Thus," states Franck,

> one should preach intensely, sharply and earnestly, and when someone does not want to reform and better himself, leave off and shake the dust from your feet,...have nothing to do with them.[73]

"They are heathens and not Christian who do not show forth the fruits of faith,"[74] asserts Franck. "Don't throw your pearls before swine."[75] Franck

---

[69] Luke 3:8. Quoted by Franck, *Trunckenheit*, p. giii.

[70] "Schad der seelen auß der Trunckenheyt vnd füllerey/ wie sie die sünde eynfürt/ allen lastern die thür auffthut/ vnd die Seel erwürgt vnd vmbbringt." *Trunckenheit*, p. giii-v.

[71] "Die vernunfft spricht/ Sälig sind die fröhlichen die guts muts lauffen vil lieber ins wein hauß/ dann ins klaghauß. Da wider spricht Christ. Matth. v. mit Salomen hie/ sälig sind die trostlosen/ die da trawen." *Trunckenheit*, p. gv.

[72] "Allso wer dem fleisch wein zu geust/ thut nicht anders/ dann...öl dem fewer zu wirffett." *Trunckenheit*, p. gvii.

[73] "Da solt man hefftig/ scharpff/ vnd mit ernst predigen/ vnnd wo man sich ye nit daran wolte keren/ vnnd sich besseren/ davon lassen/ den staub von den füssen schülten/ oder je wo jn etlich sagen liessen/ die andern in Bann thun/ nit mit jn zuthun haben..." *Trunckenheit*, p. gvii.

[74] "Heyden seyen die vnd nit Christen welche des glaubens frucht nitt beweysent." *Trunckenheit*, p. hvi-v.

[75] *Trunckenheit*, p. hviii.

is just warming to his task.

> Oh misery! We are not alone drunk from wine, but drunk, drunk with the lying spirit, error and ignorance. One should punish the public vice, preachers with the word and ban, the princes with the sword and law. For so long as no ban exists, and is in place, I recognize no Gospel or Christian community to speak of. One must remove the impure from the community of God.[76]

Franck does not think his judgements will be heeded. The ones who make the laws would be the first to break them. "Therefore I hold," continues Franck,

> the world may no longer be counseled. I would to God that I were lying, but I have entirely lost heart. It has rooted too deeply, and sin has become habitual. Everyone would first have to be born again differently, another mind must be set up. Yes, there would have to be another world, but that will occur only with difficulty, and therefore I am afraid, that no one will be able to prevent it or stamp it out other than the end times when the Lord will eradicate all offense and weeds from his domain; would to God that it happen soon.[77]

These are the words of one who is bitterly discouraged. Franck's descriptions of the wages of drinking show the jaundiced eye which he cast toward moral dissipation. He paints the picture of someone destroyed by excess.

> One receives an evil untimely old age, a wild confused mind, dizzy head, bleary eyes, a stinking breath, bad stomach, shaking hands, gout, dropsy, weeping leg sores, water on the brain.[78]

---

[76] "Ach des jamers wir seindt nit allein vol von wein/ sonder vol vol des schwindel geysts/ irrthumb vnd vnwissenheyt/ Man solt die offentliche laster straffen/ Die prediger mit dem wort vnd ban/ die Fürsten mit den schwerdt vnd gesatz. Dann weil der Ban nit gehet/ vnd auff gericht wirt/ weyß ich vonn keynem Evangelio/ odder Christlichen gemeyn zu sagen. Man muß je den Vnflat auß der gemeyn Gottes hergen." *Trunckenheit*, p. hviii-v.

[77] "Da seind die Gesatz geber die ersten/ die es verbrechen. Darum halt ich/ die welt sey nit mehr zu rathen. Gott wöll das ich lieg/ ich habe schier daran verzagt/ Es hat zu tieff eingewurtzelt/ vnd ist sünd ein gewonheyt worden/ Müsten allzumal anderst geboren werden/ Eyn andern kopf auff setzen. Ja es müst ein andere welt werden/ das wirdt schwerlich fürgehen/ darumb sorge ich/ es wirts niemandts künden weren/ vnd auß rotten/ dann der jüngsten tag wann der Hertz alle ergernuß/ vnd vnkraute/ auß deinem reich wirdt rotten/ Gott wöl das es bald geschehe." *Trunckenheit*, p. ii to ii-v.

[78] "Denn durch das fressen vnd sauffen/ wirdt die gantz natur verderbt/ eyn böß vnzeitigs alter/ blöden dollen kopff/ schindel im haupt/ treffende augen/ ein stinckender athem/ bösen mag zitterende händt/ das Podogra/ die wasser-

One tenth of the people die an early death from the effects of drinking, says Franck; they degrade themselves from the image of God to animals, having not even the understanding of a cow or donkey.[79] They become poor, in fact all of Germany becomes poor because of drinking.[80] The chief reason for revolt in the land is the fact that the rulers are all drunks, who love wine and good times more than the land and people.[81] Franck's utter disgust with drunkenness and drunkards comes through in his description of the drunks in action.

> There one sees a peculiar people; one sings; the other bewails the drunken misery; he, although defenseless, would fight; he counts money and has none; he preaches about fasting; this one laughs, no one knows what about; that one boasts about great tricks; this one speaks his own shame; he wants to yell; he speaks with Cicero; this one is shameless, strips himself bare; that one becomes courtly, and a wise guy, so that he becomes a fool for [all his] greater wisdom, and stretches out donkey ears. This one wears on himself a gold crown, is very rich, has however a distant home; this one can do it all; that one sleeps now; this one growls like a hound; that one rumbles like a bear; this one is vomiting; that one crawls into the stall with the pigs. There they talk to each other in a friendly way, make great pacts and alliances, and want to start who knows what; the next day no one knows any thing about all this. If those are not fools I don't know what a fool is.[82]

One gets a good idea of the disgust with which Franck viewed that part of vil-

---

sucht/ fliessend ölschenckel/ ein flüssig haupt kriegt..." *Trunckenheit*, p. iiii.

[79] *Trunckenheit*, p. iiv.

[80] *Trunckenheit*, p. kvi-v.

[81] *Trunckenheit*, p. li-v.

[82] "Da sicht einer seltzam leut/ Der singt/ der annder beweint das truncken ellendt/ der will nun wehrloß fechten/ der gelt zelen/ vnd hat keyns/ der prediget von fasten/ dieser lacht/ weiß niemanndt was/ diser rühmpt sich grosser streyche/ diser sagt sein eygne schand/ der will bülen/ der mit Cicerone reden/ dieser wirdt schandtloß/ enntplöst sich gar/ yener wirdt höflich/ vnnd naß-weiß/ das er vor grosser weißheit zum narren wirt/ vnnd die esels ohren herfür reckt. Diser träet ihm selber ein gülden kron/ ist sehr reich/ hat aber weit heym/ der kan es alles/ er schlafft nunn/ der murret nun wie die hunde/ der brummelt wie ein beer/ Der speyet nun/ der kreuchet in ein stall zu den sewen/ Da sprechen sie einander freuntlich zu/ machen grosse pacte vnd bünd/ wöllen weiß nit was annfahen/ zu morgen weißt keyner nichts darumb/ Sind das nit narren/ so weyß ich nit was narren sind." *Trunckenheit*, p. miii to miii-v.

lage life that was earthy or squalid.

The balance of the book is filled with demonstrations of the evil influence of alcohol, and calls for people to live in repentance and in struggle against sin.[83]   Numerous social ills—thievery, murder, even the Peasants' War,[84] as well as blasphemy and idolatry— are attributed to alcohol.   In the end Franck's advice turns away from suggestions for improving the situation and takes on a stoic tone.

> For whoever wants to live a godly life in this world must truly sacrifice all enmity...and take the cross on himself, and must not let himself err, even if he is alone like Lot in Sodom...; that means living soberly in the middle of the tavern, chastely in the middle of a whorehouse, piously in the middle of a dancehouse, amiably in the middle of a murderer's den.[85]

To complete his book Franck adds to his comments his judgement of the significance of all the drunkenness he saw around him, in a chapter titled "How boozing, gorging, and drinking are a certain sign before the end times."[86]   The day of judgment is at the door, warns Franck.   "Our destruction is nearer than we believe and the ax is already laid to the roots of the tree."[87]   Franck quotes from John the Baptist (Matthew 3:10); "Every tree that does not bear fruit is chopped down and thrown in the fire."   "In summary," Franck prophecies,

> all evil and all adventure rises to a peak, that the world itself must confess, it must break or be changed. Now it is not indeed to be imagined how it might become different, therefore it must break.[88]

---

[83] For example see *Trunckenheit*, p. oiii.

[84] *Trunckenheit*, p. ovii-v.

[85] "Dann wer...Göttlich leben will in diser welt/ der muß sich recht verwegen aller feindschafft...vnd das creutz an sich nemen muß sich nit lassen irren/ ob er gleich allein wie Loth in Sodoma...dz heißt mitten im schenkhauß nüchter/ mitten im hürhauß züchtig/ mitten im dantzhauß Göttlich/ mitten in der mördergrub gütlich leben." *Trunckenheit*, pp. piiii-v to pv.

[86] *Trunckenheit*, p. pviii.

[87] "Dann unser verderben ist neher dann wir glauben/ vnd die axt schon gelegt an die wurtzel des baums." *Trunckenheit* p. q.

[88] "Summa alle boßheyt/ vnd all abentheur auffs höchst kommen/ das die welt selbs muß bekennen/ Es muß brechen/ oder annders werden. Nu ist nit

Franck thoroughly exercises his prophetic voice before ending the book with "God help us all."[89] One leaves the book almost exhausted from Franck's exertions in these last few pages.

What does this work reveal of Franck's situation as he composed it? Intellectually he was at the same place as in the Althamer translation: a follower of Luther who puts the accent, the heavy accent, on a faith which brings forth fruits. His emphasis on these fruits, or the lack thereof, was fast becoming an obsession. Between the lines and in his depiction of drunken scenes one glimpses his shock at the life among the flock for whom he was the shepherd. The means available to Franck have not proved efficacious, thus his call for a ban and the intervention of the temporal arm of the prince. But this was a mere bow in the direction of church discipline. Perhaps Franck had talked with or heard the demands of Anabaptists who wished to see a church of visible saints. Franck's comments later in the book show that he has no real hope of reforming through those means. The world must be changed. Franck's prophetic voice was changing. He had exercised his calling by pointing the people to repentance, but he now points to the signs of the times. The end approaches.

It comes as no surprise that Franck's mind soon changed, and with that his career. Franck's demands were absolute. There can be no Church without repentance and the fruits of faith, i.e. a pure godly life that chastises the flesh in order to free the spirit to serve God. In the light of the approaching kingdom of God, Franck must speak out and condemn the world which so clearly does not repent its fallenness and seek God's kingdom. Yet when Franck's mind cast for the message to speak to this fallen world, it was still within the realm of evangelical teaching. Franck preached the law to bring about despair and repentance; he indicated the grace the Christian finds in Christ; he called upon preachers and princes to exercise their offices for the greater glory of Christ's Church. Franck cast no aspersions on the evangelical teaching of justification by faith, only on its misinterpretation. His lack of success, the church's lack of success (as Franck saw it) in reforming the flock had made his mood unsettled. Soon he would find a message more fitting the signs of the times.

There is no official record of why Franck gave up his pastorate. Later opponents would say it was because he consorted with the Anabaptists,[90] but

---

wol zu gedencken/ wie es anderst werden möcht/ darumb muß es brechen." *Trunckenheit*, p. qii-v to qiii.

[89] "Gott helff vns allen." *Trunckenheit*, p. qiii-v.

[90] See above, footnote 36.

the visitation in Brandenburg-Ansbach in 1528-29 made no mention of this. This visitation examined Franck in September 1528 and noted tersely that he had a wife and held himself well.[91] Shortly thereafter Franck gave up his pastorate and moved to Nuremberg. There is really no reason to give credence to reports of Franck consorting with Anabaptists and thus being forced from his position. Undoubtedly he knew and had talked with Anabaptists. The road between Nuremberg and Augsburg ran near to Gustenfelden, running directly by Schwabach, and those fleeing one or the other place were known to rest and organize in Schwabach.[92] Franck's account of Anabaptists in later writings displays a first hand familiarity. But though he disliked the persecution of the Anabaptists and sympathized with their moral earnestness, his developing beliefs were inimical to any sort of sect building. As for the cause of his departure from the ministry, Franck had never hid his opinion that if the people in the town prove unreformable one should shake the dust off one's feet and leave. Do not throw pearls before swine or give the treasure to the hounds. Franck was always one to practice what he preached.

It was logical that Franck, along with his wife, would gravitate toward the large Imperial city of Nuremberg. His ties were extensive. He had been appointed by the city council to his original position in Büchenbach. He had married a woman from Nuremberg, indicating, at the least, his occasional presence in the city. Through his wife he would have had entrance into Nuremberg society, most likely its religiously heterodox wing. Nuremberg in this period was one of the two or three leading cities in the Empire, an Imperial city of singular distinction. It contained around 25,000 residents,[93] and was noted for its artisans, as a trading center, and its artistic achievements, particularly of Dürer and his school. Though Willibald Pirckheimer graced the city with his knowledge of letters, literary activity was not encouraged by the wary eye of the Nuremberg city council. So, too, the city was by no means known as the free haven for reli-

---

[91] "Gustenfeld: Fruemesser herr Sebastian nürnbergisch lehen, hat ein eeweib, helt sich wol." Ansbacher Religionsakten, Staatsarchiv Nürnberg, Repertorium 111, #viii, fol. 32r. Quoted in Horst Weigelt, *Sebastian Franck*, p. 14, footnote 22. See also the comments of K. Schornbaum, *Beiträge*, p. 40.

[92] See Günther Bauer, *Anfänge täuferischer Gemeindebildungen in Francken* (Nuremberg, 1966). Pp. 153-154 speak of how the mill in Schwabach was known as a meeting place for Anabaptists.

[93] Gerald Strauss, *Nuremberg in the Sixteenth Century* (2nd ed., Bloomington, Indiana, 1976), p. 38.

gious exiles, as was the case for a time with Augsburg and Straßburg. In March 1527 the city had carried out the execution of an Anabaptist, Wolfgang Vogel, because of his seditious and heterodox views and practices.[94] This was the first known execution of an Anabaptist outside of the Swiss territories,[95] and was designed to spread fear among the populace, a technique the Nuremberg city council had used with success during the Peasants' War.[96] In fact, because of the nature of South German Anabaptism in its early stages, in the minds of the city council the Anabaptists were directly connected to the upsets and violent anti-authoritarianism of the Peasants' War. The Anabaptists of this region stood under the influence of Hans Hut, who was a sometime accomplice of Thomas Müntzer and a veteran of the Peasants' War. His hatred of the authorities, a result of his experience in the Peasants' War, and his mysticism and intense chiliastic expectation, were conveyed to a significant part of the South German Anabaptists active in and around Nuremberg. Sometime after Hut's death in late 1527 the teachings peculiar to Hut began to devolve.[97] In Nuremberg proper the Anabaptist community stemmed from Hut himself, and it appears to have reached a high-point in 1529/30, though this was still a relatively small group when compared to Augsburg or Straßburg. The influence of the more biblicist, quietistic Swiss Anabaptism becomes apparent first in 1529, though this did not mark a point of rapid reorientation.[98] It was in fact only in 1529 that the Anabaptists established themselves directly in the city in any numbers, for the most part among handworkers.[99]

This was the situation that Franck entered in late 1528 or early 1529, a wary city council and an Anabaptist sect marked by its mysticism and chiliasm. How he made his livelihood is not recorded, although it is possible that in Nuremberg's well established printing shops he first learned what would be his

---

[94] Hans-Dieter Schmid, *Täufertum und Obrigkeit in Nürnberg*, (Nuremberg, 1972), p. 149.

[95] Schmid, *Täufertum*, p. 151-152.

[96] Schmid, *Täufertum*, p. 150.

[97] See the discussion in Werner Packull, *Mysticism and the Early South German-Austrian Anabaptist Movement 1525-1531* (Scottsdale, PA, 1977), esp. chapters 4 and 5.

[98] Schmid, *Täufertum*, pp. 131-132.

[99] Schmid, *Täufertum*, p. 133.

trade.[100] It is Franck's intellectual/spiritual life which is most accessible and of interest. What were his contacts with Anabaptists and radicals? What influences shaped his thinking at this time? It appears highly unlikely that Franck threw in his lot with any Anabaptist group whose teachings were marked by Hut's thought, or which drew its members from the lower or uneducated segment of society. Though Franck would later inveigh against the learned, nowhere does he display any sympathy for chiliasm or enthusiasm on a sect level, and he shows throughout his life a fear of the "common man." So, too, the biclicism of the Swiss Anabaptists would hold little attraction for Franck. It is clear from his later writings about the Anabaptists that Franck was familiar with the variety of their beliefs. It may be safely ventured that he had contact with a variety of different groups and ideas in this time, though identifying himself with none of them. One could speculate endlessly about whom Franck might have met.[101] The writings of two figures, though, are of unquestionable importance for the development of Franck's thought in this period—those of Erasmus, especially his attack on Luther, *De Libero Arbitrio*, and of Hans Denck.

The influence of Erasmus on Franck has been long recognized. Franck, as we shall see, gave ample praise and credit to Erasmus as the best of the humanists, and as one who was a unique witness to God's indwelling Spirit in humans. Franck's own enthusiasm for the famed humanist would later lead Erasmus to turn against Franck in anger. When Franck may have first encountered Erasmus' writings is a matter of speculation. The older literature placed this encounter in his Ingolstadt days,[102] which is plausible, though the consequences of the Erasmian influence were not immediately perceptible. Some of Franck's comments about the effects of the overstatement of Luther's doctrine of justification—that it could lead to moral laxity—which are present in the *Diallage* and the tract on drunkenness may be attributable to the Erasmian influ-

---

[100] See Strauss, *Nuremberg*, p. 261.

[101] Peuckert, *Sebastian Franck*, p. 90 and following, makes a great deal out of the fact Franck mentions Paracelsus' visit to Nuremberg in 1529 in his *Chronica*, p. 243, and speculates about a close relation which forms here and continues throughout Franck's life. He considers this very important for the development of Franck's thought. It is possible Franck became acquainted with Paracelsus, but similarities between the two men's thought are of secondary importance for understanding Franck. Paracelsus had a small influence on Franck, if any. See the comments of Dejung, *Wahrheit und Häresie*, p. 113, for a similar opinion.

[102] F. Weinkauff, *Alemannia* 7 (1879), p. 4.

ence. It was in the period now under discussion that Franck finally draws the
logical conclusion from the Erasmian critique, separates from the evangelical
party, and strikes out on his own. There were two main aspects to Erasmus'
teaching, a criticism of certain dogmas, traditions and practices of the Church,
and his *philosophia Christi*, which was a mystically tinged program for practical
piety. It was Erasmus' criticisms which exercised the most influence on Franck,
for they "cleared away space" within which Franck could reconstruct his world
view.[103] This was the effect *De Libero Arbitrio* had on Franck.

Erasmus wrote *De Libero Arbitrio* in part to quiet his own critics. He
had come under increasing attack by defenders of Rome for his supposed closet
"Lutheranism." Erasmus himself desired to remain neutral, but under increasing pressure he reluctantly decided to take up his pen for the task of theological
debate. The issue between Rome and Luther centered on what both sides saw
as the heretical apostasy of the other, but for Erasmus his discussion was merely
that, a discussion of disputed, and disputable doctrine.[104] By choosing the
doctrine of free will Erasmus got to the heart of the differences between himself
and Luther. Erasmus was able, by investigating this theme, to demonstrate what
he saw as the prime function of dogma, which was to facilitate and encourage
people to follow the example of Christ. Erasmus brought to his discussion what
has been referred to as a "firmly ambivalent" attitude.[105] Erasmus states,

> As far as I am concerned, I admit that many different views about
> free choice have been handed down from the ancients about
> which I have, as yet, no fixed conviction, except that I think there
> to be a certain power of free choice.[106]

---

[103] "[R]aumschaffender" is how Rudolf Kommoß depicts the effect of Erasmian criticism on Franck, *Sebastian Franck und Erasmus von Rotterdam* (Berlin,
1935), p. 25.

[104] See the comments of Brian Gerrish, "*De Libero Arbitrio* (1524): Erasmus
on Piety, Theology, and Lutheran Dogma," *Essays on the Works of Erasmus*, ed.
Richard L. DeMolen (New Haven, 1978), pp. 187-209; pp. 191-192. Erasmus
indicates in his prefatory observations how "Inter difficultates, quae non paucae
occurrunt in divinis literas, vix ullus labyrinthus inexplicabilior quam de libero
arbitrio." Erasmus von Rotterdam, *Ausgewählte Schriften*, vol. 4, ed. Werner
Welzig (Darmstadt, 1969), p. 2.

[105] Gerrish, "*De Libero Arbitrio* (1524)," p. 191.

[106] "Itaque quod ad sensum meum attinet, fatior de libero arbitrio multa
variaque tradi a veteribus, de quibus nondum habeo certam persuasionem, nisi
quod arbitror esse aliquam liberi arbitrii vim." *Ausgewählte Schriften* 4, p. 8.

One of the reasons for these different views, according to Erasmus, is the obscurity of Scripture. "For there are some secret places in the Holy Scriptures into which God has not wished us to penetrate more deeply."[107] Some things God has not willed to be known, and the things he has willed to be known are those pertaining to the good life.[108] Free will is one of those topics which it is better not to debate beyond what serves the good life, since to do so would lead to the weakening of those who are prone to offense.[109] Having established the debate on his own terms, he turns to Luther. He concentrates on the principle expressed by Luther that whatever is done is done not by free choice but by necessity. Even conceding that there might be some truth in this, states Erasmus, "What could be more useless than to publish this paradox to the world?"[110] "What a window of impiety," he continues, "would the public avowal of such an opinion open to countless mortals?"[111] Here is essentially Erasmus' argument. He goes on to enumerate those authorities who stood on the side of free will as opposed to those few who deny free will, and to show the various shadings of freedom and determinism which are involved in various opinions. He also lines up the passages from Scripture that support free choice and then those against. He argues for the primacy of the passages favoring free will. In the end he states:

> ...since different men have assumed different opinions from the same Scripture, each must have looked at it from his own point of view, and in the light of the end he was pursuing. Those who remembered how great is the apathy of mankind in seeking godliness, and how great an evil it is to despair of salvation; those, while seeking to cure these evils, have fallen unawares into others and attributed too much to free choice. On the other hand, those

---

English in the text is from *Luther and Erasmus: On Free Will and Salvation*, eds. and trans. E. Gordon Rupp and Philip S. Watson (London, 1969), p. 37.

[107] "Sunt enim in divinis literis adyta quaedam, in quae deus noluit nos altius penetrare..." *Ausgewählte Schriften* 4, p. 10; *Luther and Erasmus*, p. 38.

[108] *Ausgewählte Schriften* 4, p. 12, 14.

[109] *Ausgewählte Schriften* 4, p. 16.

[110] "...quid inutilius, quam hoc paradoxon evulgari mundo?" *Ausgewählte Schriften* 4, p. 18; *Luther and Erasmus*, p. 41.

[111] "Quantam fenestram haec vulgo prodita vox innumeris mortalibus aperiret ad impietatem...?" *Ausgewählte Schriften* 4, p. 18; *Luther and Erasmus*, p. 41.

who ponder how destructive it is of true godliness to trust in one's
own powers and merits and how intolerable is the arrogance of
some who boast of their own works and sell them by measure and
weight, just as oil or soap is sold; in their great diligence to avoid
this evil, these either so diminish free choice that it avails nothing
whatever toward a good work, or even cut its throat entirely by
bringing in the absolute necessity of all things.[112]

Ultimately Erasmus has turned the question into a subjective one; people read
according to their concerns. Erasmus seeks to find the middle way by conceding enough to free will to motivate people while pointing to God's grace as the
source of the initial impetus toward, and consummation of, salvation. Erasmus
uses free will and judgment to inculcate piety or virtue; he will not use it to
plumb the depths of God's nature.

In one sense Erasmus is very far from Franck in this tract. Erasmus
publicly eschews hyperbole and speculative mysticism and heads always toward
the subjective ethical center of the problem of free will. When Franck took up
the very same issue later in his own writings the structure and style of the argument were very much different. But Erasmus had put his finger on something
that had greatly bothered Franck. Why had the reform of the Church not led to
the reform of behavior? According to Erasmus, because the very message
which had been preached inculcated laxness regarding piety and virtue. Further, the Scripture, whose clarity is essential in resolving the matter, seems to
speak contradictorily. These thoughts penetrated Franck's consciousness, de-
stroying his confidence in the evangelical message. Erasmus' solution of moderation and practical utilization of these themes to instill piety, did not, however, satisfy Franck. Or perhaps Franck, with his eclectic mind, combined Erasmus' criticisms with those of another critic of Luther, Hans Denck.

If Erasmus knocked out many of the supports that had held up Franck's
world view, Denck provided the material for reconstruction. Denck has entered

---

[112] "...ut ex eadem scriptura alii aliam sumerunt opinionem, in causa fuit,
quod alius alio spectaret et ad suum quemque scopum interpretabatur, quod
legebat. Qui secum reputabunt, quanta esset in hominibus ad studium pietatis
socordia, deinde quantum esset malum desperatio salutis, dum his malis mederi
student, incauti in aliud incidere malum ac plus satis tribuerunt libero hominis
arbitrio. Rersus alii perpendentes, quanta sit pestis verae pietatis hominem suis
viribus ac meritas fidere, quam intolerabilis quorundam arrogantia, qui sua
benefacta iactant atque etiam ad mensuram ac pondus vendunt aliis, quemad-
modum venditur oleum et sapo, dum hoc malum magno studio vitant, aut dimi-
diarunt liberum arbitrium, sic ut ad bonum opus nihil prorsus ageret, aut in
totum iugularunt inducta rerum omnium absoluta necessitate." *Ausgewählte
Schriften* 4, p. 156-158; *Luther and Erasmus*, pp. 85-86.

the story already, as one implicated with the "godless painters," and the object of the *Diallage's* refutation.[113] Though Denck was already dead by 1529 (he had succumbed to the plague in 1527), he had left behind him a number of writings, with which Franck was intimately acquainted. In his *Chronica* Franck devoted three pages to recapitulating Denck's opinions.[114] It is likely that Franck encountered Denck's writings while still in Nuremberg, perhaps before he gave up his church office. It was through Denck that Franck first encountered many of the ideas which would mark his own thought.

Denck himself has been the subject of much attention by scholars. Like Franck he has been greatly admired by liberal church historians.[115] He is one of the more attractive figures of dissent in the Reformation period, though one who, like Franck, is difficult to categorize. Recent research has emphasized the influence of Thomas Müntzer on Denck—as a source for Denck's mysticism—and has traced Denck's legacy in the actions and thought of Johannes Bünderlin and Christian Entfelder.[116] Denck's first public profession of faith was in the confession he provided for the city council in Nuremberg after being implicated with the "godless painters." Denck spoke here of his spiritual poverty, but stated, "I sense however besides this something in me that resists powerfully my inborn malice."[117] It was this inborn "something" that Denck would attempt to understand and act on in his life and writings. This inward spark of God put Denck in direct conflict with the forms of salvation established by the historical church and with the authorities of Denck's own day, and he found himself an unwelcome guest, first in Nuremberg, later in other places.[118] The conflicts in

---

[113] Denck and Franck had both attended Ingolstadt, their stays overlapping by about two months. There is no evidence, though, that they knew each other personally.

[114] *Chronica*, p. ddii-v and following.

[115] Representative of this would the biography by F.L. Weis, *The Life, Teachings and Works of Hans Denck 1495-1527* (Strasbourg, 1924).

[116] See Werner O. Packull, *Mysticism...*, es. chaps. 2 and 7. See also James M. Stayer, Werner O. Packull and Klaus Deppermann, "From Monogenesis to Polygenesis: The Historical Discussion of Anabaptist Origins," *The Mennonite Quarterly Review* 49 (1975), pp. 83-121; esp. pp. 100-111.

[117] Hans Denck, *Schriften*, part 2, ed. Walter Fellmann (Gütersloh, 1956), p. 20.

[118] For Denck's Nuremberg troubles see T. Kolde, "Hans Denck."

Denck's life foreshadowed those in Franck's.

Denck's first two publications, and for understanding Franck his most important writings, were published in Augsburg in 1526, *Was geredt sei, daß die Schrift sagt, Gott tue and mache Gutes und Böses* and *Vom Gesetz Gottes.*[119] These two writings have been described as,

> a frontal assault on the three Lutheran *solae*: *sola scriptura* as authoritative revelation; *solus Christus incarnatus* as the agent of salvation; and *sola fides ex auditu verbi* as the narrow gate to Christian life.[120]

Indeed Denck's teaching was a much more radical dissent from Luther than was Erasmus'. Again, though, at the center of his argument stands the question of free will. In his first writing Denck shows himself to be greatly influenced by Neo-platonic conceptions. God created in order to have his majesty known outside himself, and yet he covered over his knowledge of human sin, for if he had known about this sin, it would be as if he had forced them to do what they did, just as if humanity were a stone or a block.[121] Denck understood sin two ways. In one sense sin is evil, in that it is created by men, without God, but in that sense it is nothing before God, for by definition God is all in all, and all that is outside him is evil and nothing. That which is called sin is good, to the extent that it is used by God as punishment, to turn humans toward God, to break down their evil self will.[122] For one learns from God only to the extent that one is passive, receptive, surrendered (*gelassen*),[123] which is brought about when the self will is broken through suffering. In this way humans contribute to their salvation, in that they surrender. It is at this point that what is in us from God can be united again with God.[124] This whole process takes place inside of us. What we hear and obtain from outside is only of use in that it confirms

---

[119] *Was geredt sei...* (Augsburg: Silvan Otmar, 1526); *Vom Gestz Gottes* (Augsburg: Philip Ulhart, 1526). See the bibliography by Georg Baring; Hans Denck, *Schriften*, part 1 (Gütersloh, 1955) pp. 22-23.

[120] S. Ozment, *Mysticism and Dissent*, pp. 125-126.

[121] *Schriften*, part 2, pp. 28-29.

[122] *Schriften*, part 2, p. 29.

[123] *Schriften*, part 2, p. 30.

[124] *Schriften*, part 2, p. 32.

the witness to truth which God has already given us.[125] Denck states that:

> The word that is in the heart one should not ignore, but hear with
> diligence and earnestness what God wishes to speak in us; further
> no outer witness should be simply rejected, but everything listened
> to and tested and in the fear of the Spirit, held one against the
> other; thus the understanding becomes purer the longer this is
> done, until we would hear God speaking with us directly, and we
> would become certain of his will, which is to leave behind all
> selfhood and yield oneself to the freedom which is God.[126]

Denck then asks the rhetorical question, whether this would not be setting
Christians equal to Christ, as if they need nothing of Christ.[127] This he
answers by saying Christians are to a certain degree like Christ. It is not that
they are complete as Christ was, but that they seek that completeness which
Christ never lost. Christ is the most complete mirror of his father.[128] In the
incarnate Christ is displayed that means which God had prepared from the
beginning of the world. With Jesus humanity has an outward witness to what is
received inwardly from the Spirit. For Denck Jesus is a witness of the perfection in spirit for which the individual strives also. Denck sums up his message
this way:

> Whoever truly and in the depth of his soul wants to sacrifice to
> the Lord, so that he wants to put aside his will and seek God's
> will, should give attention to the work of God, thus the merciful
> father will receive him with great joy, and take him up, regardless
> of how he behaved in the past, however basely he has wasted his
> inheritance; indeed regardless of what the father had resolved
> against him.[129]

---

[125] *Schriften*, part 2, p. 34.

[126] "Das wort, das im hertzen ist, solt man nit verleügknen, sonnder fleissig
und ernstlich horen, was Gott in unns reden wolt, darneben auch kain eüsserlich gezeügknuß schlecht dahin verwerffen, sonnder alles hören und brüfen und
in der forcht des gaists gegeneinannder halten, da wurd der verstand von tag zu
tag ye lennger ye rainer, biß das wir Gott aufs allerblössist höreten mit unns
reden, und wir seines willens gewiß wurden, welcher ist, alle aigenschafft ver-
lassen und sich der freyhait, die Gott ist, ergeben." *Schriften*, part 2, p. 37.

[127] *Schriften*, part 2, p. 37.

[128] *Schriften*, part 2, p. 37.

[129] "Welcher sich dem herren im grund seiner seel und in der warhait opf-
fern will, also das ir seinen willen suchen will, der hab achtung auf das werck
Gottes, so wirt in der barmherzig vatter mit grossen freüden empfahen und

Denck's is a voluntarism of the spirit which points to the written word of Scripture as witness to the Word planted by God in our heart, to the life of Christ as a witness to what God seeks to work in us. For Denck, Christ's suffering and death thus signify the perfect obedience to the will of God; there is no discussion or possibility of atonement. The Word of God, which is Christ, was put forth by God from the beginning of the world, was present in perfection in Jesus of Nazereth, and is present to one extent or another in every Christian. All these ideas are seminal for the development of Franck's thought.

Denck's tract *Vom Gesetz Gottes* extends the arguments against Luther's teachings. In this case, the obvious target is the perceived moral laxity of Denck's age. He speaks of the evilness of the world, particularly of the latter days, as it is revealed in history and chronicles.[130] Many people say they wish to do God's will and yet do not, something that is happening more and more according to Denck. But if someone wants to be a Christian, they must walk the way Christ walked.[131] Christ came to fulfill the law, not to do away with it. This means Christians, too, must fulfill the law. Christ announced and wrote this law to his own not only outwardly, as Moses, but speaks and writes to them from the beginning of the world to the end in their heart.[132] The fulfillment of the law, for Denck, is not in ceremonies but in a spotless life. This does not mean there will be no temptations, but one resists, does not give in to sin. "Indeed, the more strife in the flesh, the more peace in God."[133] There may be fleshly minded ones though (Denck is referring to the followers of Luther), who might oppose this through learned quotation from Scripture. Denck has this to say:

> Whoever has received the new covenant of God, that is to whom the law is written in his heart through the holy spirit, he is truly righteous. Whoever thinks he wants to obtain it out of the book, so that he keeps the law, he ascribes to the dead letter that which

---

aufnehmen, unangesehen wie er sich vorhin gehalten, wie schnöd er sein erbtail verthon habe; ja, unangesehen weß sich der vatter gegen im entschlossen hab." *Schriften*, part 2, p. 46.

[130] *Schriften*, part 2, pp. 48-49.

[131] *Schriften*, part 2, p. 50.

[132] *Schriften*, part 2, p. 50.

[133] "Ja, ye mer streyt im flaisch, ye mer fryd in Gott." *Schriften*, part 2, p. 55.

belongs to the living spirit.[134]

The very means of arguing from the dead letter of Scripture shows that one will not keep God's laws: this is one way in which Denck preempts the Scriptural arguments of his opponents. "Whoever honors the Scripture," he states, "and is cold in godly love, watch that he does not make an idol out of the Scripture, which all the learned in Scripture do, who are not educated for the kingdom of God."[135] Denck even limits the efficacy of the outward word in bringing about the instruction of the unbeliever, saying that if you are promised a great good in a letter, and you do not know how good and rich this good is, it would be foolish to depend on the letter.

> The Scripture and the law are in themselves holy and good;
> however in an upside-down heart all things will be upside down,
> thus nothing is of use to him, except that God himself without
> mediation help.[136]

On a larger scale, the law is of no use to a world turned upside down, since to that world the law itself will be stood on its head. Thus God must write directly in the human heart. This is a point that will be of particular importance for Franck's thought, one which he will extend further.

Denck's writing must have taken on a particular relevance for Franck in that they were aimed directly against some of the main tenets of Luther's teaching. Again, as with Erasmus, free will is promoted. Unlike Erasmus, though, Denck does not look back. Where Erasmus engaged the Church fathers, scholastic theology, and the word of Scripture, Denck undercuts these authorities by direct recourse to the Spirit. For Franck, who had been deeply disillusioned by the inefficacy of his pastoral efforts, Denck's writings must have explained the reason for the putative failure of the reformers' efforts. The outward means which were used—preaching, Scripture, exhortation—were of little use if one was

---

[134] "...Wer den newen bund Gottes empfangen hatt, das ist, welchem das gsatz durch den hailigen gayst in sein hertz geschriben ist, der ist warlich gerecht. Welcher maint, er wöll es auß dem buch zuwegen bringen, das er das gsatz halte, der schreybt dem todten buchstaben zu, das dem lebendigen gayst zugehört." *Schriften*, part 2, p. 59.

[135] "Wer die schrifft eeret und in göttlicher liebe kalt ist, der sehe, das er nitt auß der schrifft ainen abgott mache, welches alle schriftgelerten thund, die nit zum reych Gottes geleert seind." *Schriften*, part 2, p. 61.

[136] "Die schrifft und gsatz seind an inen selb hailig und gut; aber in ains verkerten hertzen wird doch alle ding verkert, so vermag im auch sunst nichts, dann Gott selb on mittel zu helffen." *Schriften*, part 2, p. 63.

not touched directly by God in one's heart, where the seed or ember which was implanted by God still lay. And if one was touched by God in this way, then Scripture and all outward means were not necessary, serving only as witnesses to what has already been grasped more perfectly within. So Franck's intense prophetic call to repentance in his drunkenness tract, his ethical demands, attracted him to a position where only God, and God alone, would or could effect the change which was considered essential. The extreme rejection of all outward means might seem a recipe for quietude and resignation. But in Franck's case it led him to intense literary activity. Perhaps the effect reading Denck and Erasmus had on Franck led him to recognize the value of the outward witness, the isolated light shining in the darkness. Franck would no longer call for princes to institute the ban, nor would he call on people to repent their drunken ways. He would now pronounce judgment on the world, all its history, institutions, and practices. Franck may not have considered outward forms to hold much hope for turning people from the corruption of the world to the light of God, but he absolutely could not keep himself from speaking to this world, condemning it, showing it its error. The career Franck took up was as prophet of judgment.

Franck's specific occupation after his move to Nuremberg may not be clear, but he must have given every moment possible to his literary activities. His first publication was a translation of that seminal tract of the English Reformation, Simon Fish's *A Supplicacyon for the Beggars*.[137] The *Klagbrieff*, as Franck called it,[138] shows signs of a shift in Franck's thinking.[139] The text

---

[137] *A supplicacyon for the beggars* (Antwerp: J. Grapheus?, 1528). See William Clebsch, *England's Earliest Protestants 1520-1535* (New Haven, 1964), pp. 240-245, for the history of this tract. Clebsch mistakenly places Franck in Straßburg at this point.

[138] *Klagbrieff* (Nuremberg: Friedrich Peypus, 1529). Franck does not give Fish as the author, which has led to some confusion among Franck's biographers. Peuckert does not name an author (p. 67), Teufel states, "Franck hat die Schrift als übersetzung bezeichnet, aber man vermutete bald ihn selbst als Verfasser," (p. 33).

[139] The translation of the work raises questions about Franck's linguistic training. Franck states the book was "erstlich in Englischer sprach außgangen/ vnd yetz zu letst durch mich verteutscht." *Klagbrieff*, p. A-v. There is a Latin translation, *Supplicatorius libellus pauperum...*, which is dated 1530. It is possible a manuscript of a Latin translation fell into Franck's hands. There is no other evidence that Franck knew English.

itself is a broad condemnation of the Roman clergy for their comfortable spiri-
tuality, which allows them to steal from the poor to satisfy their own appetites.
Whereas the text itself points specifically to the clergy, Franck, in his introduction, broadens the scope somewhat. He starts by noting that in the tract one
sees those things that the Lord finds abominable. "No one should think,"
states Franck,

> that this alone is the Devil, and point with the finger to them, as
> if they had alone sinned. Christ will say no to that. Thus when
> we do not all better ourselves and do penance, we will all alike
> die...There are yet many Antichrists who have gone out in the
> world, even out of us, and the devil sits even among the children
> of God, and Judas among the Apostles.[140]

Here solidarity with the reforming party seems to be breaking down. His condemnation extends now to those in whom he had previously invested his hopes
for reform.

Franck's next publication gives ample evidence of his change of heart. It
is again a translation, entitled *Chronica vnnd Beschreibung der Türckey*.[141]
Included is a foreword by Luther which he wrote in Latin for a Wittenberg
publication of the original Latin tract.[142] The tract itself was written by an

---

[140] "Doch sol niemant mainen/ das dise allein der Teufel sind/ vnd mit
finger auff sie deuten/ als haben sie allein gesündiget. Christus wirt nein darzu
sagen. Darumb wo wir uns nit allzumal besseren vnd büß thund/ werden wir
all zu gleich vmbkommen...Es sind noch vil Anti Christi in die welt außgangen/
auch auß vns/ vnd sitzt der Teufel auch unter den kindern gottis/ vnnd Judas
vnter der Aposteln." *Klagbrieff*, p A-v.

[141] (Nuremberg: Friedrich Peypus, 1530). There is an earlier partial translation of this work which appeared in Straßburg from the publisher Christian
Egenolph. Though some have considered this evidence that Franck was already
in Straßburg, this is not necessarily the case. Why did the full edition appear
then in Nuremberg? In any case the topic of the Turks was on people's minds
because of the siege of Vienna and Franck was not the only one to take an
interest in this tract. See the editions listed in Carl Göllner, "Die Auflagen des
'Tractatus de ritu et moribus Turcorum'," *Deutsche Forschung im Südosten* 3
(1944), pp. 129-151; pp. 143-149.
 The original Nuremberg translation of Franck has been reprinted; *Chronica vnnd Beschreibung der Türckey...Unveränderter Nachdruck der Ausgabe Nürnberg 1530 sowie fünf weiterer 'Turkendrucke" des 15. und 16. Jahrhunderts*, ed.
Carl Göllner (Cologne, 1983), pp. 1-106.

[142] *Libellus de ritu et moribus Turcorum...* (Wittenberg: Johann Lufft, 1530).
See *Luthers Werke* 30, part 2, pp. 198-208.

unknown person of Transylvanian origin (referred to as Capitivus Septemca-strensis), who was captured by the Turks in the 1430's and lived in servitude to them for twenty-two years. He eventually escaped to Rome, where he became a Dominican and published his account around 1480. As with all his later translations, Franck used the material in this tract to his own ends. He explains his method of selection in an afterword:

> In the translation of this Chronicle, my reader, we have acted so that we have neither added nor subtracted anything from the truth of the history without a reason, as it deserved, but, where the author recounts and relates the history [we have] diligently copied, imitated, and translated; where he is however a theologian, and, seeking to strengthen our faith, has disputed...the Turks, we have omitted for clarity's sake.[143]

It would seem Franck found the author's theology to be distasteful. Franck notes, too, that he has introduced his opinions in only a few small points.[144] But a comparison with the original leaves little doubt but that Franck was being modest here.[145]

What direction did these changes take? Perhaps the best example comes in the section entitled "on the Turkish wars, weapons, victories, and manner of fighting."[146] The Turkish threat was on the minds of many in 1530, with the siege of Vienna fresh in memory. Franck has this in mind as he interjects his own voice concerning the Turkish victories. He notes that the great power and might of the Turks have led many Christians to fall away from the faith, as if

---

[143] "In verteutschung diser Chronica/ mein leser/ haben wir uns also ge-halten/ das wir der warheyt der histori nichts vergeben/ vnd wie sich gebürt/ weder genommen noch geben/ sonder/ wo der author die histori anzeucht vnd erzelt/ fleyssig angemasset/ immitirt vnd verteuscht haben/ wo er aber ein Theologus ist/ vnd vnsern glauben zu befestigen/ er Türcken...disputirt/ haben wir zu verteuschen gern unterlassen..." *Chronica der Türckey*, p. Liii-v.

[144] *Chronica der Türckey*, p. Liii-v.

[145] Bernhard Capesius, "Sebastian Franck's Verdeutschung des 'Tractatus de ritu et moribus Turcorum'," *Deutsche Forschung im Südosten* 3 (1944), pp. 103-128; "Wenn wir also feststellen können, daß nur etwas über die Hälfte des Urtextes als solcher bei Franck erscheint und anderseits nicht einmal drei Vier-tal des Franckischen Textes Eigentum des Mühlbachers sind, so kann man wohl in der Tat kaum von einer einfachen übersetzung sprechen, sondern es handelt sich um eine ausgesprochene überarbeitung" (p. 115).

[146] *Chronica der Türckey*, p. E.

the true belief must lead to riches and outward triumph.[147]   He points out that the true triumph is inward, in belief and patience.

> God hides the victory of the Christian, so that they rule in the midst of their enemies, live in death, have peace in turmoil, triumph even as they are laid low, are free even as they are captured, as the entire Scripture professes. Especially the New Testament in this judges from the outer to the inner, from flesh to spirit; that the outer victory, order, and circumcision of the Old Testament no longer is valid; only one thing is valid; turn from the figure to the truth, from the outer into the inner.[148]

He goes on to note that there are very few who actually enter on the right way, as even some of the pagans, such as Cato, Socrates, and Pythagoras, have recognized. The Turks, though, are associated with those apes who judge according to the Old Testament.[149] This is a typical piece of Franckian exegesis, where the text provides a convenient forum in which to interject his own concerns. Such error is not limited, though, to the Turks.

The Latin original ends with an observation on the ten divisions in Christendom: Latins, Greeks, etc. Franck feels compelled to add,

> Look alone at the Latin belief, which is most familiar to us, and how many sects it is divided into; such as Picards, Hussites...Lutherans, Zwinglians, Baptists, and so many hundreds of orders and sects; certainly other nations will not lack this either, so that I believe, error goes through the entire world...[150]

Here is the first indication that it is the division of Christianity that weighs heavily on Franck's mind.

---

[147] *Chronica der Türckey*, p. E-v.

[148] "Also verbirgt Got auch dem sig der Christen/ Das sie herschen mitten vnter yhren feinden/ leben ym tod/ fryd haben yn vnfried/ sigen so sie unterligenn/ frey seind/ so sie gefangen werden, etc. wie die gantz schrift bezeugt/ besunder das Neü Testament gar dohin gericht ist von eusern yn das ynner/ vom fleysch yn geyst/ also das die eussern sig regiment/ benedeyung des Alten Testaments nicht mehr gelten sonder eins seind/ kert von der figur yn die warheit/ von dem eusern yn das ynner." *Chronica der Türckey*, p. Eii.

[149] *Chronica der Türckey*, p. Eii-v.

[150] "Sihe nun allein der Latiner glauben an/ der vns basten bewist ist/ yn wie vil sect er yn ym selb zertrent ist/ als in Beham Pickarden/ Hußiten/ Luterisch/ Zwinglisch/ Teufferisch/ vnd so vil hundert örden vnd secten/ Es wird freylich anderen Nationen auch nit felen/ Das ich glaub/ irthum gee durch die gantze Welt aus" *Chronica der Türckey*, p. Kii-v.

The comment about the true inwardness of Christianity and the concern about Christendom's division are brought together in a statement tucked in at the end of a small section Franck appended on the "Moscobiter." Franck relates:

> Three main beliefs have originated in our times, which have large followings: Lutherans, Zwinglians and Baptists; the fourth is coming, that will clear out of the way all outward preaching, ceremonies, sacraments, the ban, and callings as unnecessary, and simply collect an invisible, spiritual Church in unity of the Spirit and belief among all people, which will be set up and ruled alone through the unseen Word, by God without any outward means, just as if the apostolic Church, soon after the time of the Apostles, were laid to waste through the abomination and fell; and if the times are particularly dangerous, God help us all, and grant us that in fear of him we grasp what is right, and walk the straight path in this darkness.[151]

All error has been brought about by the concentration on the outward church and all that goes with it. The division of Christianity, wars, vice, these are all signs of the movement of history towards its end. The statement that the fourth Church, the Church of the spirit, is "auff der ban" conveys this expectancy. No longer is Franck's concern simply with moral lassitude. He sees this now as one of many signs of the time. The Turks, too, are one of these signs. Franck states in his conclusion that it was with this small book on the Turks "that I first see that the Devil can be more that just the Pope and monks, and alone pull the Christians along by the nose...Here I see that he is in all happenings."[152] Franck extends his comments to denounce the Turks, and all those who live seemingly upright lives but who are in reality without faith, deceivers.

---

[151] "Weyter seind zu unsern zeyten drey fürnemlich glauben auffgestanden/ die grossen anhang haben/ als Lutherisch/ Zwinglisch/ vnd Taufferisch/ der vierd ist schon auff der ban/ das man alle eusserlich predig/ Ceremoni/ Sacrament/ ban/ beruff/ als vnnötig/ wil auß dem weg raumen/ vnd glat ein vnsichtpar geystlich kirchen in ainigkeit des geyst vnd glauben versamlet/ vnter allen völckern/ vnd allein durchs ewig vnsichtbar wort/ von Got on aynich eusserlich mittel regiert will anrichten/ als sey die Apolstolich kirch bald nach der apostel abgang/ durch den grewel verwüst/ gefallen/ vnd seind zumal geferlich zeyt/ Got helff vns allen/ vnd geb vns/ das wir in seine forcht ergreyffen das recht ist/ vnd rechten weg in diser finsternuß wandeln. Amen." *Chronica Der Türckey*, p. Kiii-v.

[152] "...ich erst sihe/ das der teuffel mehr kan dann allein ein Bapst vnd münich sein/ vnd allein die Christen bey der nasen zuführen...Hie sihe ich/ wie er in allen spilen ist..." *Chronica der Türckey*, p. Liii-v.

This they will not hide from God. He shows how true belief is the emptying of self will and being taken over by God's will. Without that change one will never be able to read the signs of history, Scripture, or anything else. "In summary, to those on the left and turned about, everything appears to the left and turned about,"[153] he states, using one of his favorite sayings. Little is useful for those who cannot see.

Franck's comments in this translation mark his complete break with Luther and the movement for reform. Though he included the introduction by Luther, Franck no longer takes his stand with Luther's movement. Lutherans, Zwinglians, and Anabaptists are all superseded by the Church of the Spirit.

> The Pope, the Turks and all unbelievers have an appearance without essence, do works without faith; thus we supposed Christians and evangelicals have much belief without works, the essence...without the appearance, truth without expression...becoming confused in a shameless, rough, wild life, letting the appearance, the works die with the faith, that we are now neither Turks nor Christians.[154]

Franck gives vent here to disappointed hopes. Though the evangelicals will never come in for the massive broadsides he directs against Rome, Franck himself is no longer of the reform party. He witnesses for the truth that the Spirit of God sets in the individual's heart when they yield themselves to him.

This tract is only a small part of that witness, "a foretaste of my main Chronicle,"[155] as Franck states in closing. Here history and the amazing work of God from the beginning of the world will be shown. Though Franck would finish one other translation, plus a revision of the tract on Turkey during this period, most of his energy was going into what would be his master work.[156]

---

[153] "ynn Summa dem linkenn vnd verkerten alle ding linck vnd verkert ...scheint." *Chronica der Türckey*, p. Ni-v.

[154] "Also füren der Bapst/ Türcken/ vnd alle vnglaubigen/ schein on wesen/ werck on glauben/ So füren wir vermainten Christen vnd Evangelischen vil glauben on werck/ wesen...on schein/ warheyt on ausspruch...geradten also in ein frech/ rauch/ wild leben/ vnd lassen den schein/ die werck mit dem glauben faren/ Also das wir weder Türcken noch Christen nun seind." *Chronica der Türckey*, p. Oiii.

[155] "...ein vorschmack...meiner hauptchronick." *Chronica der Türckey*, p. Oiii.

[156] The revision of the Chronicle of Turkey, *Cronica/ Abconterfayung vnd entwerffung der Türckey* (Augsburg: Heinrich Steiner, 1530) appeared on Octo-

The reasons for Franck's removal from Nuremberg are uncertain, as is the date. There is no record of any legal action against him by the council. His publications to that point had stirred no protest, as far as is known. As noted earlier, though, the environment of Nuremberg may have proved stifling under the watchful eye of the city council. Franck had thrown all his efforts into this promised Chronicle. If he were looking for a likelier spot to publish, certainly the city of Straßburg would have stood out. Radicals of every stripe had gathered there, a fact that surely did not escape his eye as he gathered materials for his Chronicle. It is most likely for this reason that Franck, probably in the second half of 1530, moved with his wife to Straßburg.[157] Here he would learn first hand what happens to prophets who speak their truth too loudly, when God's absolute inner Word confronts Satan's kingdom of the world.

---

ber 10th. Franck scrapped the Luther introduction and his own conclusion, and substituted a very pithy introduction of his own. Perhaps because he was out from under the eye of the Nuremberg censor, or perhaps because his own thoughts were now more sharply focussed, Franck lays out clearly how Chronicles expose the world as God's carnival, how the world is ruled by the devil, that the divisions and upsets of the world force men to God and into his school. B. Capesius, "Sebastian Franck's Verdeutschung...," pp. 127-128, has ventured that this second edition marks Franck's final break with Lutheranism, that the intervening Diet of Augsburg had finally thoroughly disillusioned Franck. There is no basis for this. The first edition contains the same material as the second, except as already noted. One suspects the Luther foreword was there only for name recognition and to ally any fears the Nuremberg censors might have had. In the freer air of Augsburg Franck merely focussed his message more.

[157] Judging by his publication record Franck remained in Nuremberg into 1530. His *Klagbrieff* and the Turkish chronicle were published in Nuremberg, as was the Beroaldus translation of 1531. Franck's first Straßburg publication is not until the second half of 1531.

CHAPTER TWO: FRANCK IN STRAßBURG

"Especially in Straßburg one is not asked where he is from, who he may be, or how he is leaving."[1] "Where elsewhere one would hang, in Straßburg one is flogged."[2] With these words Franck revealed the attraction Straßburg held for religious radicals of all stripes in the years between 1525 and 1535. Heterodox religious movements were not the city's only distinction. According to Franck's description, "the fields and region around this city are fertile for wine, corn, and every sort of fruit: the river is full of fish and ships."[3] Indeed during the bad harvests and crop failures that hit Europe in the years surrounding 1530 Straßburg's harvests were sufficient, though prices still rose.[4] Franck also praised the unity and good order of the city, the lack of unneeded laws and compulsory statutes.[5] When one adds to this picture an active printing industry, it is understandable why Franck made his way to Straßburg.

Straßburg was one of the most important cities of the Empire. Though it was not the center of a far flung trading network, as was Nuremberg, its position on the upper Rhine meant that much of the shipping on the river originated or passed through Straßburg. The city was also the site of the last bridge over the Rhine before it found the sea.[6] Trade coming from Italy bound for the Rhine valley passed through Straßburg.[7] For the most part Straßburg's economy was based on regional trade within the area of the upper Rhine. The city did not have a dominant industry which depended on distant markets. As a consequence the limited political autonomy which was granted most Imperial

---

[1] "...sunderlich zu Straßburg/ fragt man nit/ von wannen einer sy/ wes er sey oder wie er abgeschieden." Sebastian Franck, *Weltbuch* (Tübingen: Ulrich Morhart d.Ä., 1534), p. 64-v.

[2] ..."Was man anderswo henckt/ dz streicht man zu Straßburg mit ruten auß." Sebastian Franck, *Germaniae Chronicon* (Frankfurt a.M.: Christian Egenolff, 1538), p. Aa vi.

[3] "Der acker vnd regent umb dise statt ist fruchtbar vonn wein/ korn/ vnnd allerley frücht/ die fluß visch/ schiffreich..." *Germaniae Chronicon*, p. Aa vi.

[4] Klaus Deppermann, *Melchior Hoffmann* (Göttingen, 1979), pp. 237-238.

[5] *Germaniae Chronicon*, p. Aa vi.

[6] Jacques Ungerer, *Le Pont du Rhin à Strasbourg* (Strasbourg, 1952), p. 8.

[7] Miriam Chrisman, *Strasbourg and the Reform* (New Haven, 1967), p. 4.

cities might be wielded less cautiously in Straßburg than was the case in some other cities. The disfavor of the Emperor was not quite so fearsome a threat. Or to put it in less negative terms, the ties that bound Straßburg to the Emperor were not so sturdy as were those of Nuremberg.[8] Though it is unlikely Franck took into account the relative economic and geographic isolation of Straßburg when he decided on his move, these conditions, in part, help explain the city's unique policy toward religious heterodoxy.

While these conditions make Straßburg's lenient policy comprehensible, it was a complicated set of particular circumstances and personalities which gave this policy its content and character.[9] Like many cities, Straßburg's status as an Imperial city developed over a period of years during the Middle Ages. Rather than emphasizing its connection to the Emperor, like Nuremberg, Straßburg stressed its own status as a "Free City." Though originally referring, constitutionally, to the city's relationship to the bishop, it came to imply a less close dependence on the Emperor. In their oath "Free Cities" did not swear obedience and subjugation to the Emperor as their lawful sovereign.[10] Thus constitutionally Straßburg had a store of arguments to resist those policies promoted by the Empire which seemed inimical to the city's own perceived concerns. In the Reformation one of those concerns was religion.

The currents of reform were given voice in Straßburg early on. The most vocal proponent was Johann Geiler von Kayserberg, preacher in Straßburg from 1478 to his death in 1510;[11] the influence of Jacob Wimpfeling and Sebastian Brant should also be noted.[12] This reform current, however, was more marked by its moral earnestness than by any true theological innovation. Its

---

[8] Hans Baron, "Religion and Politics in the German Imperial Cities during the Reformation," *English Historical Review* 52 (1937), pp. 405-427, 614-633; esp. p. 614 and following.

[9] The sources for the following discussion are: Miriam Chrisman, *Strasbourg and the Reform*; Lorna Jane Abray, *The People's Reformation* (Ithaca, NY, 1985); Thomas A. Brady, Jr., *Ruling Class, Regime and Reformation at Strasbourg 1525-1555* (Leiden, 1978); Hans Baron, "Religion and Politics..."; Klaus Deppermann, *Melchior Hoffmann*.

[10] Baron, "Religion and Politics...," pp. 622-623.

[11] See Johann Adam, *Evangelische Kirchengeschichte der Stadt Straßburg* (Straßburg, 1922), p. 16 and following.

[12] On Wimpfeling see Lewis W. Spitz, *The Religious Renaissance of the German Humanists* (Cambridge, MA, 1963), chapter 3.

vision of change was limited to reform instituted from above by sumptuary laws. While this specific current of reform does not qualify its advocates as "anticipators" or "reformers before the Reform," the theme of moral reform carried over into the Reformation, expressing itself in the earnest attempts of the city's reformers to have strict church discipline imposed on the community. As Franck's career shows, the moral themes could take on cosmic significance which vitiated the claim of the reformers to have instituted proper teaching. In Straßburg the impetus for the evangelical reform came from outside, from Mathäus Zell, Martin Bucer, Wolfgang Capito, and Caspar Hedio.[13] Though these reformers were all originally moved by Luther's message, their own background and social setting influenced the way in which they came to appropriate and realize the message of justification by faith. The city setting led to a different sort of reform campaign than in the princely territories, and to a modulation of theological opinion. For the Straßburg theologians reform came not just through the spiritual sword, through teaching, but the uniting of both church and temporal authority in the attempt to lead humanity to Christ.[14] Thus we find the calls for discipline. But the reformers, while perhaps the formal advocates and guardians of reform, were not the only ones who had an interest or influence in the channeling of these currents. Though the vision of the Christian society may have fueled the city reformers' ideas and attempts at reform, it may also have masked a profound unease concerning the actual unity of purpose within the city walls. For the aristocracy and the common man found in the reform hopes and dangers which were not pertinent to the reformers.[15]

---

[13] For an overview of these figures see Miriam Chrisman, *Strasbourg and the Reform*, chapter 6. On Capito see James Kittelson, *Wolfgang Capito* (Leiden, 1975).

[14] On the whole question of the Reformation in the cities see the seminal article by Bernd Moeller, *Reichstadt und Reformation* (Gütersloh, 1962); for Bucer see p. 43 and following. This touched off a literature too extensive to discuss here. See the review articles of Hans-Christoph Rublack, "Forschungsbericht Stadt und Reformation," *Stadt und Kirche im 16. Jahrhundert*, ed. Bernd Moeller (Gütersloh, 1978), pp. 9-26; and Kaspar von Greyerz, "Stadt und Reformation: Stand und Aufgaben der Forschung," *Archiv für Reformationsgeschichte* 76 (1985), pp. 6-63.

[15] Lorna Jane Abray emphasizes in her study the different trajectories which were envisioned for the reforms by the religious reformers, the magistrates, and the people; pp. 10-11. In actuality her book has much more to say about the competing interest of magistrates and reformers than the role of the people in the reforms, their role being difficult to grasp in the surviving records.

The Peasants' War and the Straßburg magistrates' response to it are a good example of the uses of reform among the various social orders. The peasants saw the evangelical message as the justification for their movement to effect reform in the social order. The aristocracy used it to appease sentiment in the city.[16] Indeed the attempt to impose reform without setting loose chaos, both in the social and political world, provided a formidable challenge to the rulers of early modern Europe. More often than not the standards for judging heresy in Straßburg were directly related to the heresy's potential for dissolving the existing social and political bonds.

In the 1520's, the evangelical movement was still involved in the process of definition and institution of reform. While there was broad popular support for the reform of the church, this did not translate into a settlement. The reformers were forced to work through the secular magistrates in order to effect reforms. For their part the magistrates did not wish to cede authority to the religious reformers, and in fact the reform movement provided the opportunity to bring the control of religion more firmly under the council's jurisdiction. The reformers had to fight a long battle against the secular magistrates, who were ultimately very reluctant to see a reform of morals instituted through the religious authorities. In the end Bucer was a frustrated man. While the Mass was discontinued and the evangelical message rang forth from the pulpit, it was not until the second half of the century, after Bucer's departure, that the church successfully claimed authority over church discipline and began a more rigorous enforcement of the reform of morals.

One of the most difficult areas for the new church order was the treatment of religious radicals. Clearly the religious authorities believed those people who endangered the emerging church order must be eliminated, but it was not always easy to distinguish friend from foe, especially in the early years. The names of those who found a home in Straßburg, at least for a while, reads like an honor role of sixteenth-century radicalism— Clemens Ziegler, Hans Denck, Michel Servetus, Melchior Hoffmann, Martin Cellarius, Michael Sattler, Johannes Bünderlin, Christian Entfelder, Jacob Kautz, Caspar Schwenckfeld, Pilgrim Marpeck, to name only the most prominent. The reasons for this hospitality are many. For one, in Straßburg it was a tradition to allow each person accused of heresy to explain her or his case, a common practice in many places, and one on which both the clergy and city council frequently agreed. The clergy

---

[16] See Brady's analysis in *Ruling Class...*, chapter 6. Brady stresses the losses also incurred by aristocratic rule with the dismantling of the late medieval church in Straßburg.

saw it as an opportunity to refute the particular heresy. The council, though, often tended toward leniency, all the better to maintain their prerogative in the enforcement of religion.[17]

In the early Reformation period, up to 1532 or 1533, Bucer and especially Capito were inclined toward a mild policy when dealing with heterodoxy. They generally inclined toward tolerance for those of differing opinions, except in cases where individuals sought to form sects outside the church or were too vocal or public in the expression of their ideas. Capito's own sentiments inclined, for a time, strongly in the direction of the spiritualists.[18] He accentuated the memorial and pedagogical function of the sacraments even more than Zwingli or Bucer. He harbored numerous radical figures in his house, including Cellarius, Schwenckfeld, and allegedly even Michel Servetus. Capito remained faithful to the reform of the institutional church of Straßburg, and hoped by his irenic efforts to win dissenters to the position of the reformers. Ultimately Capito's efforts were in vain, as no major figure was won to the reform. Indeed the Anabaptists charged that Capito lacked the courage to withdraw from the church. Bucer, who worried over the turn in Capito's thought, increasingly took over the leadership of the church in Straßburg.

With the split, beginning in 1524, in the ranks of the evangelical movement which came with the sacramentarian controversy, the Straßburg preachers took their stand with Zwingli. This eventually led to a bitter split between the Straßburg reformers and Luther, which was not healed for many years. Thus some of Luther's foes, such as Hoffmann and Schwenckfeld, were welcomed into the city. Karlstadt, Luther's arch foe, was recommended for special care to Zwingli since the Straßburg council, on political grounds, would not permit him residence in the city.[19] In general the Straßburg reformers' experience of the Reformation had impressed upon them the importance of popular support when carrying out changes in the face of a reluctant city council, and a policy of persuasion rather than force seemed, at least for a time, the most promising avenue to control reform. Events, personalities, and traditions converged in the late

---

[17] Abray, *The People's Reformation*, p. 106.

[18] See Deppermann, *Melchior Hoffmann*, p. 169 and following, where he discusses Capito's turn, after 1527, toward apocalyptic spiritualism under the influence of Martin Cellarius, a tendency in Capito's thought which is regarded by Kittelson, *Wolfgang Capito*, p. 183 and following, as being more a "matter of language than substance" (p. 184).

[19] Deppermann, *Melchior Hoffmann*, p. 154.

1520's to turn Straßburg into a relatively safe haven of dissent.

This did not mean that every dissident was greeted with open arms. Sect building and the spread of ideas which detracted from the authority of the reformers were looked upon askance. As early as 1526 the council dealt with those who would not allow the baptism of their children.[20] And while certain Anabaptists, such as Michael Sattler, earned the admiration and sympathy, if not the agreement, of the reformers, certain other persons earned their hearty condemnation, and were summarily expelled. Two such expulsions, that of Hans Denck and Jacob Kautz, foreshadow what would happen to Franck in Straßburg. Denck, who came to the city in 1526, did not last even two months before he was expelled. Bucer took particular exception to Denck's *Von dem gesatz gottes*, and his inner Word mysticism. Both Capito and Bucer felt Denck's teachings would potentially throw the church into disorder. Bucer held a disputation with Denck, and soon after Denck was ordered to leave the city.[21] Though expelled Denck's teachings left an imprint on Straßburg's Anabaptist community in the 1530's.[22] Kautz, who was one of Denck's disciples, encountered similar problems in Straßburg. Kautz's public teaching of Denck's spiritualizing theology earned a vigorous rebuke from Bucer.[23] Bucer's rebuke was all the more sharp because Johann Cochlaeus had attacked the evangelical party over Kautz's teachings, holding them up as an example of the threat to order represented by reform teachings.[24] Bucer is especially carefully to rebuke Kautz for the implications his theology had for authority and the legitimacy of outward institutions, both ecclesiastical and secular. Such teachings go entirely against Bucer's understanding of the community of love, in which the office of authority is instituted by God to provide order. For Bucer the city is

---

[20] See the council record in *Quellen zur Geschichte der Täufer*, vol 7: *Elsaß I; Stadt Straßburg, 1522-1532*, eds. Manfred Krebs and Hans Georg Rott (Gütersloh, 1959), p. 51.

[21] See the documentary record of Denck's stay in Straßburg, *QGT* 7, pp. 58-62.

[22] Deppermann, *Melchior Hoffmann*, p. 163 and following.

[23] For a documentary record of Kautz's activities see *Quellen zur Geschichte der Täufer*, vol. 4: *Baden und Pfalz*, ed. Manfred Hoffmann (Gütersloh, 1951), pp. 113-115. For Bucer's refutation see *QGT* 7, pp. 91-115.

[24] Jacob Kautz [Johann Cochlaeus], *Syben artickel zu Wormbs von Jacob Kautzen angeschlagen vnnd gepredigt. Verworffen vnd widerlegt mit schrifften vnd vrsachen auff zwen weg* (Without publisher or location, 1527).

the setting of the Christian society, and the authorities have the command to order and punish. The authorities play a role which God in his mercy established, and which can serve his kingdom.[25] The followers of Denck would accuse Bucer of setting up a new papacy to destroy evangelical freedom, an accusation which irritated Bucer intensely. Bucer, in return, thought that by restricting salvation to their own small circle and damning those outside their authority, the sects set up the new papacy.

Bucer's refutation of Kautz points up the attitude of the Straßburg reformers toward the so-called radicals. Bucer and Capito would find points of agreement with them, but would feel that their attitude toward authority was the gravest of errors. In this they were at one with the city council. On July 27, 1527 the council issued its first ordinance against the Anabaptists, condemning only their attitude toward authority and warning the populace against them. Kautz, who came to the city in 1528, was prosecuted according to these laws, and ordered to be placed in the tower.[26] After a long period, in which the preachers sought to change his opinions supporting adult baptism, Kautz was expelled from the city in November 1529, under pain of physical punishment should he return.[27] For the reformers of Straßburg the inner church of the spirit as promoted by Denck and Kautz denied the legitimacy of the outward church in the world, which is made up of pious holy people whose new and eternal life is indeed inward and unseen, but who always live with others who are not born of God. The community of love, which is formed in the world with unbelievers in its midst, is threatened by Denck's and Kautz's split between the true inner Church and the outward church, as well as by adult baptism and sect building. The Straßburg reformers were willing to go to great lengths to insure their teaching against this threat.[28] The council did not share the reformers' theological sensitivities, but was equally concerned about any threats to order. Had Franck been fully aware of the experiences of Denck and Kautz in Straßburg he might not have been so bold in his own publications, or at least have foreseen what awaited him. The air may have been freer in Straßburg, but

---

[25] *QGT* 7, p. 109. For an analysis of Bucer's views on authority see Marijn de Kroon, *Studien zu Martin Bucers Obrigkeitsverständnis* (Gütersloh, 1984), esp. p. 9 and following and pp. 24-36.

[26] *QGT* 7, p. 163.

[27] *QGT* 7, p. 250.

[28] See the refutation of Kautz in *QGT* 7, pp. 201-218.

there was a reform to defend, and the reformers saw enemies on many sides.

In 1527 the council expelled large numbers of Anabaptists because of their threat to authority. In 1528 the first Imperial mandate was issued against Anabaptism, making rebaptism punishable by death. In south and middle Germany two hundred Anabaptists were executed.[29] Numerous Anabaptists chose Straßburg as a refuge,[30] many of these coming from Augsburg and bringing with them the apocalyptic ideas of Hans Hut. In 1529 Melchior Hoffmann entered the city, and though originally welcomed by the reformers as an ally against Luther in the Eucharistic controversy, he soon came into conflict with Bucer. It was in Straßburg that Hoffmann developed his apocalyptic teachings, and it is likely the Augsburg Anabaptists became some of the followers of Hoffmann. The city council may have contributed to the spread of these ideas with their expulsion of more moderate Anabaptist leaders such as Kautz. This, coupled with the food shortages and inflation that hit Europe in the late 1520's contributed to the reception the apocalyptic ideas of Hoffmann found among the Anabaptists of Straßburg.[31] These Anabaptists would be perceived as an even more extreme threat by the reformers of Straßburg. In addition to the increasingly radical character of Anabaptist sects in Straßburg, there were also external pressures which rigidified Straßburg's treatment of heterodoxy. The sacramentarian controversy, and the defeat of Zurich and the death of Zwingli in 1531 began to move Straßburg into closer alliance with Wittenberg and the evangelical princes, which also worked against the policy of relative tolerance.[32] The council, while attempting a reconciliation with the Lutheran princes, was more susceptible to the arguments for sterner measures against the Anabaptists. This policy did not fully emerge until 1533, but as Franck was entering the city, changes were gradually taking place which would make the city magistrates less tolerant of heterodox ideas and movements. Franck's first experience, however, was with the various groups and personalities of Straßburg's dissenting fringe.

Franck had very little sympathy with the great majority of Straßburg's dissenting community. These were split up into as many as seven main groups,

---

[29] Claus-Peter Clasen, "Executions of Anabaptists, 1527-1618," *Mennonite Quarterly Review* 47 (1973), pp. 115-153; p. 119.

[30] See Deppermann, *Melchior Hoffmann*, pp. 236-237.

[31] See Deppermann, *Melchior Hoffmann*, p. 238 and following.

[32] Klaus Deppermann, "Sebastian Francks Straßburger Aufenthalt," *Mennonitische Geschichtsblätter* 46 (1989), pp. 145-160; p 157-158.

including the followers of Denck and Kautz, the Augsburg refugees, some of whom were gathered around Hoffmann, and the followers of Caspar Schwenckfeld. Hoffmann's circle was stamped by its apocalypticism and the dream visions of some of its members. In many places in his writings Franck speaks scornfully of this sort of visionary enthusiasm, though his own teachings have points in common with Hoffmann's.[33] Franck held many ideas in common with Denck and Kautz, though he was always critical of Denck for setting his faith in the outward act of baptism. Franck praised Denck because at the end of his life he had regretted and recanted his promotion of adult baptism.[34] Kautz, too, by 1532 had given up promoting adult baptism and supported only a spiritual baptism.[35] That group of Anabaptists who had been followers of Denck and Kautz appears to have died out by 1532. Any remaining sectarian group which practiced outward baptism would not have attracted Franck in any case. Whether Franck might have interacted with the followers of Schwenckfeld is difficult to judge. Since Schwenckfeld and his followers sought to institute no sacramental practice or ban, Franck may have felt at home in their company, though it is hard to imagine him participating in a Schwenckfeldian conventicle.[36] It is doubtful Franck gave allegiance to any Straßburg group.

In keeping with his individualistic belief, Franck limited his sectarian activity to exchanges with various individuals whom he found either like-minded or susceptible to his message.[37] Among these people were Schwenckfeld and

---

[33] Sebastian Franck, *Chronica, zeytbuch und geschichtbibell* (Ulm: Hans Varnier, 1536), p. ZZv.

[34] Franck states in his *Chronica* that he hopes Denck will stand as an example to the Anabaptists as one who regretted his foolish enthusiasm, which was without a calling (p. kkiii-v). See also Franck's discussion of Denck's teachings, p. ddii-v and following, where he cites Denck as one of the founders of Anabaptism.

[35] See *QGT* 7 pp. 557-562 for documents concerning Kautz's change of heart.

[36] On these conventicles see R. Emmet McLaughlin, *Caspar Schwenckfeld, Reluctant Radical* (New Haven, 1986), p. 140, esp. footnote 71.

[37] Franck states in his letter to Johannes Campanus, "Lieber Bruder, ich kan nit all mit feder anzeygen das ich durch gottes gnad im hertzen wol begreifen hab, vnd wölt wol, das ich einmal selbst bey dir sein möcht vnd mündtlich mit dir reden. Denn ich verhoffte vil mit dir außzurichten: du hast die ohren noch nit verschlossen vnd bist noch im süchen." *QGT* 7, p. 319.

Johannes Bünderlin, most likely Christian Entfelder, and possibly even Michel Servetus. It is likely Franck first met Schwenckfeld in Straßburg in 1530 or 1531.[38] This was the beginning of a long association. It must have been something of a strained relationship, since these men were quite different. Schwenckfeld was a Silesian noble of impressively dignified bearing, accustomed to having the ear of ruling society, at first at the ducal court at Liegnitz, then of city council members and wealthy members of society in the southern German cities. He was never at home in the city setting, and after his exile in 1529 he never settled permanently in any of the cities he frequented.[39] Franck, on the other hand, was a product of these southern cities, and though educated, eked out his subsistence on the margins of society. While Schwenckfeld was reserved and temperate in his discussions of theological questions, Franck was vehement and unreserved, though both shared, in the reformers' view, an annoying persistence in the face of official disapproval. Thus they shared many of the same legal problems, and were ultimately condemned together at Schmalkald in 1540. In the minds of the reformers they were brothers in arms. Although they shared, on the surface, many beliefs concerning the spiritual nature of the Church, they came to recognize that they were basically at odds in their anthropology. Schwenckfeld was more formally influenced by Luther, and held to the belief in a completely fallen human nature before spiritual regeneration, while Franck, more directly influenced by Denck and the medieval mystics, looked to that one spark (*Fünklein, scintilla*) in the human heart which was susceptible to the fanning ministrations of God. It was over this basic difference that the two men fell out. Franck would eventually list Schwenckfeld with the Pope, Luther, and Zwingli, as people who have their own church, opinions and beliefs.[40]

---

[38] Horst Weigelt, "Sebastian Franck und Caspar Schwenckfeld in ihren Beziehungen zueinander," *Zeitschrift für bayerische Kirchengeschichte* 39 (1970), pp. 3-19; p. 3, places the meeting in 1531, though he states, pp. 3-4, footnote 4, that Schwenckfeld traveled from Silesia to Straßburg in 1529, possibly by way of Nuremberg, and the two may have met at this time. R. Emmet McLaughlin, "Schwenckfeld and the Straßburg Radicals," *Mennonite Quarterly Review* 59 (1985), pp. 268-278; p. 270 places the meeting in 1529, using as evidence the statement in *QGT* 7, p. 301 that Franck was in Straßburg from autumn 1529 and forward. As stated earlier there is no hard evidence that Franck was in Straßburg before 1531, though it seems likely he arrived sometime in 1530.

[39] See the depiction of McLaughlin, *Caspar Schwenckfeld*, pp. 123-125.

[40] Sebastian Franck, *Weltbuch*, p. hii-v. Though published in 1534, Franck mentions the volume in the first edition of the *Chronica* (1531), raising the

Though many have considered Schwenckfeld a great influence on Franck,[41] it is hard to lend much credence to this view. Franck's views on the spiritual church and on tolerance were already set by 1531, as evidenced by his *Chronica*. As stated, his beliefs shared many points of contact with Schwenckfeld's, not surprisingly as both were deeply influenced by Johannes Tauler and by Luther's early writings. However Franck's most distinctive ideas came from Denck and Erasmus. Franck's only mention of Schwenckfeld in his published writing is in the *Weltbuch*. Still the two men retained a certain respect for each other, and found a certain commonality of purpose. Franck was not one to associate with those he considered beyond the appeal of his message. They shared a spiritual and political exile, first from the church formations of the day, and then from the principalities and powers. This alone would have created a certain understanding.

With Johannes Bünderlin, Franck shared not only exile, but a common spiritual faith. Bünderlin had fled his native Austria in the face of the persecution of the new heresy by Ferdinand; he was baptized in Augsburg, perhaps by Denck himself, and eventually made his way to Straßburg.[42] On March 16, 1529 he was interrogated, along with a number of other Anabaptists, concerning their gathering.[43] Previous to this he had published two books in Straßburg,[44] and later would send to press two more.[45] It is not clear how long he stayed

---

possibility that he came to his opinions on Schwenckfeld early on. Of course this comment may be a later addition made in the light of Franck's Straßburg experience and later interactions with Schwenckfeld.

[41] Most recently Meinulf Barbers, *Toleranz bei Sebastian Franck* (Bonn, 1964), pp. 33-38, 98-104, esp. p. 104.

[42] Alexander Nicoladoni, *Johannes Bünderlin von Linz* (Berlin, 1893), p. 105; *QGT* 7, pp. 231-232.

[43] *QGT* 7, pp. 232.

[44] *Ein gemeyne berechnung vber der heyligen schrifft innhalt* (Straßburg: Balthasar Beck, 1529); *Ausz was vrsach sich Gott in die nyder gelassen vnd in Christo vermenschet ist* (Straßburg: Balthasar Beck, 1529).

[45] *Ein gemayne einlayttung in den aygentlichen verstand Mosi vnd der Propheten* (Straßburg: Balthasar Beck, 1529); *Erklerung durch vergleichung der Biblischen geschrifft* (Straßburg: Balthasar Beck, 1530). For a bibliography of materials on and works by Bünderlin see Ulrich Gabler, "Johannes Bünderlin," *Bibliotheca Dissidentium*, vol 3, ed. André Séguenny (Baden-Baden, 1982), pp. 9-42.

in the city. He was in Constance in early 1530, though his movements otherwise are not known. He made a great impact on Franck, partly through his writings, but also, it appears, through personal contact. In his 1531 letter to Campanus, Franck recommended Bünderlin and his books in glowing terms.

> I am sending you here a book [probably the one published in 1530] by my brother in faith...I promise you, he is a marvelously learned, God-fearing person, entirely dead to the world, who has a baptism that I with my entire heart wish also to receive.[46]

Franck goes on to say how Bünderlin has seen through the pharisaical learned, and has learned to see beyond the letter of the Scripture. This is all fairly remarkable for Franck, who spoke coolly, when at all, about his contemporaries. Only Erasmus receives accolades of similar warmth. A perusal of Bünderlin's writings explains Franck's enthusiasm. Many of Franck's most closely held beliefs were put forward by Bünderlin, particularly in the *Erklerung* of 1530, which Franck most likely was recommending to Campanus.

Bünderlin's writings betray the influence of Denck. His first published work, *Ein gemeyne berechnung*, is his longest, and puts forward many of the themes particular to Denck's spiritualism. According to Bünderlin God is spirit and life, and humans have his image, his seed, his son, his kingdom, in them. God must be understood according to the spirit. He distinguishes the inner from the outer word, which determines his method of interpreting the Scripture. The Word of God is not equivalent to the letter of Scripture, but must be understood according to its inward revelation. Christ came not to set us free through his physical life and death. We must observe the basis and cause of his mission. Christ points to the fullness of God, which can be in us just as it was in him.[47] Bünderlin's second work betrays his Neo-platonic world-view, not unexpected in a disciple of Hans Denck. Here Bünderlin lays out his version of salvation history. God created out of himself, first making the angels, then, a little lower and later, humans. In them he set his image, and warned them against sin. Adam forgot this warning, and brought about evil. The image of God in man suffered. God, though, was in no way responsible for this evil.

---

[46] "Ich sende dir hie meines bruders im glauben büchlein...Ich sag dir zu: er ist ein wunderbarlich gelehrter, gotforchtiger mensch vnd der welt gantz abgestorben, mit wölches tauff begere ich auch von gantzen hertzen geteufft zu werden." *QGT* 7, pp. 317-318.

[47] Ulrich Gäbler, "Johannes Bünderlin," gives a synopsis of each of Bünderlin's works. I have used this for the discussion of Bünderlin's first three works; for *Ein gemeyne berechnung*, pp. 27-31.

The problem now for humans is their flesh, which distracts them from the Spirit of God speaking within them. In the Old Testament God gave outward judgment through the law, and pointed humans to the inner spiritual gift. Christ, too, gave this outward witness. God's purpose, though, is to speak to us inwardly through his true Word. This has been made clear outwardly by the example of Christ, though it was known inwardly, albeit hidden from view, in the Old Testament, just as the law still operates inwardly through the New Testament.[48] Bünderlin's third book, *Ein gemayne einlayttung...*, is a good example of the allegorical interpretations used by the spiritualists, as he lays out the meaning of Moses and the prophets as an allegory of the New Testament.

It was in his fourth work that Bünderlin definitively turned his back on his former Anabaptist colleagues. He begins by stressing the primacy of the inward revelation, the outward standing only as a witness. God allows the physical world and human desire for the things of the world in order to bring judgment and suffering, so that humans will turn away from the flesh to the spirit.[49] Christ came as a witness to this, for Israel needed this outward sign that the law was done away with in the spirit. The outward practices are no longer needed, not even those of the Apostles, for the spirit has been given. The Church fell into ruin soon after the Apostles' time as it set up all sorts of outward practices and a gathered community. The outward practices, such as baptism, are of no use, but should be understood spiritually. The godly belong to no outward group or sect, but will remain unrecognized till the end of the world.[50] Bünderlin's books stand as a condemnation of any sectarian activity, physical baptism—adult or infant—and all attempts to gather the community of God. Like Denck before him, Bünderlin's spiritualism led him to separate from all sectarian groups.

Most of Bünderlin's ideas resonated with Franck's own thought. Bünderlin is much more programmatic than Franck, but at one point or another Franck would repeat ideas on God's act of creation, the fall of Adam, the Old Testament and the function of law, Christ's earthly mission, the distinction between outward and inward, the spark of the soul, and many other points which were at one with Bünderlin. As we shall see, with Franck these ideas were developed much more extensively, and given a more complicated historical perspective, but it is clear that he learned a great deal from Bünderlin.

---

[48] Gäbler, "Johannes Bünderlin," p. 31-35.

[49] Johannes Bünderlin, *Erklerung*, pp. Av-v, Biiii-v to Bv, Bvi.

[50] Gäbler, "Johannes Bünderlin," pp. 41-42.

Franck's eclectic mind collected ideas from thinkers of various traditions and with various purposes, throwing them in the pot and trusting in God's Spirit to provide the higher meaning. In Bünderlin, though, he encountered, and recognized, a mind truly sympathetic to his own. One cannot make any definite statement concerning which ideas came from Bünderlin, since they shared so many common influences—Denck, Tauler, Neo-platonism—but the direction of Franck's thought could only have been reinforced by his encounter with Bünderlin.

The other noted spiritualist whose stay in Straßburg coincided with Franck's was Christian Entfelder. Entfelder's life is even more obscure than Bünderlin's. This is a tribute to his ability to avoid the eye of the authorities. His name does not appear in the Straßburg records, but a note in what was likely his first book places him in Straßburg as of January 1530.[51] Most likely he came there from Moravia in 1529, where in 1526 he had served as preacher to an Anabaptist gathering.[52] Though it is mentioned that he was associated with Bünderlin,[53] evidence is lacking. Certainly, though, their faith was compatible. Entfelder's name does not show up in Franck's writings until 1538, when Franck quotes a long passage from the book *On the Recognition of Christ and God*.[54] It is safe to assume that Franck, at the very least, became familiar

---

[51] Christian Entfelder, *Von den manigfalten im glauben zerspaltungen* (Straßburg?, 1530?). "Geben zu Straßburg/ den 24 Januarii Anno 1530." P. Eviii. For a bibliography on Entfelder see André Séguenny, "Christian Entfelder," *Bibliotheca Dissidentium*, vol. 1, ed. André Séguenny (Baden-Baden, 1980), pp. 37-48. For a brief discussion of Entfelder's works, and the few details known of his life see André Séguenny, "A l'origine de la philosophie et de la théologie spirituelles en Allemagne au seizième siècle: Christian Entfelder," *Revue D'histoire et de philosophie religieuses* 57 (1977), pp. 167-182.

[52] George Williams, *The Radical Reformation* (Philadelphia, 1962), p. 267. See also Entfelder's own "Beschlußred/ an die brüder zu Eywarschütz..." in *...zerspaltungen*, p. Evi to Evi-v, where he apologizes for his withdrawal from this place.

[53] Williams, *Radical Reformation*, p. 267, "Entfelder removed to Strassburg, where he was briefly associated with Bünderlin." Williams does not say on what basis he makes this statement.

[54] "Christianus Entfelder im Büchle/ von der Erkanntnus Christi vnnd Gottes/ im druck außgangen." Sebastian Franck, *Die Guldin Arch* (Augsburg: Heinrich Steiner, 1538), p. Eeiii-v; a long quote follows. The book referred to is Entfelder's *Von Gottes vnd Christi Jesu vnnsers Herren erkandtnuß* (Without date, location or publisher).

with Entfelder's writings during his stay in Straßburg, if not with Entfelder himself. Even more than Bünderlin's, Entfelder's ideas have direct correspondence with Franck's. Some have depicted Franck as the most consistent spiritualist of the sixteenth century, but really this title should go to Entfelder, who develops in his work a Neo-platonic spiritualism of remarkable consistency.

Entfelder's first book, on the fragmentation of belief, develops a theme we have already encountered in Franck's translation of the Turkish chronicle. Here, however, Entfelder concentrates on the division of baptism. Entfelder was not oblivious to the danger to life and limb to which the Anabaptists subjected themselves when they withdrew from the world. According to Entfelder, the Anabaptists direct themselves toward God, in and for the sake of grace, more earnestly than others, yet they do not wait for the true grace. That is a main cause of many errors.[55] Entfelder saw them as being drawn by Satan from their superior place of passivity (*gelassenheit*).[56] Then they become tied to outward ceremonies, so that it appears they have never received God.[57] Entfelder recommends patience rather than action. Just as God waits for each person's surrender with great forbearance, so also should everyone await their reception by God with patience, in spiritual poverty.[58] This leads Entfelder to observe how many who wish to be learned never enter the school of the true master, but mix human and godly artifice and do not distinguish God's Word from man's, taking in much more than is offered and thus falling into all kinds of errors.[59] Entfelder states, "the kingdom of God does not stand, to be sure, in words, and much less in the writing of the dead letter."[60] This leads him into a denunciation of the learned.

> When, however, human reason, with its earthly cleverness, comes over the Holy Scripture, like a spider over the flower, then understanding does not remain one. For there will be as many senses

---

[55] Entfelder, ...*zerspaltungen*, p. Aii-v to Aiii.

[56] Entfelder, ...*zerspaltungen*, p. Aiii.

[57] Entfelder, ...*zerspaltungen*, p. Aiii.

[58] Entfelder, ...*zerspaltungen*, p. Av-v

[59] Entfelder, ...*zerspaltungen*, p. Av-v.

[60] "Das reich Gottes steht ja nit inn worten/ vil weniger inn der schrifft des todten buchstaben." Entfelder, ...*zerspaltungen*, p. Avi.

and understandings as there are heads.[61]
He emphatically distinguishes the living Word from the written word, and states
that the living Word does not only open the written word, but also the mysteries
of God.[62] The written word is merely a witness to the living Word. When it is
used as something more than a witness contradictions arise within Scripture, just
as they do in all human endeavors.[63] Spirit must speak with spirit.

He now moves on to speak of the four most prominent sects which have
arisen among those that call themselves Christian. He indicates the spiritual
meaning of baptism and Eucharist, and then relates how the various sects get
caught up in debate over the words, creating a virtual Babel.[64]

> Meanwhile everything that is not united with the one God,
> through the one Jesus Christ, in the one Holy Spirit, is divided;
> each refers first to themselves, is a Papist, a Lutheran, a Zwing-
> lian, or a Baptist (as they are called by the world). If his heart
> knows nothing about this division, then which among us has never
> been attached to one or more of these parties?[65]

Entfelder concludes with his only solution, to be still before the Lord, test all
things and in godly fear retain what is good, avoiding all heated human enthusi-
asms. The truth is itself strong enough.[66]

> I have therefore not wanted to state this, as if people did not al-
> ready know what abominable inverted religion, what dangerous
> times, what a powerful danger we are in; for the world has sung
> and spoke, preached and written for ten years now without any
> betterment. But I would wish that all who read this be provoked

---

[61] "Wann aber nun die erd klug menschliche vernunft über die hailigen
schrift kumpt/ wie die spinn über die blumen/ so kan jr verstand nit ainig
bleiben/ Dann als vil köpff/ als vil sinn/ als vil sinn/ als manigerley verstand."
Entfelder, ...*zerspaltungen*, p. Avi-v.

[62] Entfelder, ...*zerspaltungen*, p. Avii.

[63] Entfelder, ...*zerspaltungen*, p. Avii.

[64] Entfelder, ...*zerspaltungen*, p. Biiii-v.

[65] "Dieweyl alles das nit mit dem aynigen Got durch den ainigen Herren
Jesum Christum/ In den ainigen Hailigen gaist warhafft verainigt/ zerspalten
ist/ so merck ain yeder zum ersten auff sich selbst/ Er sey Bäptisch/ Luterisch/
Zwinglisch oder Taufferisch (also werden sy ja bey der welt genannt). Ob sein
hertz vmb kain zerspaltung wiß/ Dann wellicher vnter vns war nye mitt disen
partheyen/ ainer oder mehr verhafftet?" Entfelder, ...*zerspaltungen*, p. Bvii.

[66] Entfelder, ...*zerspaltungen*, pp. Cv to Cv-v.

to think more earnestly with me, how they are headed into spiritual and physical danger, how one might ease the wicked times and might moderate the evil days in the Lord.[67]

Except for its mild tone one might mistake this tract for one of Franck's.

Entfelder's tract *Von Gott vnd Christi Jesu...Erkantnuß*, which Franck quoted in his *Guldin Arch*, gives a Neo-platonic account of creation, which is only hinted at in Denck, and nowhere clearly stated in Franck. His aim is to absolve God from all responsibility for sin, a theme dear to both Denck and Franck. According to Entfelder, God desires to be recognized, though he forces no one to do this, for this would be against the model of love, which he himself is. God is good, and desires that this good be spread, not in himself, but in others. Thus creation occurred, both of things seen and unseen.[68] Humans, though, became divided, hence God, in order that his creating be not in vain, must portray himself as divided, so that humans might again be brought into unity.[69] God works in the world in order to draw all things back to him.[70] God does this through his Word.[71] Entfelder goes on to discuss the human way of understanding, which is captive always to the physical visible world; this world can help humans understand what the real is, as a painted picture does, though it is not the thing itself.[72] However, humanity becomes used to the visible, and elevates it above God himself.

Thus also these people, the more learned they become, the more turned about they are, when they look upon the spiritual things

---

[67] "Vnd das hab ich nit darumb wöllen erzölen/ als man es zuvor nit wüßte/ inn was grewlicher verkerter religion/ inn was gefärlichen zeit/ inn was strenger gefängknuß wir seind/ weils die welt nun wol zehen jar singt vnd sagt/ schreibt vnd predigt on alle besserung/ sonder damit ich alle die dises lesen werden/ verursachte/ mitsampt mir ernstlicher zu bedencken/ wie sich doch in solchen seel vnnd leib gefär zuhalten sey/ wie man die arge zeit lösen/ vnd die bösen täg im Herrn miltern möchte." Entfelder, *...zerspaltungen*, p. Eii.

[68] Entfelder, *Von Gott vnd Christi Jesu...*, p. Aiii.

[69] Entfelder, *Von Gott vnd Christi Jesu...*, p. Aiii.

[70] Entfelder, *Von Gott vnd Christi Jesu...*, p. Avi.

[71] Entfelder, *Von Gott vnd Christi Jesu...*, p. Avi-v.

[72] Entfelder, *Von Gott vnd Christi Jesu...*, p. Bii-v.

with an entirely earthly understanding.[73]

"For I have had to experience, unexpectedly, praise God," says Entfelder,

> through all sects, what the letter without the spirit, enthusiasm without understanding, is capable of ...Seek the Lord himself, without any mediator, in the Lord himself; for as he is to himself, thus approach him.[74]

This attitude Entfelder promotes in his third book, *Von warer Gotseligkayt*, enjoining people to renounce the world, be still before God, and suffer for God, as Christ did, awaiting the day of the Lord.[75]

Entfelder, along with Bünderlin, has been recently depicted as developing the spiritualist dimension of Denck's thought in a highly consistent manner, a development which Denck's ideas favored.[76] Thus one movement within south German Anabaptism favored a religious world view which came to deny the relevance of any outward forms of church life. Entfelder and Bünderlin reflect very well this influence of Denck. But their importance for understanding Franck is more than simply as an exemplification of the spiritualist strain in the thought of sectarian and extra-church movements of the period. Entfelder's version of salvation history was most congenial to Franck's own spiritualist creed. Specific formulations in Entfelder—the depiction of the learned as turned about, the definition of all churches, including the Roman, as sectarian, and the condemnation of this, the exhortation to test the spirit of all things, and to watchful vigilance—are similarly formulated and expressed in Franck's writings. Franck's faith must have been fairly well developed when he first encountered Entfelder's writings, but these would have provided for him a powerful reinforcement of his views, one more witness of the inner spark. Entfelder's influ-

---

[73] "Also auch die/ so ye gelerter/ ye verkerter werden/ wann sy sich am gaistlichsten achten/ gar irdisch gesinnet werden..." *Von Gott vnd Christi Jesu...*, p. Bv.

[74] "Dann ich/ Gott lob/ durch alle Sect/ vnversehens erfaren muß/ was buchstab on gaist/ eyfer on verstand vermögen...Such ain yeder den herren selbst/ on all Element/ in jm selbst/ weyl er jm ist so nahent." *Von Gott vnd Christi Jesu...*, p. Cvi.

[75] "Wacht/ betet/ seind nüchter/ dann jr wissend weder tag noch stunde." *Von warer Gotseligkayt*, p. Aviii.

[76] See Packull, *Mysticism*, chapter 7, esp. p. 156.

ence has frequently been passed over in discussions of Franck,[77] but his thought corresponds as closely to Franck's as any figure of the period. It is difficult not to come to the conclusion that Entfelder's writings, along with Bünderlin's, served to reinforce and clarify Franck's own thought during his Straßburg period.

Another figure who is mentioned often in the same breath with Franck is the controversial Spaniard, Michel Servetus.[78] Franck mentioned Servetus' tract on the errors of the Trinity to Campanus, stating that he favored the Spaniard over the view of the Roman church.[79] Given Franck's theology of the inner Word, coupled with his conviction that the church fell from the truth soon after the time of the Apostles, his inclination toward Servetus is not surprising. Certain emphases in the two men's thought are similar. Servetus conceived of Christ as being eternal as the Word of God, which animated and supported all of nature, and which was present in Jesus the man in its fullness. In the same way we too can share in God's being. We can be deified as Jesus was, though not as perfectly. Servetus saw the early church fathers, such as Irenaeus and Tertullian, promoting his own view of the Trinity, though he felt that by the Council of Nicea the church had fallen into corruption with its abominable view of the Trinity. Franck's own view of church history followed the same lines, though he took these ideas to greater extremes. Servetus' anthropology was to a certain extent congenial with Franck's. The idea of the human capacity for regeneration which has its locus in the soul—the soul sharing with God a capacity of being—is not dissimilar to Franck's emphasis on the inner spark. We shall see that Franck even on occasion promotes a view of Christ as the animator of the natural world, the essence of all essences, which may be a borrowing from Servetus, though he could have received it from other sources. He never fully coordinated or reconciled this view with his polemic against the physical world as the kingdom of the Devil, and with his radical spirit/world split. While the

---

[77] Peuckert does not mention Entfelder in his study, nor does Teufel or Dejung. On the other hand André Séguenny, *Spiritualistische Philosophie als Antwort auf die religiöse Frage des XVI. Jahrhunderts* (Wiesbaden, 1978) traces the influence of Denck on Franck, and the development of spiritualism, through Entfelder; see esp. p. 23.

[78] My discussion of Servetus' thought is drawn from Roland Bainton, *Hunted Heretic: The Life and Death of Michael Servetus* (Boston, 1953), esp. chapters 2 and 3.

[79] "Die römischen kirch stelt drey personen in einem wesen. Ich wolt lieber mit dem Spanger halten." *QGT* 7, p. 322.

concerns of Servetus, or Paracelsus, attract Franck's attention, they never stand at the center of his vision. Thus, as with Paracelsus, the influence of Servetus must be judged marginal. Franck does not bring Servetus' name up in his publications, though this may be only a reticence in the face of the authorities' unanimous disapproval of Servetus' highly unorthodox opinions. Bünderlin and Entfelder, of all the Straßburg radicals, spoke most directly to Franck's concerns.

The environment of Straßburg had the effect of ripening Franck's views. Franck had doubtless encountered most of the opinions entertained by the Straßburg sectarians. The sheer variety in this city, though, must have impressed upon him the extent of the breakup of the visible church, and the presence of like-minded spirits must have provided the opportunity to sharpen his own convictions and formulations. Though Straßburg did not harbor a multitude of witnesses to Franck's own faith, the few it did harbor provided adamant arguments against all the visible sects. During his Straßburg period Franck composed a number of expressions of his own thought, the most forthright being his letter to Johannes Campanus.

By 1531 the considerations and influences which had been moving Franck away from all outward forms of religion had been fully absorbed. As Franck wrote his letter to Campanus in February of that year, he had come to some very extreme views about the history of the church, the legitimacy of all the gathered bodies of believers, and the value of all the fathers and saints of the church. Servetus' theologizing, his attack on the dogma of the Trinity which had involved the person of Christ and the legitimacy of the church's earthly form, had caused great consternation among the learned. He managed to offend the whole spectrum of theological opinion, from the staunch defender of Rome, Cochlaeus, to Luther, and the irenic Oecolampadius, his onetime host. Franck's criticism went beyond dogma. The problem in Franck's view was that the church was hopelessly fallen, from the Apostles' time to Franck's own day, and fell progressively further every day. Had the full breadth of Franck's teaching reached the ears of the learned, his fate might have been that which eventually overcame Servetus, a possibility of which Franck was aware. Thus he wrote plainly only to someone such as Campanus, a person whose writings placed him completely outside the orthodox school.[80] We are fortunate this letter was preserved, as it provides great insight into Franck's mood as he embarked on

---

[80] For a bibliography of works by and on Campanus see André Séguenny, "Johannes Campanus," *Bibliotheca Dissidentium*, vol. 1, pp. 13-35.

his idiosyncratic career as a lone witness to the truth.[81] Franck opens his letter by congratulating Campanus that he has spoken out against the doctors of the church rather than share in their errors.[82]

> For all the renowned doctors whose writings now remain are the wolves whom Paul, in the spirit, foresaw would rush in soon after his own departure into the company of the Lord, and whom John calls Antichrists, who departed from the Apostles while they yet lived, and marched out, indeed are not from them, to which likewise their actions especially testify; I do not doubt this. For the works of Clement, Irenaeus, Tertullian, Cyprian, Chrysostomum, Hilary, Cyril, Origin, and others are full of nonsense, having a different commission that the spirit of the Apostles, being full of laws, earthly things, and things wholly of human invention.[83]

Franck states his certainty that everything became turned about, such that the

---

[81] The transmission of this document is complicated. Two translations have come down, a middle Dutch and a high German. These are published in *QGT* 7, pp. 301-325. More recently a copy of part of the Latin original was found in the Austrian National Library, codex 10364, and was published; Bruno Becker, "Fragment van Francks Latijnse Brief aan Campanus," *Nederlands Archief voor Kerkgeschiedenis* N.S. 46 (1963-1965), pp. 197-205. This contains a little over half the text, up to the middle of page 315 in the *QGT* 7 documents. The Dutch tract dates the letter Feb. 4, 1541, the German tract simply 1531. Though at one time in dispute, the date can be placed with some certainty in 1531. Franck's references to Campanus own book, to Bünderlin's book, and to Servetus' book would make little sense in a letter written in 1541, ten years after the fact. Also the opinions expressed by Franck in the letter accord well with his views expressed in other writings around the year 1531. Peuckert's arguments for a 1541 dating, p. 594 and following in his biography, are not persuasive. For other opinions placing the letter in 1531 see *QGT* 7, p. 325; Hegler, *Geist und Schrift*, p. 50 and following; and Ozment, *Mysticism and Dissent*, p. 145.

[82] Bruno Becker, "Fragment van Francks Latijnse Brief," pp. 199-200; *QGT* 7, p. 302. I will quote from the Latin when possible. As the Latin text is only a copy, of unknown distance from the original, I will also refer to the Dutch and German translations and indicate any variance in their rendering of the text.

[83] "Nam omnes iactari doctores quorum exemplaria nunc restant, lupos esse quos Paulus mox post suum discessum in gregem domini irruituros, spiritu praevidit, et quos Ioannes Antichristos vocat, qui iamiam vivis adhuc apostolis, ab ipsis desinentes egressi sunt, sed qui non erant ex ipsis, non ambigo, id quid vel eorum factus testantur. Nam mox Clementi, Iranaei, Tertulliani, Cypriani, Chrysostomi, Hilarii, Cyrilli, Origenis et aliorum opera plena sunt deliramentes, et plane humanis inventis." Becker, p. 200; *QGT* 7, pp. 302-303.

outward church of the Lord was laid to waste by Antichrist and soon after the time of the Apostles was taken up into heaven, lying hidden in the Spirit and the truth, so that there has been no external collected church nor sacraments for fourteen hundred years.[84] The misuse and abuses of the church show the Antichrist's work. Franck explains to Campanus how the original sacraments which were instituted by God must now be known in the Spirit.

> For as one spirit is the teacher of the New Testament, so he alone baptizes and ministers to all things, namely in spirit and in truth.[85] And as the things of the Church are pure spirit, and everything consists in spirit, so law, father, spirit, clothes, bread, wine, sword, kingdom, life and everything consist in spirit, but nothing externally.[86]

He speaks now of the one Spirit who baptizes with fire and spirit those who believe and are obedient to the inward Word, wherever they may be.[87] Franck includes here Turks and Greeks, barbarians, lord and servants—all who perceive the light.[88] Franck is blunt— all outward things and ceremonies have been done away with and are not to be reerected, although many attempt just that. The Church will remain till the end scattered among the heathen.[89] Franck upbraids the learned—"the wolfish doctors of true ignorance and apes of the apostles of the Antichrist"—for their errors.[90] Franck does not limit his comments to the doctors and fathers of the Roman church. Many today numbered

---

[84] Becker, p. 200; *QGT* 7, p. 303.

[85] There is a problem with the Latin text. One or more lines have been lost, as both the Dutch and German texts give similar readings which cannot be gained from the Latin. I have consequently translated from the German at this point.

[86] "Iam ipsum ut doctor est Novi Testamenti unus spiritus, ita baptisator et omnia, [German: "eben also teuffet er auch allein vnd bedienet all ding allein, nemlich in geist vnd warheyt."] et ut ecclesia res est mera spiritualis, et tota consistit in spiritu, ita legem, patrem, spiritum, vestem, cibum, vinum, gladium, regnum, vitam et omnia in spiritu, nihil autem externe." Becker, p. 201; *QGT* 7, p. 305.

[87] Becker, p. 201; *QGT* 7, p. 306.

[88] Becker, p. 201; *QGT* 7, p. 306.

[89] Becker, p. 201; *QGT* 7, p. 306.

[90] "Quae omnia ignoravere lupi illi doctores et simiae apostolorum Antichristi." Becker, p. 202; *QGT* 7, p. 307.

among the evangelicals, he says, would restore the Mosaic kingdom in place of the Pope's priesthood.[91] With their teaching, certain evangelicals at the court put the sword into the hand and thus throw oil in the fire.[92] Franck sees this as a grave error, as it introduces force into religion, a theme he would pursue throughout his later writings.

Franck points out the problem posed by the continued existence of division in the outward church.

> Supposing that the outward baptism, Eucharist, and the whole Church of Christ still stood, or it be possible to retrieve; without doubt there is one Eucharist, faith, Gospel, God, and Christ in the one Church, which is his bride. For it is not possible that the one and indivisible God, with Christ, grace, and his sacraments be in dissimilar churches. Thus it is certain, if Luther baptizes, then Zwingli does not baptize in his church. If the Pope Baptizes, or certain Anabaptists, then none of the other who are not of their party or church baptize, or for that matter do anything but scatter, since they are not gathered with Christ.[93]

"If one [Church baptizes]" Franck states,

> I ask, where is it? Is it not that which is in India, Greece, Armenia, the German lands, Rome, Saxony, or in the Alps? I believe therefore it is none of those, but all have run without being called.

Franck's conclusion is that they are all true servants of the Antichrist.[94] Why would God reinstitute a sacrament that is against his essential nature, which is inward and spiritual, Franck asks, when he himself has been for over fourteen-

---

[91] Becker, p. 202; *QGT* 7, p. 307.

[92] Becker, p. 202; *QGT* 7, p. 308-309.

[93] "Deinde si baptismum, coena et tota ecclesia Christi externa stat adhuc, aut ea repetere licet, certe una est altem, eucharistia, fides, Evangelium, Deus, Christus in una illa sponsa ecclesia. Neque fieri potest ut unus idem et individuus Deus cum Christo, gratia et sacrementis suis in disparibus sit ecclesiis. Unde certum est, si Luther baptisat, Zuinglius in sua ecclesia non baptisat. Si Papa baptisat, aut certe anabaptistae, certe nullus aliorum qui non sunt de eo numero et ecclesia baptisat, vel aliquod facit, sed dispergit, ut qui cum Christo non colligit." Becker, p. 204; *QGT* 7, pp. 312-313.

[94] "Si una: rogo quae? Non ea quae in India, Graecia, Armenia, Germania, Roma, Saxonia vel in Alpibus est? Credo ergo nullam eorum, sed omnes current non vocate...deinde ex propriis ut loquunter ita baptisant quoque et ecclesiam dispersam colligunt ex propriis non iussi, Antichristi veri." Becker, p. 204-205; *QGT* 7, p. 313.

hundred years the teacher, bread, baptizer, in spirit and in truth.[95] "Now all occurs in truth, which previously symbols signified."[96] When things are fully known in the spirit, of what use are the external things, which are for children? Franck scolds Campanus for concerning himself with the outward church, a fruitless undertaking.[97] "Let the Church stand in spirit," says Franck.

> View as your brother all Turks and heathens, wherever they may be, who fear God and act righteously, and are taught and inwardly drawn by God, even if they have never heard of baptism or even any history or words of Christ himself, but have only received his power through the inward Word.[98]

It is at this point he recommends to Campanus Bünderlin's book.

The preceding is Franck's constructive effort. But Franck receives much of his energy from his conviction of the corruption of the church and the world, and he ends his letter with a spirited denunciation of those in the pulpit. Franck informs Campanus that no true word of Christ is recognized on earth by those who present the falsified word to the swine and hounds, the common folk. Thus their sermons bear no fruit.[99]

> [They] spew out the word according only to the letter, not according to the godly understanding, and foul it with human filth. For they know no other word to speak except the written, and of no other teaching but their evangelical.[100]

Franck's hope is in the movement of history toward its consummation.

---

[95] Becker, p. 205; *QGT* 7, p. 314.

[96] "iam omnia in veritate fiant, quae priora symbola saltem significarunt." Becker, p. 205; *QGT* 7, p. 315. The Latin breaks off at this point, so I shall be quoting from the German henceforth.

[97] *QGT* 7, p. 316.

[98] "Darum stehe ab von solchem fürnemen vnd laß die kirch gottes im geist bleiben vnter allen völckern vnd heiden...Achte auch für deine brüder all türcken vnd heiden wo sie seien, die gott förchten vnd wircken gerechtigkeit, gelehrt vnd inwendig gezogen von gott, ob sie schon nimmer von dem tauff, jha von Christo selbst nimmer kein history oder schrifft gehort, sonder allein sein krafft durch das innerlich wort in sich vernommen." *QGT* 7, p. 317.

[99] *QGT* 7, p. 320-321.

[100] "kotzen das wort aus allein nach dem buchstab vnd mit menschendreck besudelt, nit nach göttlichen sinn. Denn sie wissen auch von kein ander wort zu sagen denn das schrifftlich ist, vnd von keinen andren lehrern denn von ihnen euangelisten." *QGT* 7, p 321.

For light, resurrection, Christ, truth, last judgement, damnation, recognition of God, Gospel, belief, love, and all things are very different or have a much different meaning than has been taught up to this time; but in the end learned ones will arise among the people and shall give understanding to many. Daniel 12.[101]

Here is Franck's hope and his vision of his prophetic mission. But first, as he tells Campanus, everything learned from the Papists, or Luther, or Zwingli must be put behind. God has hidden his truth in parables and similes so that only those taught of God may understand.[102] Franck's view of the church sweeps away all religious authority and all the teachings of the church, and constructs the temple of God in the human heart. A new priesthood emerges which finds its witness not in outward sacraments but in a life lived upright before God. Franck is well aware that his teaching will find no sympathy among the authorities. He concludes his letter by warning Campanus not to let his letter come before the swine or hounds and thereby prepare an untimely cross or make an untimely harvest out of him. "Many have brought themselves to the gallows through their thoughtless or untimely chatter," cautions Franck.[103] Though Franck's public actions were often bold, there was no martyr complex at work in him.

The letter portrays well the mature views of Franck. He would go on to explore the consequences of his faith in the inward Word, but he would never significantly change his views. The church fathers would be used as authorities in his later writings, but Franck used them for his own purposes, to promote his own message, to defeat the apologists of the Roman church on their own terms. His denunciation of history, sacred and profane, evident in all his writings, was in fact imbedded in his splitting of the physical and the spiritual. Franck's literary activity was motivated by the regenerate seed which lies hidden at the center of the human soul. The letter shows his own expectations for the few en-

---

[101] "Denn hell, aufferstentnus, Christus, warheit, letzt gericht, verdamnus, erkentnus gottes, evangelium, glaub, lieb vnd alle ding seint vil ein anders oder haben vil ein ander meinung denn biß anher alle gelehrt haben, sonder am end werden gelehrte aufstehen im volck vnd sollen vilen verstant geben, Daniel xij." *QGT* 7, p. 321.

[102] *QGT* 7, pp. 323-324.

[103] "laß doch diesen brieff nit für die hundt vnd säwe kommen, das du mir nit ein vnzeitlich creutz bereitest vnd machest ein vnzeitlich ernd aus mir. Denn vil durch ihr vnbesünnen vnd vnzeitlich schwetzen brengen sich selbst an galgen." *QGT* 7, p. 324.

lightened souls who have listened to the word within themselves: they will bring about the new teaching which will mark the end of time. The letter also exhibits Franck's pessimism about the historical process as a continuum. For Franck the church has been laid to waste; he hints at the corruption of the political powers. The seed of regeneration may lie in humans, but it is completely covered over by the outer world, and the world witnesses to nothing but the absence of God's truth and spirit. When Franck wrote this letter he must have been well advanced in his study of the course of history, which, in Franck's mind, was the testimony to this absence.

Franck published this testimony, the *Chronica, Zeytbuch vnd geschychtbibel* on September 9, 1531.[104] The final product was the result of up to a year's worth of printing activity,[105] for the *Chronica* is a huge work, running five hundred thirty-six folio leaves. It was Franck's labor of love, and one can only imagine how pleased he was with the results. Especially compared to today, when book production is completely mechanized, the time and effort put into a volume the size of the *Chronica* would be prodigious. And if Franck is remembered for any work, it should be for his *Chronica*. In terms of its content it is not a book of great originality. Franck borrowed his material from other chronicles, especially from Hartmann Schedel's famous *Nuremberg Chronicle*, a fact Franck clearly acknowledged.[106] But the story of the movement of history from Adam forward offers Franck the opportunity to provide the marginal gloss which opens up the text of history. For Franck history, like Scripture, is not just the dead letter of events which occurred in the past, but is a living sign of God, there to instruct those who know how to read it. Franck is convinced he has the insight to look upon the events and read their significance.

Franck opens the book with a wide-ranging introduction. He carries no great hope that his *Chronicle* would open the eyes of the world. As he explains, the world never learns before it is too late to recognize or be concerned for its condition, or, as he picturesquely states in the margin, "the world first shuts the

---

[104] "Getruckt zu Straßburg. Durch Balthassar Beck vnd vollendet am fünfften tag des Herbstmonats. Im Jar MDXXXI." *Chronica, Zeytbuch vnd geschychtbibel* (Straßburg: Balthasar Beck, 1531), p. VViiii. I have used both the 1531 and the 1536 editions of the *Chronica*. Most quotes are drawn from the 1536 edition, but have been checked against the 1531.

[105] For a discussion of the time involved in printing a book see Miriam Chrisman, *Lay Culture, Learned Culture* (New Haven, 1982), p. 5.

[106] Franck includes a full list of his sources at the beginning of the book.

barn when the cow is outside."[107]   Nevertheless he exhorts his reader to see "here in this chronicle, through God's agency, the wonders of the wondrous God and learn to recognize the nature of his work."[108]   His work is nothing else but what Mary sings,

> He has shown strength with his arm, he has scattered the proud in the imagination of their hearts, he has put down the mighty from their thrones, and exalted those of low degree, he has filled the hungry with good things, and the rich he has sent away empty.[109]

Such is God's work in history. This is no partisan judgment, says Franck. He will present everything in his *Chronicle* temperately and without judgment.

> We write neither against nor for anyone, but of foreign acts and words presented out of foreign books...I also do not want to show what I believe or hold of anyone, nor add my judgment, but simply recount the acts of everyone, and offer them up for the reader to decide.[110]

Franck considered himself to be impartial, in the sense that he belonged to no party or sect—Lutheran, Zwinglian, Papist, etc. He is bound only to Christ, to which his reason is obedient.[111]   What Franck means by this is that Christ is the inner Word which interprets all the he, Franck, comes to know. Christ's Word is the enlightened center of his heart which allows him to read the mes-

---

[107] "Die welt that erst den stall zu wenn die ku heraus ist." *Chronica* (Ulm: Hans Varnier, 1536), p. aii.

[108] "Demnach sihe doch durch Gott hie in diser Chronick wunder von dem wunderbarlichen Got vnd lerne die art seiner werck erkennen." *Chronica* (1536), p. aii.

[109] "Da finstu nichts dann das Maria singt Lu. 1.   Er hat gewalt geubt mit seinem arm vnd die hoffartigen in ires hertzen sinn zerstrewet.   Er hat die gewaltigen vom stul gestossen vnd die nidrigen erhoben.   Die hungrigen hat er mit güttern erfult vnnd die reichen leer gelassen." *Chronica* (1536), p. aii. The passage is Luke 1: 51-53.

[110] "wir weder wider oder für niemand schreiben/ sonder frembde that vnd red/ aus frembden büchern anzeigen. Will auch hiemit niemandt...auch nit/ was ich glaub/ oder von yemand hatte/ anzeigen/ vnd mein urteil/ zu sich setzen/ sonder bloß/ ...eines yeden geschicht erzelen/ vnd dem leser zu urteiln auffopffern..." *Chronica* (1536), p. aii-v.

[111] "Ich kan/ Gott hab lob/ als ein unpartheischer/ vngefanger/ ein yeden lesen vnd bin keiner sect oder menschen auff erden gfangen...vnnd bin in keines menschen wort geschworen/ dann Christi meines Gottes vnd mitlers/ in des gehorsam ich mein vernunfft allein gefangen nimm." *Chronica* (1536), p. aiii-v.

sage of God's acts in history unfettered by the outward world which holds all others enchanted.

Another cause for Franck's confessed impartiality is involved in his search for the witnesses to the truth.

> For there is scarcely a heathen, philosopher, or heretic who has not made at least one good guess; thus I do not reject them but worship as refined gold and likewise find, love and honor also something of my God in heathens and heretics. For as he lets his sun shine on good and evil, so he pours out his good out over all the children of men.[112]

It is for Franck a principle of history that God's indwelling Word finds a reception within all people, so that one must investigate even heretics and heathens to find the truth. Franck is not exactly forthright in formulating the principle here. What he really believes, as shown by his letter to Campanus, is that God is most manifestly revealed in heretics, who stand as witnesses to the fleshly depravity of all institutional churches. This theme will be thoroughly discussed in his *Chronicle*.

Franck has a number of concerns he urgently wishes to address with his *Chronicle*, though the most urgent is the divisions of Christendom. As he observes in the introduction "it has now come so far that no one wants or is able to be pious for himself, but each thinks he must erect his own church, sect and separation."[113] Franck advises all to be pious for themselves and look to God's Word and works. Indeed this is the secret of viewing history.

> Look on the works of God, as David did, in silence, listening to what he is speaking inside of you; thus you will find the exegesis in the works themselves,...the results and resolution. He will lead you as Abraham from one place to another and with the acts preach in and through all creatures, so that the entire world and all creatures will be nothing but an open book and living Bible for

---

[112] "Dan es ist kaum ein heyd/ Philosophus oder ketzer/ der nit etwa ein gut stuck erraten hab/ dz ich nicht darumb verwirff sonder als feingold anbett/ vnd gleich etwas auch mein Gott in heiden vnd ketzern find/ lieb vnd ehre. Der wie er sein Sonn lesset scheinen über gut vnd böß/ also schüt er seine gute aus über alle menschen kinder..." *Chronica* (1536), p. aiii-v.

[113] "seind yetz dahin kommen/ das keiner für sich selbs mer kan oder will frumb sein/ sonder ein yeder meint/ er müß mit seinem glauben vnd frumbkeit in eigen kirchen/ sect vnd absünderung anrichten." *Chronica* (1536), p. aiiii.

you...[114]

This passage explains why Franck entitled his book a historical Bible. If instead of striving to set up churches, the learned passively experienced God in his acts in history and in people, then they would see the folly and blindness of their ways. "For in acts one finds an open example, which in Scripture is often only taught with dark words."[115] "Because now so much rests in experience," states Franck, "and we do not believe before we see, I value history far above all books of instruction; for history lives, and teaching is only a dead letter."[116] In history one can experience the judgment of God on the flesh, one learns of the folly of humankind in a living example. Defined negatively, history is the suffering and death of Christ on the cross writ large. Positively, it gives witness to the fruits of faith, and the lack thereof among the unfaithful.[117] Of course the problem still remains of seeing history with the eyes of the spirit. Whatever one is or seeks—rich and powerful or fearful and pious—one will find in the *Chronicle*.[118] The dynamic witness of history—the living sign of God's relationship to the world, both as his judgment of the flesh and his presence in the human soul—is the center of Franck's investigation.

As will be amply demonstrated in Franck's account of the past, his impartiality is not of the modern variety. He will tell you what history means. He sees it with the eyes of the spirit. But to see it this way is exactly not to be party to its outer development. The Papists, Lutherans, Zwinglians, etc., are all party to the flesh and to the history of the flesh. So are the rich, the powerful, the mob. They find in the outer course of history just what their fleshly eyes

---

[114] "Derhalb hab du auff die werck Gottes acht mit David in der stil/ zulosende was er in dir rede, Psalm lviii. so wirtt sich die auß lesung selbs finden im werck/ dem folg vnd los/ so wirdt er dich/ wie Abraham sein von einen zu dem anderen füren/ vnd mit dem werck durch vnd in allen creaturn predigen/ das dir die gantze welt vnnd alle creaturen nichts dann ein offen buch vnd lebendige bibel sein wirt..." *Chronica* (1536), p. aiiii-v.

[115] "dann im werck findt man offentlich/ was die schrifft offt mit dunckeln worten leert/..." *Chronica* (1536), p. av.

[116] "Weil nun sovil an der erfarung ligt/ vnd wir nit ee glaub/ wir sehen dann/ achte ich/ die historien weit für alle leer bucher vrsach/ die historien lebt/ die leer ist allein ein todter buchstab." *Chronica* (1536), p. av-v.

[117] "Da wirt in der that der lebendig glaub oder vnglaub im werck mit jrem früchten für die augen gestelt." *Chronica* (1536), p. av-v. "Weiter sihe auch hierinn/ wie die welt durchaus Gottes fastnacht spil sei." *Chronica* (1536), p. av-v.

[118] *Chronica* (1536), p. av-v.

will allow them to see. Franck sees the course of history without this fleshly engagement. Thus he presents what is there without the partisanship of all the churches and sects. For Franck every age is equidistant from God, in that they are all utterly turned away from him. Only the individual witnesses to the truth will stand out. This he demonstrates in the whole history of the world, from Adam to Christ, in the history of the emperors and rulers of the earth, and most glaringly, in the history of the church. Only those who are transformed in their mind by the Word of God spoken at the center of their heart—at that point where all humans are susceptible to the ministrations of God's spirit—will realize the clear message of history. Ultimately Franck writes to those who can and will see and hear.

Following the introduction, Franck divides his *Chronicle* into three main parts: the history of the time from Adam to Christ; a history of temporal rulership from Rome to 1531, focussed mainly on a chronicle of emperors; and a many sectioned account of "spiritual" affairs. The first section, dealing with the time before Christ, is a whirlwind tour, its focus divided between the Jewish and pagan world. As is his habit, Franck starts this section with an introduction. Here Franck repeats many of the same ideas offered in other places regarding the split between spirit and flesh, but he brings up some interesting witnesses for the defense of this split. "Many heathen have written very well of the one God, by means of the implanted Word and illuminating light," confesses Franck, "such as Plotinus, Hermes Trimegistus, Socrates, Diogenes, Plato, Orpheus, Sibulla, Sophocles."[119] It is revealing of Franck's sympathies the predominance of Platonic and Neo-platonic philosophers in this list. At the same time Franck introduces God, Christ, and the Holy Spirit. He describes Christ role as that of the stone tablets on which were written the Ten Commandments, which call people back to God by reminding them of the error of their ways. Christ is best known, though, according to his divine nature, since this is the best part of him.[120] Franck's discussion of the Trinity reveals just how little regard he has for any formal doctrine. The Holy Spirit is referred to as God himself, or the sweet revelation of God to the conscience, as opposed to the bitter Christ who martyrs the conscience.[121] "Christ is the beginning, his spirit

---

[119] *Chronica* (1536), p. bii.

[120] *Chronica* (1536), pp. bii-b to biii.

[121] "Der heilig geist der vom vatter durch den Sun außgeet/ ist nach viler meinung nichts anders dann gottes gnad geist vnd gunst/ ja Gott selb der ein geist ist/" *Chronica* (1536) p. biii-v. "Durch Christum ist Gott erstlich saur

the end of all things,"[122] summarizes Franck. For Franck, Trinitarian formulae are just words used to describe the Spirit which is God. Still there is no explicit denial of the creedal formulae, such as marked Servetus' work.

Having introduced the creator, Franck turns to his creation. As would be expected, Franck stresses that God set a picture of himself in all things.[123] Here he differentiates between the flesh which is created from nothing, and the spirit, the inner person, which comes from God.[124] The soul of the inner man, which is born of the spirit through the Word of God, may not sin.[125] Christians carry this new person in their flesh with great travail their life long until they die, and are thus born into eternal life through God's grace.[126] Franck differentiates, however, between the spirit which is blown into the flesh and gives it life, and the spirit which Christ gives us, and which works against the flesh. Franck provisionally distinguishes between the soul (*seel*) which is fleshly, and the spirit (*geist*), a distinction known in late medieval theology.[127] It is provisional because Franck immediately provides the disclaimer:

> concerning the soul, in summary, as with other spiritual, unseen things, nothing is certain with the fleshly, earthly, mundane, visible human being.[128]

Franck demonstrates the truth of his comments on the uncertainty of knowledge

---

vnd martert das gewissen vnd fleisch. Durch den heiligen geist ist Gott süß senfft vnd stilt das gewissen vnd geist." *Chronica* (1536), p. biiii.

[122] *Chronica* (1536), p. biiii.

[123] *Chronica* (1536), p. c.

[124] *Chronica* (1536), p. c-b.

[125] "darumb ist es war das die seel der inner Mensch vom geist durchs wort aus Got geborn ist so müs folgen das er nit sündigen mag." *Chronica* (1536), p. c-v.

[126] "Disen neüwen menschen tragen die Christen in jrem fleisch jr lebenlang mit grosser muh...bis sie im tod...durch Gotes gnad gebern zum ewigen leben." *Chronica*, (1536), p. cii.

[127] See the discussion of Karl-Heinz zur Mühlen, *Nos extra nos: Luthers Theologie zwischen Mystik und Scholastik* (Tübingen, 1972) pp. 1-8.

[128] "Von der seel ist in summa/ wie von andern geistlichen/ unsichtbaren dingen nichts gewiß bei den fleischlichen/ irdischen/ sichtigen menschen." *Chronica* (1536), p. cii.

by citing the conflicting opinions of numerous philosophers on this very question.[129] Franck has little faith that language can capture the truth which is grasped inwardly. Throughout this and other works he sets disclaimers by his speculations and compiles conflicting witnesses, knowing that those who are able to see, will see.

The great expanse of time between Adam and Moses' written account— 3686 years by Franck's reckoning—is convincing proof for Franck that God deals directly with humans without any outward means. For if Moses' is the first written account of God's dealings with humans, how did the pious before that time come to know God except through the Word of God spoken directly within them?[130] Franck would use this argument repeatedly.

Franck is not only interested in the foundation of the inner Word in humans. He also looks to the outer world of power and rulership.

> It is here to be noted that rulership comes forth from the left, godless side and evil straying children of Noah, and not from the line of Christ nor from the members of the righteous...Therefore I say, the origin of rulers is not nearly honorable and they have little praise in Scripture; and they have almost all kept a thoroughly evil house, as one sees still, that a pious prince is venison in heaven. Thus there is the saying, one could engrave all the faces of the pious princes on a ring.[131]

Franck goes on to present the evidence for this view, showing "how the authorities are a vengeance, ordered by God, and the servants of God."[132] This view is not unique to Franck; Luther, too, talks of wicked princes as a punishment for sin. The nobility, being heathens who would lift up their own name, receive the same treatment. "Virtue alone makes one noble before God, and, contrari-

---

[129] *Chronica* (1536), p. cii-v.

[130] *Chronica* (1536), p. ciii-v.

[131] This comes under the heading "wie die gewalt vnd herrschafft sey auffkommen." "Es ist auch hie zu mercken/ das die herrschafft von der lincken/ gotlosen seitten vnd übel geraten kinder Noe herkumpt/ vnd nicht von der linien Christi/ noch von den glidern der gerechten...Darumb sprich ich ist der Herren herkommen nicht fast ehrlich/ vnd haben allzumal ein klein lob in der schrifft/ vnnd haben fast all durch aus übel hauß gehalten/ wie man noch sihet/ das ein frummer Fürst wiltpret im himel ist/ also das daher ein sprichwort kommen ist/ Aller frummen Fürsten angesicht möcht man auff ein ring stechen..." *Chronica* (1536), p. cv.

[132] "Das oberkait ein raach sey/ von Gott geordnet/ vnd Gott dienerin." *Chronica* (1536), p. cv-v.

wise, what is high, noble, great, etc. before the world, that is an abomination in God's eyes."[133] The history of power is the history of God's judgment. Franck tells the Germans the use of this history: the story of the fall of Jerusalem teaches the evanescence of human power, how it cannot resist God if he chooses to punish us; weapons will not avail for anything.[134] He places all these evil deeds and acts of the powerful in the *Chronica*, not as an example, but so that people will shy away from sin.[135]

At times Franck appears to see a prescriptive use for his history writing, as witnessed by the above passage. Rulers are evil, but perhaps they can be taught. So, too, he can put up the distant past as an example over against more recent times, a relative Golden Age, as it were. This despite drawing his account of the origins of evil from the account of Genesis. He talks about the old holy fathers who were simple farmers, and how to be a farmer was considered honorable. By contrast Franck sees his age as no longer desiring to farm, half the people being idle. He adds a criticism of the traders for their actions.[136] Cutting across any prescriptive effort is his bleak eschatological vision and his understanding of humans in the flesh, which renders moot any reform effort or vision of the Golden Age. For Franck follows his comment on farming and trade with this expostulation.

> But what is one to say, the world simply must have such people, otherwise it would not be the world. Indeed one can wish that it were different, however nothing other will result than the same murderer's grave and robber's house...Therefore this history is being told now as a judgment of and witness to the world, not that it will be changed or bettered—I am certain that won't occur—but the situation will become ever more evil the longer it persists; afterwards we have to prepare ourselves, the end nears, the Lord will put an end to the world. I say this to counter certain foolish enthusiasts, those who hope with singing, speaking, writing and hard effort to persuade the world, that it become pious, and that

---

[133] "Tugen macht allein edel vor Gott/ widerumb/ was hoch/ edel/ gros/ etc. vor der welt ist/ das ist ein greüwel vor Gottes augen." *Chronica* (1536), p. diii-v.

[134] *Chronica* (1536), p. i-v to ii

[135] "Darumb setzt man gemeinlich die fürtrefflichen bösen in die Chronick/ nit zu einem exempel/...sunder als ein vogel scheühe vnd garttenleutzen/ daran wir scheühen vnd vns stossen sollen." *Chronica* (1536), p. viii-v.

[136] *Chronica* (1536), p. Bii.

it not lust, wanting to make a school of discipline and paradise out of it...In summary all is lost with the world, especially with these frantic (*ungelaßnen*) recent times; one only can let it go its way, it helps neither to anoint nor baptize until it goes to ruin.[137]

Though Franck makes various sorts of comments on the course of history, here is the most persistent vision in his works.[138] History wends its way inevitably toward destruction, because flesh will always be flesh, the world will always be the world. Though this theme will be somewhat muted in his later historical works, it is the dominant theme in the *Chronica*. The pessimism of the tract on drunkenness has only deepened.

One may condemn the sins of the ancient fathers with less danger of offending those who are living. Franck perhaps was treading on thin ice with some of his comments in his first section, but politically it was unlikely they would be cause for alarm. Franck had indicated, however, that his condemnation of rulership had universal application and in his second section he demonstrates the pertinence of his views for his own time.

The second chronicle is the yearbook of the Emperors, from Julius Caesar to Charles V, "named the new world," states Franck, which deals with "all the Roman Emperors, worldly dealings, memorable, worthy and choice histories, stories, signs, wondrous acts, wars, slaughters, campaigns, defeats, victories,

---

[137] "Aber wz sagt man/ die welt muß eitel solch leüt haben/ sy wer sunst nit welt. Es laßt sich wol an ds wünschen/ aber es wirt nit anders darauß/ als diser mördergrüb und raubhaus...Darumb sei dise histori nun zum gericht und zeugnis über sy erzelt/ nit dz sy sich endern oder bessern werden/ das ich gewiß bin dz nit geschehen wirt/ sonder die sach wirt je lenger je böser werden/ darnach haben wir uns zurichten/ es nahet zum end/ der Herr will mit der welt den garauß machen. Das sag ich wider etlicher torechten eifer/ dz sy sich mit singen/ sagen/ schreiben/ hart bemühen vnd verhoffen/ die welt zubereden/ dz sy frumm werd/ dz sy nit gelust/ wolten gern auß der welt ein zuchtschul vnd paradeiß machen/...Es ist in summa alles verloren mit der welt/ sonderlich mit diser ungelaßnen letsten/ man las sie nur jren weg anhin geen/ es hilfft doch weder crisam noch tauff/ biß sy selbs zutrümern wirt gehn." *Chronica* (1536), p. Bii.

[138] Philip Kintner's dissertation, "Studies in the Historical Writings of Sebastian Franck (1499-1542)" (Yale, 1958), gives a good discussion of the various systems which Franck employs to present the course of history. He emphasizes the lack of unity in Franck's depictions. See esp. his introductory comments, pp. 1-2.

rulerships, and regiments of the sixth and last age."[139] Franck starts his account with an introduction, where he discusses the nature of the eagle "and other wild, untamed, terrible animals" and why they are displayed on weapons and shields.[140] Franck chooses to discuss the eagle for two reasons. One, it is the form displayed on the shield of the Emperor, and thus provides a not very subtle way of depicting the character of rulers. Two, the German words for eagle (*Adler*) and aristocracy or nobility (*Adel*) bear a striking similarity, a fact Franck does not let pass unnoted. The idea is not Franck's own. For the most part Franck is translating from Erasmus' *Adagia*.[141] By setting this discussion here, at the beginning of his history of Emperors, Franck gives new emphasis to Erasmus' material. He starts by noting how the present rulers are following their heathen ancestors, as is reflected by their weapons, and he calls on them to change their heathenish nobility of the flesh into a Christian nobility of the spirit and virtue.[142] He launches then into a description of the bird.

> The eagle is alone incapable of any discipline, nor may it be domesticated or tamed by any training...The flesh feeding bird is hateful and hostile to peace, born, as it were, to rob, murder, and fight, as if it was not enough for the bloodthirsty bird that he lives from the flesh and blood of other birds.[143]

For those who ask what this bird has to do with the model of the prince as the philosophers have depicted them, Franck can only say that, while the depiction

---

[139] "der Keyser jarbuch/ oder die new welt genant/ von allen Römischen keisern/ weltliche händeln/ gedechtnüs wirdigen außerleßnen historien/ geschichten/ zeychen/ wunderwercken/ kriegen/ schlachten/ heerzügen/ niderlagen/ sygen/ herschafften/ regimenten/ des sechsten letsten Alters..." *Chronica* (1536), p. Biii.

[140] "von des adlers vnd andern wilden vnzämen freisamen thieren/ ...warum dise eben in die wappen/ schildt vnd auff die helm seien gezuckt." *Chronica* (1536), p. Biiii.

[141] "Scarabeus aquilem quaerit." See Kommoß, *Erasmus von Rotterdam*, p. 31.

[142] "damit sy jren heydinischen adel des fleisches/ in ein Christilichen adel des geystes vnd tugent verwechßlen." *Chronica* (1536), p. Cii.

[143] "Allein der adler ist zu einicher zucht nicht düchtig/ mag auch mit keyner übung gezämt oder heimlich gemacht werden...der fleisch fressend vogel des frides hassig vnd feindselig/ gleichsam zurauben/ mörden/ streitten geboren ist/ vnd gleichsam als sei es dem blutgirigen vogel zuwenig/ dz er von der andern vögel blüt vnd fleysch lebt." *Chronica* (1536), p. Cii.

is praiseworthy, one will find scarcely one or two in the chronicles who hold to this example.[144] Franck proceeds from here to lambaste further the habits and nature of eagles and princes. "The princes of this world," states Franck, "have ever persecuted the truth and right wisdom of God, as they themselves confess...has indeed even one prince believed in him? Thus not a spark of wisdom is in them."[145] Franck does not desist from this condemnation until he has made quite clear the low estate occupied by rulers. This is not the vision of a social revolutionary of Müntzer's or Hans Hut's stripe. Franck does not believe these problems will be redressed in the flesh. He pronounces judgment in order to turn the eye of the ruler away from riches and power to the Word of God within, if such a thing were possible. As Franck learned from his reading of chronicles, not much evidence existed to give one hope of convincing the princes. In fact his introduction would have far from the desired results. Franck's account of the Emperors is organized much the same as his first chronicle. The various Emperor's lives are recounted, interspersed with the few individual voices Franck considered witnesses to the truth. He starts with Christ, who ushers in the sixth age of grace, which will last till the end of the world.[146] Franck moves quickly into his account. Most of the historical depiction of the Emperors is derivative and of little interest. There are a few places of note where Franck's own voice is clear. Seneca provides the occasion for complimentary comments; he is even included in a list of Christian martyrs, undoubtedly because of his correspondence with the apostle Paul.[147] The story of Christ, the Apostles, and the early Christians provides much material to pillory the Christians of Franck's day for their soft living. Even Pilate, and Festus and Felix can be used as examples of good magistrates, who did not judge without a hearing.[148] Franck sees his own time dominated by the devil,

---

[144] "ist gleich wol lobswert/...ja in den Chronicken findt man kaum ein oder zwen/ den du zu disem exemplar darfft behalten." *Chronica* (1536), p. Cii.

[145] "...die Fürsten diser welt die warheyt vnd recht weißheyt Gottes allzeit verfolgt haben/ wie sy selbs bekennen/...Hab auch je ein furst an yn glaubt? Sogar ist kein füncklin weißheit in jn." *Chronica* (1536), p. D-v.

[146] *Chronica* (1536), p. Diii.

[147] *Chronica* (1536), p. E-v.

[148] *Chronica* (1536), p. Eiii to Eiii-v.

such that not even a breath of the truth may be heard.[149] The Donation of Constantine causes Franck to lose his impartial voice, his rage directed at the Pope, whose whole history is denounced as "sealed with lies."[150] Franck has a lower view of the Popes than of the Emperor;[151] at least the Emperor has been instituted by God to keep order and thus we should be obedient to him even if he were a Turk.[152] The Pope has no real reason or right to exist. Franck sounds very much like Luther at this point.

Franck's account of the invention of book publishing betrays his trade and his hopes.

> Through the art of printing will the long stopped up spring of godly and inexpressible wisdom and art be distributed into the community. Therefore the Germans, especially the inventors of this art, are worthy of all praise, indeed God in them, through whom God has given us this art.[153]

As Franck approaches his own age this is one of the few positive developments he finds. Mercenaries (*Landesknecht*) and syphilis, the fantastic superstitions of the papists, all reveal the darkness of the world.[154] The sack of Rome shows how God uses rogues to punish rogues.[155] The Peasant's War too shows how

---

[149] "Es seind fürwar yetzt die geferlichen zeit/ darin der zornig teüfel so zarte oren hat/ das er von der warheit nit mag hören husten..." *Chronica* (1536), p. Eiii-v.

[150] "wie fast alle bäpstliche historien mitt lugen versigelt seind." *Chronica* (1536), p. Hiiii-v.

[151] *Chronica* (1536), p. Hv-v.

[152] *Chronica* (1536),p. Mv-v.

[153] "Durch dise kunst der truckerey wirt der lang verschlossen brunn Göt-licher vnd vnaußsprechlicher weißheit/ vnnd kunst in die gemeyn außgeteylt. Darumb die Teütschen/ bsunder der erfinder diser kunst alles lobs werdt ist/ ja Gott in jm/ durch den uns Gott dise kunst geben hat." *Chronica* (1536), p. Riiii-v.

[154] For Franck's comments of the "Landesknecht" and syphilis see *Chronica* (1536), pp. Tii-v to Tiiii. For the superstitious church see the story of the Bernese monks recounted on p. Viii-v.

[155] "Also ist Gott offt mit ein buben/ den er für ein rut vnd geysel braucht/ ein andern buben straffen." *Chronica* (1536), p. Yiii-v.

God punishes those who do evil under the name of God and the Gospel.[156]

> God will truly not forget nor exempt the tyrant, as little as he has
> the peasants; he is already judged,...When we do not turn our-
> selves about, then he has his bow already drawn taut, his sword
> sharpened, and aimed...[157]

Comment on the diet of Augsburg and the inflation of the time of Charles V
leads to Franck's most explicit eschatological statements. This Diet show the
futility of all Diets, the misplaced faith of humans.

> Love has grown cold in all humans, the ax is laid to the roots of
> the tree, the punishment is already started, no one marks it, for
> the world is stricken with a deep blindness...[158]

Franck conveys a message that could compete with any prophet of doom. "All
prophecies and signs of the judgment day," cries Franck, "point with a finger to
this time of ours."[159] This last evangelical world is the worst, according to
Franck. But though Franck himself plays the role of prophet of Doom, he adds
this caution: one must test prophecies and decide if they are from God or not,
"for every age and world has its hypocrites, learned pedants, and dissemblers,
so also its prophets."[160] Still, if one will only stand silent before God, he may
speak through us. He ends on this note.

It is difficult to summarize the mass of material Franck includes in his
history. His method is compilatory, not systematic, his organization chronologi-
cal. He changes his message often, depending on what he is presenting. One
gets the sense of a mind whose mood is tied very directly to what he is presenting and the thought of the moment. His comments on printing exemplify this.
The predominant mood is clearly apocalyptic. The contemplation of rulers and

---

[156] *Chronica* (1536), p. Yiiii-v.

[157] "Gott wirt der tyrannen warlich nit vergessen noch verschonen/ so wenig
als der pauren/ vnnd ist schon im gericht...Wa wir uns nit bekeren/ so hat er
sin bogen schon gspant/ sein schwert gewetzt/ vnnd zilet schon." *Chronica*
(1536), p. Yiiii-v.

[158] "dann alle lieb ist in allen menschen erkalt/ die axt ligt an der wurtzel
des baums/ die straff ist schon angangen/ niemant merckts/ dann die welt ist so
mit dicker blindtheit...geschlagen." *Chronica* (1536), p. AAiii-v.

[159] "Alle propheceien vnd zeichen des Jüngsten tags deütten mit fingern auf
dise vnsere zeit." *Chronica* (1536), p. AAvi-v.

[160] "Dann wie alle zeit vnd welt jr gleißner/ schrifftgelerten vnd heüchler
hat/ also auch sein propheten..." *Chronica* (1536), p. BBii.

politics directs Franck to one conclusion, the age is coming to a close, the end times are near. Occasionally he will talk of the values with which one can evaluate rulers, but these qualities are always compromised, in Franck's mind, by their involvement in the visible, physical, corporeal world. Franck does not speak specifically of the next age. There is no strong Joachite influence (though he knows of Joachim and his prophecies) or Müntzerite expectation. God's spiritual kingdom will not be set in the physical world. Force will not institute the kingdom of God. And that fate which lies hidden in the providence of God will not be revealed by human words. Franck's demands for political rulers are essentially those for the Christian—enlightenment by God. The social order that would result from enlightened rule, judging by his comments in the section on inflation, would be communism based on the New Testament model. We will have occasion to discuss Franck's social thought further. But rulers who read Franck might be excused if they did not find themselves inspired. Any practical suggestions which the *Chronica* might contain are overwhelmed by pessimism about the inevitable corruption and downfall of all political forms.

Franck's *Chronica* may have been offensive to the power and the honor of political rulers. But it may have had a certain saving grace in the eyes of rulers struggling with an aggressive ecclesiastical leadership. For Franck turns next to the spiritual sword, and as he did with Emperors, lays out in bald detail the many sins and abominations of the princes of the church. This is Franck's "Third chronicle of the Popes and spiritual dealings, from Peter up to Clement VII, of faith and all sorts of spiritual things, concerning heresies, orders, councils and Popes."[161] As Franck explains in his foreword;

> Up to now we have heard, my God-believing reader, the dealings, history and tragedy of the outer world and its movements, which has been nothing but war, squabbling, blood letting, hacking and stabbing, ruling, need and all sorts of outward disasters, sword, kingdoms, and everything. Now we want to turn with God to the spiritual double world, to the devil who creeps in midday, to the pestilence and arrows which fly and destroy the day; indeed to the lost flock, which thinks itself pure and clean, and yet is not washed of its own filth, among whom go about a few Christians, like some kernels of grain in a pile of husks, like Lot in Sodom,

---

[161] "Die Drit Chronica der Bapst vnd Geystlichen handel/ von Petro biß auff Clementem den sibenden/ des glaubens vnd allerley geystlichen sachen/ kätzereien/ örden/ Concilien vnd Bäpsten betreffende..." *Chronica* (1536), p. Aa.

Moses in Egypt, and a rose among the thorns.[162]
Clearly for Franck the church is in no better shape than the world.

First of all, it seems to Franck that there are so many sects, beliefs, and judgments among the Christians, that one might begin to wonder about the one faith.[163]   Still, Franck reports on them all, "for there is scarcely a heretic so evil that he has not guessed one good thing among his errors...We all, with David, have to confess and pray, Lord would you not consider our ignorance."[164]   The uncertainty of outward things should bring a measure of humility to what we say. Yet everyone wants to damn the other, be everywhere master, the student of no one, especially of Christ.[165]   Unfortunately the inner world has the same turmoils as the outer; however it is more dangerous, for in it you may murder Christ's spirit.[166]

Franck leaves it to the reader to judge what is heretical or not, though he has included in his chronicle of heretics the best that could be obtained from the councils and the fathers, "so that I dare name the third part of my *Chronicle*...a theology and sermon in which the kernel from the fathers, councils and Popes is included."[167]   Still some of the teaching is not so good, warns

---

[162] "Biß hie her haben wir/ gottgleübigen leser/ die händel/ historien vnd Tragedi der eüsserlichen welt vnd bewegnissen gehört/ das ist nichts gewesen dann kriegen/ zancken/ blütvergiessen/ hawen/ stechen/ regieren/ nöten vnd allerley eusserlich vnglück/ schwert/ reich vnd alles. Nun wollen wir mit Got an die geistliche doppel welt hin/ an den teüfel der im mittag schleicht/ an die seücht vnnd pfeil/ die des tags fliegen vnd verderben/ ja an den verlornen hauffen/ der sich reyn vnd sauber dunckt/ vnd doch nit von seim vnflat geweschen ist/ darunder die Christen eyngemengt vmbfaren/ wie etlich körner vnder eim hauffen sprewer/ wie Loth in Sodoma/ Daniel in Babilone/ Moses in Egipten/ vnd ein roß vnder den dornen." *Chronica* (1536), p. Aa.

[163] *Chronica* (1536), p. Aa.

[164] "Dann kaum ein ketzer so bös ist/ der nit neben sein irrigen stucken ein guts errhaten hab...wir alle mit David zu bekennen vnd zubitten haben/ vnser vnwissenheyt wollest du uns herr nit gedenken." *Chronica* (1536), p. Aa.

[165] "Noch sprich ich/ vrteylt vnd verdampt ye einer den andern/ ...vnd will jederman meister sein/ niemandt zuloser vnd schuler/ sunderlich in der schul Christi." *Chronica* (1536), p. Aa.

[166] *Chronica* (1536), p. Aa.

[167] "dz ich das drit teil meiner chronick/ wol auch ein theologia vnd predig darff nennen/ darinn der kern auß den vätern/ concilien vnd bäpsten eyngeleibt ist." *Chronica* (1536), p. Aaiii.

Franck. The reader must judge. There is only one God, belief, and baptism, who has one like-minded people; the rest belong to the Antichrist.[168] The problem is that everyone reads Scripture according to the dead letter. They should first be taught by God's spirit, then Scripture will be exegeted within them, its spirit and life being in them.[169] There are so many divisions in Christendom that,

> now there are indeed alone ten varieties of Anabaptist, so that no one can say or write anything certain about them...I say this so you do not become angry when I cannot write for everyone; who could serve so many Lords?[170]

He has not meant to offend any person, but to place before the eye the tale of man's generations, that they might see how low man is. Not even the Pope has been reproached, Franck claims, for he has presented him through his own words and acts.[171]

While the above sounds very irenic and judicious, when he comes to discuss the Popes and the Roman church there is a distinct change of tone. He starts by spending numerous pages proving that Peter could not have founded the papacy. "Now behold," Franck states in summary,

> on what the Papacy rests, namely, built on simple stinking lies, and the holy city in which the abomination sits may be named a seat of pestilence. God help us all from the darkness of all error.[172]

---

[168] *Chronica* (1536), p. Aaiii.

[169] *Chronica* (1536), p. Aaiii-v.

[170] "Nun seind doch alleyn wol zehenerlei Teüffer/ das niemant nichts gewiß von jnen schreiben oder sagen kan...Das sag ich darumb/ dz du dich nicht ärgerst/ wann ich nicht für ein yeden schreiben kan/ dann wer kan sovil Herren dienen?" *Chronica* (1536), p. Aaiiii.

[171] "Gar niemandt will ich mit diser meiner Chronick angetast haben/ alleyn die fabel menschliche geschlechts für die augen gestelt haben/ dz wir daran ersehen/ wie ein armes/ bäwfälligs/ vnstäts/ finsters/ lugenhaffigs ding vmb ein menschen sey/...dann sovil den Bapst belangt/ den ich auch nicht anders tadel/ dann mit sein eygen worten vnd wercken." *Chronica* (1536), p. Aaiii-v.

[172] "Nun sihe aber/ warauff das gantz Bapstum stand/ nemlich/ auff eitel erstuncken lugen gebawen/ dz es wol Cathedra pestilentie/ vnd die heylig statt/ darinnen der grewel sitzt/ mag genannt werden. Gott helff uns allen von der finsternüß alles irrthumb..." *Chronica* (1536), p. Bbv.

Later the Popes will be termed the apostles of the devil.[173] The traditions of the Papal church come in for hard words too:

> The holy histories and lives, which Scripture has not thought [to include] I have diligently left out, because all the books of legend wander about so much that one has absolutely nothing from them which is certain; for they stink of the lies with which they are spattered with throughout; whoever has a desire for these, go buy a legend book or *Lives of the Fathers*.[174]

Franck doubts the stories of whole lands being converted, for whole people do not turn into Christians. "Human words do not alone make a Christian, but the death of the soul. Whoever is not taught in his heart by God, is lost."[175] Franck's anti-papal sentiments do not indicate a sympathy with councils: "I speak my judgment openly, that, with the exception of the first council of the Apostles, Acts 15, I think little of all the others."[176] This leads him into a long exposure of the errors and contradictions of councils. "Not to mention," Franck states, "that in many councils the truth has been openly damned as heresy."[177] In fact, the supposed heresy which was damned by the church turns up in Franck's next section as the witness to the truth.

The so-called "Chronicle of Heretics"[178] is one of the most noted of Franck's writings, justifiably so, since it is an excellent example of how he subverted the official teachings of the church. Franck said he would damn the

---

[173] *Chronica* (1536), p. Bbv.

[174] "Der heyligen historien vnd leben/ der die schrift nit gedenckt/ hab ich mit fleiß auß gestat/ weil der legend bücher allenthalb sovil umbfaren/ darzu so gar nichts gewiß von jn haben/ das es alles von lugen/ damit es durch spickt ist/ stinckt/ wer lust darzu hab/ kauff jm ein legend buch/ oder Vitas Patrum." *Chronica* (1536), p. Bbv.

[175] "menschen wort nit alleyn Christen macht/ sunder der seelen tod ist...wer nit...vom Gott in seim hertz gelert worden ist/ der ist...verdorben." *Chronica* (1536), p. Ddii-v.

[176] "Ich sag mein vrteyl frey/ das ich außgenummen das erst der Apostel/ Act XV wenig von allen halt." *Chronica* (1536), p. Lliii-v.

[177] "Ich geschweig das in vil Concilien die warheit offentlich als ketzerey verdampt worden ist." *Chronica* (1536), p. Llv.

[178] It is referred to widely in the German literature as the "Ketzerchronick," though Franck titles it "die Chronica der Römischen ketzer." *Chronica* (1536), p. Ooiii-v.

Papacy with their own words and acts, and here he takes the *Catalogue of Heretics* of the Dominican prior Bernard of Luxembourg, which first appeared in 1522, and molds his own catalogue.[179] In the foreword to this section Franck explains his project:

> You should not therefore assume, my reader, that I consider all those as heretics who I here recount and have written in the register of heretics, for should I be the judge, perhaps I might turn the whole game around, and canonize many of those and set them among those numbered blessed; for many wholly precious people are here fouled with the Roman (*romigen*) caldron of the Pope, people I consider worthy of eternity.[180]

In fact, Franck goes on to show that it is typical of the world to persecute the truth as heresy. Frankly, he says, he could not have honored Erasmus, Luther, Zwingli, and others more highly than putting them next to Jerome and Augustine in his chronicle of heretics.[181] The church and councils of old were not so crazy as the church of today, Franck states. He puts some of the old fathers and councils in the chronicle to show how far the church of his day has strayed. Many who are considered holy—Aquinas, Scotus, many of the Popes—will be judged.[182] Yet Franck's view is not quite so simple as to imply merely a reversal of the poles, the heretics being the just and the orthodox being the damned. Franck asserts, "therefore God also allows heresy to come: the lies must be in order to help probe the truth, because every opposite brings forth

---

[179] See Hermann Oncken, "Sebastian Franck als Historiker," *Historisch-politische Aufsätze von Hermann Oncken*, vol. 1 (Munich/Berlin, 1914), pp. 273-320; esp. p. 290 and following.

[180] "Du solt nicht darfür haben/ mein leser/ das ich alle die für ketzer acht/ die ich hie erzölt/ inn das zalbuch der ketzer geschrieben hab...dann solt ich vrteilen/ ich würde villeicht das spil vmbkören/ vnd deren vil canonisieren/ vnd in der heyligen zal setzen...dann gar vil theür leüt/ seind hie mit dem romigen kessel des Bapsts beschmeißt/ die ich der vntödlicheit wirdig acht." *Chronica* (1536), p. Ooiii-v.

[181] "Es ist die yetzig welt nit besser dann die vorig/ das sy es nit auch thü/ sunder nur erger/ darinn die auff das höchst als ketzerey verfolgt müß werden." "Darumb stehn sy [Erasmus, Luther, et al.] hie mit grossen ehren in disem register/ ich het sy nit baß mögen nottieren in der gantzen Chronick/ vnd an kein eerlichere statt losieren..." *Chronica* (1536), p. Ooiii-v.

[182] *Chronica* (1536), pp. Ooiiii to Ooiiii-v.

and promotes its antithesis."[183] There is a dialectical necessity to the conflict of heresy and truth. There is no simple resolution of the matter by casting heresy as truth. Each heresy though, as a testing of the truth, is to be valued as an outward witness to God's truth. Through heresy no outward truth is allowed to set itself up as God's eternal truth. Thus the church fathers and councils are included in the "Chronicle of Heretics," since they express a truth contrary to that of the orthodoxy of Franck's day. Over and above the play of heresy and truth is the truth God reveals within the one who yields himself to God. This truth, which Franck clearly feels is revealed within himself, allows him to differentiate among the many heresies. Some heresies are valued because they counter the truth promoted by the outward church contemporary to Franck. Other heretics are witnesses to the truth which Franck himself has grasped, which resists equating any outward truth with the truth of God.

Franck turns next to the application of his theory of heresy. The writings of the church fathers such as Ambrose, Augustine and others are included, though of course only selections which serve the purpose of confounding the papists. The teaching of the councils are displayed, plus some of the communitarian teachings of the earliest Popes, though he is still not willing to concede that any of them were Christians.[184] Franck is pleased to note that the church now teaches the exact opposite of what was put forward by the early councils.[185] Part of Franck's list includes groups whom Franck himself would condemn as heretics. Jewish heretics comprise one of these condemned groups. "They are all heretics who use writings for the help of their belief and sect." This the Jews do, and Franck charges that their Talmud "is no different from the heathen Koran and the Papist's spiritual law, a book full of lies."[186] Mo-

---

[183] "Derhalb auch gott die ketzerey kummen laßt/ vnd die lug zur prob der warheyt sein muß/ darauff zu helffen/ weil yedes gegentheyl sein gegensatz herfür bringt vnd fürdert." *Chronica* (1536), p. Oov.

[184] *Chronica* (1536), p. Rr to Rrii.

[185] "So man den oberzölten capiteln entgegenwirft diser argument/ Es syen vil Canones die dz gegen teyl sagen." *Chronica* (1535), p. Zzv-v.

[186] "Ketzer seind alle die/ die falschlich jrer sect vnd glauben auß der geschrifft jren behelff nemen. Also seind die Juden billich auch ketzer zunennen/...Greg. ii vnd Inno. iiii haben beyden jren Talmut lassen verbrennen/ der mit ketzerey übersäet vnd durchspickt ist/ vnd nichts anders dann der Heyden Alcoran/ vnd der Papisten geystlich recht/ ein buch voller lugen." *Chronica* (1536), p. dd vi.

hammed is cast as the Antichrist's predecessor.[187] Magicians and necromancers are condemned for confusing the powers of God and the devil.[188] The evangelical heretics come in for denunciation also. As Franck broadly defines them,

> [they] are all the supposed evangelicals who put forward a false appearance of the Gospel (by which they want to be praised and known), and teach either hypocritical, sham, self fabricated works, or likewise the law without faith, or teach a false, cold, fruitless faith without works.[189]

These are the people who look to the letter of Scripture, and understand the Gospel in a fleshly way.[190] He groups the evangelical heretics with the Antichrist,[191] the chief of all true heresies, to whom Franck devotes a whole section. Heretics form the body of Antichrist, just as Christians form the body of Christ.[192] Some think the Antichrist will come speaking from the word and pointing to other sects, just as the Papists, Lutherans and Anabaptists do.

> God has hidden his Word, mysteries and will under the letter, and not made a path with open letters so that the swine, world, and Antichrist fall over them with unwashed feet.[193]

In Franck's view the forces of the Antichrist are widely dispersed, being all those who vest the Word of God in outward words, creeds, Scripture and law.

---

[187] "Machomet der falsch Prophet auß Arabia/ erstlich ein kauffmann/ zuletst ein teüfels Apostel/ vnd des Antichrists vorlaufer." *Chronica* (1536), p. eeiii.

[188] *Chronica* (1536), p. eeiii.

[189] "Seind alle vermeynten Euangelischen/ die einen falschen schein des Euangeliums (davon die wöllen gerümpt vnd gnent sein) füren/ vnd entweder heüchlerischen/ scheinende/ selb erdacht werck/ oder gleich das gsetz on glauben/ oder ein falschen/ kalten/ fruchtlosen glauben ohn werck leren." *Chronica* (1536) p. aavi.

[190] *Chronica* (1536), p. aavi.

[191] *Chronica* (1536), p. bb-v.

[192] "Antichristus ist das haupt aller ketzer/ welche sein leib seind/ wie Christus der seinen..." *Chronica* (1536), p. Qq.

[193] "Gott hat sein geheymniß/ willen und wort vnderm buchstaben verborgen/ vnd nit also mit offnen buchstaben an weg für die saw/ welt vnd Antichrist gelegt/ dz er mit vngewaschnen fussen fall." *Chronica* (1536), pp. Qqiii to Qqiii-v.

There are numerous heretics with whom Franck is in obvious sympathy, considering them true lights of the Church. The chief figure in this group is Erasmus. Mention has been made of Erasmus' influence on Franck. Here Franck gives a rapturous introduction to Erasmus for single-handedly bringing good letters back to Germany.[194]   He then launches into an account of the many heretical teachings of Erasmus—his casting doubt on the fully divine nature of Christ, his understanding of the Eucharist, his proof of confession as a human invention, his statement that the evangelists' memories erred in places, and so on. This goes on for almost ten pages, as Franck consistently brings out those places where Erasmus' thought is closest to his own spiritualism.[195] Franck intended this as his highest compliment, as he noted in his introduction. No inquisitor could have done a better job of demonstrating the questionable orthodoxy of numerous of Erasmus' views. Ludwig Hätzer and Hans Denck, both of whom were dead by this time, also have Franck's sympathy.[196]   Others whom one might expect to find, such as Schwenckfeld, Bünderlin or Entfelder were not included. Perhaps in their cases Franck saw the wisdom of not drawing the attention of the authorities to the living by praising their heresy, no matter how good the intentions.

There are at least two sections in the "Chronicle of Heretics" which are somewhat ambiguous in their expressions. These deal with Luther and the Anabaptists respectively. Franck devotes more pages to these two than to any other heresy. His section on Luther has been cited as the prime example of Franck's impartiality.[197]   It bespeaks Franck's own consciousness of Luther as founder of a movement which, although mired in fleshly things, points to the faith which Franck himself has achieved. Franck introduces the section by stating,

In the year 1519 arose Martin Luther, doctor of the Holy Scrip-

---

[194] *Chronica* (1536), p. Zzvi to Zz vi-v.

[195] *Chronica* (1536), pp. Zzvi-v to aav.

[196] On Hätzer see *Chronica* (1536), p. eeii; on Denck see p. ddii-v and following.

[197] See Teufel, *"Landräumig"*, pp. 42-46. Teufel's enthusiasm for Franck here (as in not a few other places) gets the best of him. His assertion that Franck has Luther "in seinem Besten und Tiefsten verstanden" (p. 45), begs the question of Franck's various expressions in the "Ketzerchronick." Teufel subsumes too much of Franck's effort and intention under the label of the impartiality and relativity of the spiritualist belief.

ture, of the Augustinian order, a man blessed of the world (*welt-selig*), richly artful, and learned of the Scripture.[198]

Though this rings of high praise, Franck usually associates learnedness with spiritual blindness, hypocrisy, and fleshly mindedness. Franck goes on to tell the story of the movement initiated by Luther, how he defied the Pope and translated the Bible into German, so that people began to read the Scripture and to see the Pope's knavery.[199] He recounts, too, the breakup of this movement around the time of the Peasants' War, as Müntzer, Karlstadt, and Zwingli began to write against Luther. They did not want the bread to be the fleshly body of Christ, but Luther would not budge from the letter of Scripture. Thus they separated from each other.[200] "Yet," Franck continues,

> these parties are, in all those things that are against the Pope, thoroughly unified; also in the main points, and almost in all facets of faith. Only in a few points, which many do not hold for articles of faith, are they at odds, such as the sacraments, baptism, original sin, images, and assurance of the spirit and faith. Now this Luther had introduced an entirely new theology and faith into the German land.[201]

Franck's analysis shows to what extent he can follow the new theology and faith. As long as it remains inward, and directed against the outward church of Rome, there is unity. Franck's list of adiaphora contains a good number of the items which make up the dogma and the outward practice of these churches, Lutheran, Zwinglian, or Roman. When he says many do not hold these for articles of faith, Franck refers to himself and only a few others. Clearly the parties at odds

---

[198] "Anno tausent fünffhundert neüntzehen/ Da entstund Martinus Luther/ der H. Schrifft Doctor/ Augustiner Ordens/ ein weltselig/ Kunst reich/ schrifftweiß Mann..." *Chronica* (1536), p. eev.

[199] *Chronica* (1536), p. eev.

[200] "Nachmals vmb die beürischen auffrur/ fieng an Thomas Müntzer/ D. Andreas Carlstatt/ Huldaricus Zwinglius wider jn zuschreiben...die wolten nicht/ das in dem brot/ oder das des herren brot der wesenlich leiblich leib Christi wer. Als nun Luther von dem Büchstaben nit wolt weichen/ sünderten sie sich von ein ander ettwas ab..." *Chronica* (1536), p. eev-v.

[201] "Doch seind dise parthei in allem dem das wider den Bapst ist/ durch auß eins/ auch sunst in der haupt sach/ vnnd schier in allen stucken des glaubens/ allein in etlichen puncten/ die will nit für Artickel des glaubens achten/ vneins/ als von Sacramenten/ Tauff/ Erbsünd/ Bildern/ vergewissung des geysts vnd Glaubens. Nun diser Lutherus hat ein gantze newe Theologie vnd glauben in Germaniam gefürt..." *Chronica* (1536), p. eevi.

held them to be essential. To the extent that Luther's new theology and faith stood in opposition to the papacy, by finding the locus of God's grace within the individual, Franck is also a spiritual co-member. To the extent, though, that this movement involved itself in the establishment of an outward church with an outward faith according to the letter, which describes, in Franck's mind, the whole movement from the period of the Peasants' War, it fell into strife and became a fleshly faith, just one of many sects.

Franck proves this point with numerous pages of quotes from Luther. These deal with various statements of Luther on God and Christ, Scripture and the Word of God, sin and grace, etc. Franck means to show flaws in Luther's teaching. First, Luther's statements are contradictory and point up the problem of faith understood according to the letter. Luther has Christ as truly Christ both according to the flesh and the spirit.[202] The Anabaptists took Luther's understanding of Scripture according to the letter and used it against him to prove the illegitimacy of infant baptism.[203] Luther made salvation dependent on faith, then promoted baptism for those without faith.[204] Franck is not promoting adult baptism but showing the contradictions of a fleshly faith. His other charge is that Luther promotes faith to the detriment of a sanctified life; "that one let all works fall away simply believe and do nothing."[205] This was also Franck's description of the "evangelical heresy." Franck here is charging Luther with one more contradiction. Faith that does no works, that does not lead to a sanctified life, is no faith at all.

Franck ends his Luther section on an irenic note. It is this statement that is normally bought forward to prove Franck's impartiality.[206]

> As I can neither understand, grasp nor believe his theology, thus I do not want to judge. For I have undertaken to write about many beliefs or heresies, not to judge, therefore I let each stand before the Lord, and allow each to be true to what he believes or teach-

---

[202] *Chronica* (1536), p. eevi.

[203] *Chronica* (1536), p. ff.

[204] *Chronica* (1536) p. ffii-v.

[205] "Das man allen werck fallen laß/ allein glaub vnd nichts thu." *Chronica* (1536), p. ffii.

[206] See Teufel, *"Landräumig"*, p. 46.

es.[207]

While this has a very appealing ring to the modern ear, Franck's impartiality is of a different sort than the word as it has been construed in the modern world. Franck is not a member of any party on which he writes. He is a party of one. Clearly, though, Franck does believe he himself has received something from God, something more true than what others have received. The evidence is in the outward witness, the contradiction of word with word, and word with deed. The grossest violators are the papal party, persecutors of truths they themselves have proclaimed in earlier times, confusing flesh and spirit. The charge is made here, too, against Luther. Franck's list of heretics contains both witnesses to the truth and transgressors. There is a certain witness in Luther's teachings, but also a great transgression of the spirit by the flesh. Franck is gingerly charging Luther with this. Franck must know the problems Karlstadt had by throwing the gauntlet at Luther's feet. Franck is using the "Chronicle of Heretics" to situate himself among the parties—member of none, judge of all.

The last section of interest in Franck's "Chronicle of Heretics" concerns the Anabaptists. Franck exhibits a measure of sympathy for this persecuted minority. He confesses that many pious people have been and are in this sect.[208] Yet many of the problems of the other sects are magnified among the Anabaptists.

> Although all sects are divided among themselves, yet especially the Anabaptists are strife-torn and disunited among themselves, such that I know nothing certain and final to write about them. Some hold their rebaptism or baptism to be so essential, that they count no one who is without it for blessed, nor offer him their hand, nor recognize him for a brother. Some hold baptism as not necessary at all, that they are happy about all pious people, and consider them as brothers; these people however are few.[209]

---

[207] "wie ich sein theologey etwan weder glauben/ fassen oder verstehn kan/ also will ichs nit vrteylen/ dann ich mir von vieler glauben oder ketzerei zuschreiben/ vnd nit zu iudirieren hab fürgenommen/ darumb laß ich jn vnd ein jeden seinem Herrn stehn/ vnnd gib eim jeden was er glaubt/ oder lert/ selbs zutreffen." *Chronica* (1536), p. gg-v.

[208] "ich für war acht vnd gantzlich halt/ das vil frommer eynfeltiger leüt in diser sect gewesen/ vnd noch seind..." *Chronica* (1536), p. kk-v.

[209] "Wie wol alle secten in jn selbs zerspalten seind/ so seind doch sunderlich die Teüffer also vndereinander vneynig vnd zerrissen/ dz ich nichts gwiß vnd endlicht von jn zuschreiben weiß. Ettlich halten jren widertauff oder tauff so nötig/ dz sy on den niemandt selig zalen/ grüssen/ die hand bieten/ oder für ein bruder erkennen. Etlich halten jn nit so gar für nötig/ dz sy auch umb

Franck likely had Bünderlin and Denck, among others, in mind as examples of the latter type of Anabaptist. With the rest of the Anabaptists, Franck's impressions are decidedly negative. He states, "there is also, as I have experienced, especially great hypocrisy with many of them."[210] These people are just like those among all sects and orders. They are exclusionists who find Christians only in their own church.[211] Some make an idol out of suffering and seek after it.[212] But not all have gone astray among them, according to Franck.

> Some speak here sharply, and to my mind not unjustly, how one must hold still before God, stand passively (*gelassen*) before all things in a free Sabbath, without any appropriation and possession, that God have his work in us, who alone recognizes that which is of him in us, and crowns nothing in us but his own work. It seems to me, though, that they could do this well without separations and sects, each for himself.[213]

Franck suggests that Denck should stand as the example of one who regretted his foolish enthusiasm.[214] He goes on to list the seven errors of the Anabaptists—that they form sects, are divided in faith, that they judge others out of self-love, make rules and promote monkishness, pronounce false prophecies, and exegete the Bible according to the letter.[215] The Anabaptist sins are practical-

---

all frumm gern seind/ vnd für die brüder achten/ der seind aber wenig." *Chronica* (1536), p. kk-v.

[210] "Es ist auch/ wie ich erfarn hab/ sunderliche grosse heuchlerei bei vilen..." *Chronica* (1536), p. kkii.

[211] *Chronica* (1536), p. kkii.

[212] *Chronica* (1536), p. kkii-v.

[213] "Ettlich reden hie scharpff/ vnd meins bedunckens nit unrecht/ wie man Got muß stilhalten/ aller ding gelassen stehn im freien Sabbath/ on alles annemen vnd eygenthumb/ das Gott sein werck in uns hab/ der alleyn das sein in uns erkenne/ vnd nichts dann sein eygen werck in uns kröne. Diß gedeücht mich aber kündten sy wol on absunderung vnd secten thun/ ein yeder für sich selbs..." *Chronica* (1536), p. kiii-v.

[214] *Chronica* (1536), p. kkiii-v.

[215] "die parteisch absünderung...jr zerißner vneiniger glaub/ in sovil secten zertrent...das frevel/ vermessen frech vrteil/ so sy meer auß eygner lieb vnd wolgefallen/ dann auß den vrteyl des geyst/ über die ander fellen...jr gesetzlich regel/ müncherei...dz jr ding nit kumpt/ das sy verheyssen...welchs eins falschen Propheten prob vnd zeychen ist...das sy die schrifft allenthalben nach dem buch-

ly the same as Luther's or the papists; all have attempted to form outward churches with the attendant fleshly error that goes with it. Ultimately the best Anabaptists are those who stop worrying about their baptism or forming sects, such as Denck. At that point they are hardly going to be Anabaptists anymore, no more than Franck was himself. Franck can sympathize with the simple earnestness of some Anabaptists, but that is about all. Those who espouse views similar to Franck's lead him to wonder why they would remain in a sect.[216] Franck distances himself from the Anabaptists as he does every other party.

With the Anabaptists in mind Franck ends his "Chronicle of Heretics" by discussing whether heretics may be legally executed. He uses Luther to prove the point that the Gospel cannot be defended with the sword. This view is inevitable considering Franck's concept of the Church:

> Let the Church remain a spiritual, unseen gathering, which we believe but do not see, free in the spirit and faith, ruled by the Holy Spirit through the Word, which is sundered from no one, as is exemplified in Christ.[217]

It is hard to imagine any outward force entering in to maintain or preserve the purity of this church.

The theory and the practice of the "Chronicle of Heretics" are somewhat at odds. Though Franck would profess to be presenting merely those voices that have spoken in the church and which have been denounced as heresy, in this way probing the papists' teaching and allowing the reader to judge if the Roman church is not hoist on its own petard, he cannot refrain from using the forum to gauge the heresies themselves. For the most part Franck does present without comment. But especially concerning contemporaries, in those parts of the "Chronicle" he composed himself, Franck measures the distance between his own spiritual belief and the heresy in question. Heresy does stand as a witness to the fleshly corruption of the church, as embodied in the party

---

staben...außlegen..." *Chronica* (1536), p. llii-v.

[216] In fact most did leave behind all organized religion. Bünderlin, Entfelder, Denck, Kautz all rejected the Anabaptist sect building of their past. Schwenckfeld was a special case. Even Schwenckfeld's attenuated conventicle building was deemed illegitimate by Franck, and led eventually to their mutual rejection of each other.

[217] "Derhalb laß man die kirche ein geistliche/ vnsichtbare versamlung/ die wir glauben vnd nit sehen/ frei im geist vnd glauben vom H. geyst durchs wort regiert/ bleiben/ die von niemant abgsündert ist/ wie wir in Christo ein fürbild haben..." *Chronica* (1536), p. lliiii.

that defined heresy, the Papal church. Franck's own inner revelation stands as the gauge of the heresy, its own fleshly/worldly corruption. Perhaps Franck's intention was merely to present the material, but he sets up a scale: the true fleshly heresy is the fleshly Antichrist and the so-called spiritual heresy is Christ. Franck does not leave readers without a guide by which to judge heresy. All sects are truly heretical,[218] and the one true spiritual Church is heresy in the eyes of the world.

Franck moves from his "Chronicle of Heretics" to a chronicle of the genealogy of the various sects and orders, practices and rites, and institutions of the Roman church. On occasion he turns to the Jews to show how they, too, are divided. Franck's intent is always to show how the church—all faiths and sects—have deviated away from their original charge and purpose, have fallen, and been divided up, especially the church of Rome. The downward curve of history and the church is given its significance in Franck's final section,

> the eighth and last part of the Pope's chronicle, of the preceding
> signs, prophecies, and visions, signifying the Pope, the great day of
> the Lord, and the Antichrist with his body; also on the death and
> end of all things.[219]

Reading the signs of the time is just as with a pregnant woman, says Franck, who knows neither the day nor the hour, yet she knows enough so that she prepares.[220] Franck then gives thirty-six signs of the end times, all of which have correspondence to an account in the *Chronica*. "It seems to me," Franck states, "that everything is now vacillating."[221] Franck confesses a reluctance to speak too specifically about these things because of their uncertainty, but maintains that there will be a perfect spiritual, heavenly kingdom.[222] These things are hidden in God, speculation is fruitless. On this note he ends the book, reminding his readers of the two deaths, one that is physical and awaits

---

[218] *Chronica* (1536), p. nniii.

[219] "Das acht vnd letst teyl diser Bapstilichen Chronica/ von den vor-gehenden zeychen/ Propheceyen/ vnd gesichten/ den Bapst/ den grossen tag des Herren/ vnd den Antichrist mit seinem leib bedeüttend/ auch von dem todt vnd endtschafft aller ding." *Chronica* (1536), p. zzii.

[220] "wie eyn schwanger weib weder stund noch tag weyß/ so weyß sie doch die refier/ darauff sie sich dann richt/ einkaufft/ vnd mit allen dingen darzu nötig/ versihet." *Chronica* (1536), p. zziii.

[221] "Ich meyn/ es ghe yetz im schwanck." *Chronica* (1536), p. zzv.

[222] *Chronica* (1536), p. zzv.

all, one that is spiritual and awaits the godless.[223]

Franck's *Chronica* ultimately works as a dark prophesy and condemnation of human history and the supposed earthly Church of Christ. The former is judged as the school of sorrows and judgment of God to turn humans toward the spirit, the latter is the body of the Antichrist which mistakes flesh for spirit and thus vests in outward things what is only to be found in the spirit. Both realms are completely turned about in themselves, so that all which they value is the opposite of the truly good. This reversal is expressed when humans appropriate all things to themselves rather than passively allow God to work all things within. Thus history heads downward, with perhaps a brief hiatus with Christ and the Apostles, and hope for a change resides in the day of the Lord, the Judgment Day, when God will create a new spiritual kingdom. As with so many things, Franck does not investigate this idea, but leaves it simply as the denouement of the entire work.

The *Chronica* is the largest of Franck's many large works, and it would require many volumes to investigate all its various references and angles. In order to comprehend the events surrounding the publication of this work, however, it is most important to recognize the confusing range of perspectives in the work, and its power to offend the sensibilities of the ecclesiastical and secular authorities. No casual reading will reveal the entire denunciatory effect of the work. One must read each of the introductions to the various sections in order to perceive the subversive possibilities of the work. Franck, though, did not write unaware of the potential problems his work might cause him. His letter to Campanus shows him aware of the dangers involved in his views. His policy, voiced often in the *Chronica*, of allowing the reader to judge, though frequently violated, was partly a matter of prudence, albeit also expressive of his own independence and conviction that words were in vain without first having an enlightened listener. The church of Rome was an open target, thus his vehement denunciation. His equation of political rulers and the eagle was perhaps impolitic, but he was only saying what was already published in Erasmus' *Adagia*. The "Chronicle of Heretics" was aimed mostly against the papal party, though any follower of Luther reading the section on "evangelical heretics" would recognize the target. His section on Luther is judiciously understated, though on careful reading the rebuke is clear. His words on Zwingli are strictly

---

[223] "von zweyerley tod/ einen deß fleischs/ den alle menschen versuchen müssen/ den andern des geists/ vor Gott sterben nach des seel...vnd diß ist der ander todt/ der dem leiblichen folgt/ allen gottlosen..." *Chronica* (1536), p. zzv-v.

neutral,[224] on Erasmus highly laudatory. Franck must have considered the work safe from charges of subversion. He made no attempt to hide his authorship or the printer. In this Franck and his printer made a serious misjudgment.

The reaction to the publication of the *Chronica* was not long in coming. On December 18, 1531 the city council resolved, in response to a complaint by Erasmus, to put Franck in the tower. The specific complaint is twofold; first, the Emperor's majesty was dishonored, a charge in which Erasmus was implicated, and second, that Erasmus was quoted as a heretic. The council ordered that Erasmus' letter be read to Franck, and that he be asked who had allowed him to publish. The answer would be sent to Erasmus. Moreover if Franck had not been allowed to publish, punishment was to be set by the council.[225] The council's order is free of any questions about orthodoxy. The charges have been brought by Erasmus and concern the honor of the emperor and the besmirching of Erasmus' character. This was not a matter of the ministers pursuing a suspected disrupter of the church. Such a scenario might have been more promising for Franck's case, since at least he could have contested this with the council, which did not always follow the reformers' advice. The main question was who allowed the printing. Straßburg had censors, but they were known on occasion to be less that rigorous in their monitoring of publications.[226] Bucer claimed, in 1535, that Franck had told the censors that the book contained nothing but history drawn from old history books.[227] Jacob Sturm attributed it to an oversight of the censors.[228] It is likely Franck would tell the censors that the book was only pure history. That is what he claims in the book itself. One could hardly expect him to warn them against his own book. Unfortunate-

---

[224] See *Chronica* (1536), p. Pii and following.

[225] *QGT* 7, pp. 358-359. The original letter of Erasmus has not been preserved.

[226] See Abray, *The People's Reformation*, p. 63, for an example from 1563, where only the titles of books were read.

[227] "Er [Franck]...versprochen hat, es wären in diesem buch nichts dann lautter Historien auß den alten Historien außgezogen." Martin Bucer, *Deutsche Schriften*, vol. 6.2 (Gütersloh, 1984), p. 133.

[228] [Sturm speaking] "Ich weisz ouch dovon und ist bi uns gedruckt, [referring to the *Chronica*] aber durch den bevelchhaber ubersehen worden." *Politische Correspondenz der Stadt Straßburg im Zeitalter der Reformation*, vol. 2, *1531-1539*, ed. Otto Winckelmann (Straßburg, ?), p. 118.

ly for Franck, the burden of guilt fell on him.

On December 30 the council published another decision. Franck had in the meantime issued a supplication seeking pardon from the council. This the council was not willing to grant, citing not only his offensive statements concerning authority, but his promise of great things in the title and foreword which he had not achieved in the book. He had lied to the censors and put into the published edition more than he had given to the censors.[229] The council took two steps. One was to expel Franck from the city, an act whose date is not recorded. The other was to send a letter to Erasmus explaining what had been done. Bucer, too, sent a letter to Erasmus.[230] Erasmus had, in his original letter, suspected Bucer of being behind the *Chronica*. His original reaction on hearing of the *Chronica* (which at that time he had not seen) was that certain evangelicals were trying to ruin his reputation with the Emperor and Ferdinand of Austria.[231] The letters of Bucer and the council disabused him of that suspicion. In a letter dated March 6, 1533, to Ambrosius Blarer, Bucer himself referred to Franck's book as that "most faulty history."[232] Erasmus' reply, dated March 2, 1533, is not conciliatory. Bucer's letter had dealt with more that just Franck, pursuing a debate between Erasmus and the evangelicals that went back two years. Erasmus' tone, therefore, is very unapologetic, though he does state that he has written the city council withdrawing the charge. He had

---

[229] *QGT* 7, p. 395.

[230] Neither of the letters to Erasmus is preserved. Erasmus in his letter of March 2, 1532 to Bucer speaks of receiving "tres epistolas," one obviously from Bucer, to which Erasmus is responding, another which, from Erasmus discussion in the letter, was from the council. *Opus Epistolarum Des. Erasmi Roterodami*, vol. 9, eds. P.S. Allen and H.W. Garrod (Oxford, 1938), p. 446.

[231] Erasmus states in a letter to Conrad Goclenius dated December 14, 1531, "Euangelici quidam, quorum magister scelorosus ille Gelrius, miris technis hoc agunt, vt Caesaris ac Fernandi animum in me irritant. Argentorati excuderunt libellum Teutonice contra Caesaream maiestatem, in quo subinde citant autoritatem Erasmi, locis aliquot, vt suspicor, decerptis e proverbio Scarabeus aquilam, et praefatione in Suetonium. Non dubito, quin haec agant Capito et Bucerus...Librum nondum vidi, sed rem hodie cognoui ex litteris Cardin. Tridentini..." *Opus Epistolarum* 9, p. 406.

[232] "historiam mendossisimum." *Blarer Briefwechsel* 1, p. 330.

not suspected Bucer of writing the book, but of having favored it by editing.[233] He charges Bucer, however, with sharing the same bad habits.[234] Erasmus complains bitterly about Franck's book, stating that Bucer has trivialized the seriousness of the injury. He refers to Franck as a fool, who has written not only intemperately but also perversely.[235] Worse, the fool Franck

> has written to me, to me apparently from his imprisonment (I might judge sooner from an inn), not to seek pardon for his faults, but to ask from me thanks for his honoring of me. Such impudence does not come from other cities.[236]

Clearly Erasmus, though he states his forgiveness for the council, considers Franck to be another expression of Straßburg's misguided, even hypocritical, evangelical fervor.

Though Franck was expelled from the city, this did not stop all the repercussions. At the Diet of Speyer the Bishop of Mainz questioned Jacob Sturm about the publication of both Servetus' and Franck's books, telling him that these had been brought to the attention of the Emperor. The Bishop described Franck's book particularly as "harmful and evil."[237] Sturm carefully circumscribed Straßburg's culpability in each case. Servetus had not published in Straßburg, and when he proved unbending in his views, he was expelled. Franck had been able to publish through an oversight; he had been punished and expelled, Sturm reported to the Bishop.[238] In the face of a sensitive polit-

---

[233] "Nec tamen suspicabar librum abs te scriptum sed te fauente editum." *Opus Epistolarum* 9, p. 453.

[234] Having charged Bucer with proclaiming tranquility and then creating a storm, Erasmus states, "quanquam ab hac nota non ita multum abest vester iste Sebastianus, siue illi stultitia siue malicia fuit consilio." *Opus Epistolarum* 9, p. 446.

[235] "Nugonis istius factum extenuas, vt omnia, at ille non solum intemptiue scripsit verum etiam peruerse." *Opus Epistolarum* 9, p. 454.

[236] "qui sic ad me scripsit, ad me e vinculis scilicet, e popina magis arbitror, non vt petat gratiam delicti, sed vt a me pro honore mihi habito gratiam postulet. Ista petulantia non venit ab aliis ciuitatibus." *Opus Epistolarum* 9, p. 454.

[237] "mer gesagt, wie von der kronik, so bei uch gedruckt, die hab ich durchlesen, und ist ein vast schedlich und bes buoch." *Politische Correspondenz* 2, p. 118.

[238] "doruf Butzer mit im [Servetus] gesprech gehalten, aber kein frucht bi im brocht, doruf er der stat bietlich verwisen...her Jocob gesagt ich weisz ouch

Franck had been able to publish through an oversight; he had been punished and expelled, Sturm reported to the Bishop.[238] In the face of a sensitive political situation, with the Emperor's suspicions already aroused because of Straßburg's dealings with the protesting German princes, the attention attracted by Franck's book was most unwelcome. Two weeks after Sturm's chat with the Bishop, Franck, who had moved across the river to Kehl, requested permission to print the fourth book of his *Chronica*, the *Weltbuch*. He was turned down by the city council in no uncertain terms. Two men of the council were to be sent to the publisher to remind him of his oath, and to warn him not to republish the *Chronica* or this new book. Franck was to be told that if there was anything disruptive in the book, he would be punished. His expulsion would stand. The order did not fail to refer, with no further comment, to Sturm's conversation with the Bishop.[239]

For Franck, as well as for his publisher Balthasar Beck, the entire incident was an unqualified disaster. The object of Franck's efforts for the last three years, a project he had seen as his witness to the world, was confiscated by the city council. He himself was expelled permanently from the city, his publishing connections in Straßburg rendered useless. The venture must have been financially ruinous. Beck, sometime after the council forbade the publication in Straßburg, had tried to print the *Weltbuch* in Hagenau; the city council there, after purportedly giving their permission, changed their minds, and confiscated the nearly completed copies.[240]

It might be tempting to say Franck was the victim of an unfortunate

---

[238] "doruf Butzer mit im [Servetus] gesprech gehalten, aber kein frucht bi im brocht, doruf er der stat bietlich verwisen...her Jocob gesagt ich weisz ouch dovon und ist bi uns gedruckt, aber durch den bevelchhaber ubersehen worden; es ist ouch der cronickschreiber doruber gestroft und der stat deshalb verwisen." *Politische Correspondenz* 2, p. 118.

[239] *QGT* 7, p. 543.

[240] See Beck's supplication to the Hagenau city council in which he seeks the return of the almost completed copies, if only for the scrap paper. *QGT* 8, pp. 284-285. It is possible Beck may have saved some of the copies of the *Chronica* from destruction by the city council by hiding them. This is the conjecture of François Ritter, "Elsässische Buchdrucker im Dienste der Strassburger Sektenbewengungen zur Zeit der Reformation," *Gutenberg Jahrbuch* (1962), pp. 225-233; (1963), pp. 97-108. Ritter notes the numerous copies which have survived. Kaczerowsky lists at least twenty-eight copies in German libraries alone, pp. 46-49.

Franck had intended his work to be an eye catcher, and it achieved that effect. Not surprisingly, the papal party and the authorities of the empire, as well as their supporters, were the most upset. Erasmus himself had been informed of the *Chronica* passages dealing with him by the Bishop of Trent, a court advisor to King Ferdinand of Austria.[242] No less than that fervent defender of the true Church, Cochlaeus, was moved to write two separate refutations of Franck's work.[243] Melanchthon, on the Wittenberg front, delivered a negative judgment.[244] Both the city of Straßburg and Ulm felt themselves poorly treated by Franck's work.[245] As Servetus with his book, Franck created many enemies and few allies with his publication. The political repercussions were too serious for Straßburg to have any inclination to permit Franck's continued presence. Pressure by the Straßburg reformers was not even necessary to obtain the expulsion of Franck, though Bucer had little enough sympathy for spiritualism of the type promoted by Denck, Kautz, or Franck. Straßburg's tolerance for heterodoxy had always been provisional, as the cases of Denck and Kautz show,

---

noted above, plus the letter to Erasmus which is now lost, he had little to do with Franck's expulsion. The city council had its own reasons for wanting a good distance between the city and Franck's work. See Teufel, *"Landräumig"*, pp. 34-38. See Deppermann's analysis of Franck's expulsion, "Sebastian Francks Straßburger Aufenhalt."

[242] Erasmus mentions this both in his letter to Conrad Goclinius and to Bucer. See *Opus Epistolarum* 9, pp. 406, 453.

[243] Johannes Cochläus, *Was von Kayser Sigismunds Reformation zu halten sei, ain disputation Johannes Coclei. Was auch von der newen Chroniken Sebastiani Franck zu halten sei* (Dresden, 1533), and *Von ankunfft der Meß vnnd der wandlung brots vnnd weins im hochwürdigen Sacrament des Alters. Ain disputation Sebastiani Francken/ mit antwort Johannis Coclei auff 88. artickeln auß der newen Chronica* (Dresden, 1533). Both were published in January of the year. The second book was dedicated to Margrave Joachim of Brandenburg; Cochlaeus makes a point of stressing to the Margrave the subversive possibilities of the *Chronica* for authority.

[244] See *Corpus Reformatorum* 3, p. 884.

[245] The end of the council decree of Straßburg from May 18, 1532 gives as one reason for letting the expulsion stand "dieweil er von einer stadt Strassburg darin schrieb, das viel anders in der wahrheit sey;" this is in reference to the *Weltbuch*, which the council had apparently already perused. The Ulm city council would complain, on Franck's arrival there, about his depiction in the *Chronica* of the city falling away from Lutheranism (p. ffiiii and following of the 1531 edition). Ulm's complaint will be discussed below.

and from 1532 forward, with the publications of Servetus, Hoffmann, and Franck, plus the aforementioned influx of Anabaptists, Straßburg's ministers took an increasingly intransigent stand against sectarianism and heterodoxy. Discipline became the watchword. Franck's only possible allies within Straßburg who had any power were the council members. Schwenckfeld found sympathy among them with his anti-ecclesiastical spiritualism and message of political obedience. He avoided official expulsion in the face of heavy pressure from the spiritual magistrates.[246] Franck, however, had not learned how to cultivate ties with people of influence or to use his own message to appeal to authority, as he would in the future. Franck's personality was such that he would never be able truly to dampen the force of his published statements. As he said many times, what he received from God, he wanted to share, to display as a witness. Franck could take comfort in the fact that the universal rejection of his views by the world was, in his own view, proof of their divine pedigree. Official disapproval would never serve to change his mind. He was apparently convinced that the Straßburg magistrates were not going to change their minds. Sometime after their rejection of his publication request, he and his family moved from Kehl to take up residence in the Imperial city of Esslingen, where Franck found a new trade as soapmaker.

---

[246] See R.E. McLaughlin, *Caspar Schwenckfeld*, pp. 142-146 for Schwenckfeld's political views; pp. 146-159 for his successful battle with Bucer and the other reformers of the city.

Though the exact date is not recorded, sometime in the fall of 1532 Franck moved to the city of Esslingen.[1] According to Franck he made the move in order to earn his living with his hands.[2] No inquiry was made into Franck's past, but alone on his oral report he was allowed entry and residence by the city council without any recommendation, application, or plea, a development which Franck saw as God's hand at work.[3] Very little that is concrete can be said about Franck's life in this period. He apparently gave up publishing his works for the moment, though he must have continued to compose, judging from his later publishing activity. He plied the trade of soap-maker, seeking to hawk his wares at weekly markets in Württemberg, though he was not very successful. As Franck explained it,

> My trade and handiwork were not customary in Württemberg,
> where almost alone the nobility, and very few of the citizens, are
> in the habit of washing with soap.[4]

Thus because of the personal habits of the local population, Franck lived a somewhat impoverished life.[5]

Esslingen itself was an Imperial city of about 7,000 residents which lay on the banks of the Neckar river south and east of Stuttgart. It was completely surrounded by Württemberg. When Franck arrived the church in Esslingen had

---

[1] Franck's supplication to the city council of Ulm from the fall of 1533 reads, "Ich habe mich vor einem jar zu Eßling nidergelaßnen..." "Brief Sebastian Franck an der Bürgermaister und Rat der Stadt Ulm." Stadtarchiv Ulm, Tresor. Franz Weinkauff published a version of this letter in *Alemannia* 4 (1877), p. 24.

[2] "jm willen mich alda mit meinem hender zu nären." Ulm Archive, Tresor.

[3] "darzu hatt mir Gott...das fenster auffthon/ vnd das hertz eines erbern Raths der maß bereyt vnd geneigt gemacht.../ das sy mich on alle fürderung/ fürschrifft/ oder supplication ja on alle forschung meins namens/ wer ich sey/ alein auff mein ploß müntlich anpringen/ ein zeytlang haben angenommen vnd freygesetzt..." Ulm Archive, Tresor.

[4] "mein handtierung vnd handwerck nit gattung im land zw wirtenburg ist/ da dast allein der adel vnd gar wenig Burgerin/ auß saiffen zw waschen pflegen vnd gewon seind." Ulm Archive, Tresor.

[5] "vnd in armut ja vmb alles kommen bin." Ulm Archive, Tresor.

just recently been reorganized according to evangelical precepts, this being above all the work of Ambrosius Blarer. Jakob Otter was installed in 1532 as pastor in Esslingen, but soon fell into a two-year controversy with his colleagues.[6] It is perhaps under these conditions that little attention was paid to Franck and his previous career. Otter himself seems to have had a certain sympathy for Schwenckfeld, and thus may also have been favorably impressed by Franck.[7] In any event, there was no known conflict between Franck and either the religious or secular authorities of the city.

While in Esslingen Franck met once again the Silesian nobleman, Caspar Schwenckfeld, who arrived in Esslingen in September 1533 and lodged with Otter.[8] It is possible Franck was present at a meeting where Schwenckfeld presented his views.[9] At the end of September Franck and Schwenckfeld together visited the *Obervogt* of Kirchheim, Hans-Friedrich Thumb, a visit that is known because of Ambrosius Blarer's letter warning Thumb against the bad influence of these two men of such peculiar views.[10] The warning had little effect, as Thumb became one of Schwenckfeld's truest supporters, though no other interaction between him and Franck is recorded.

From here Franck travelled with Schwenckfeld to Ulm, where Franck arranged for him to stay with an acquaintance. Schwenckfeld met with Martin

---

[6] For a sketch of Esslingen's reforms see Martin Brecht and Hermann Ehmer, *Südwestdeutsche Reformationsgeschichte* (Stuttgart, 1984), pp. 174-177. See also Otto Schuster, *Kirchengeschichte von Stadt und Bezirk Esslingen* (Stuttgart, 1946), pp. 150-171.

[7] See the letter of Otter's to Bucer dated January 1, 1534, *QGT* 8, pp. 248-249. For a possible connection to Franck see the letter of Ambrosius Blarer to Bucer dated October 6, 1533, *Blarer Briefwechsel* 1, pp. 429-431.

[8] Horst Weigelt, "Sebastian Franck und Caspar Schwenckfeld in ihren Beziehungen zueinander," *Zeitschrift für bayerischen Kirchengeschichte* 39 (1970), pp. 3-19; p. 8.

[9] *Corpus Schwenckfeldianorum* 4, pp. 844-845.

[10] This is appended to a letter written by A. Blarer to Johann Machtolf dated October 3, 1533. "Junckher Friderich Thummen wellen mein christlichen gruß und dienst sagen und im getrulich von meinen wegen warnen, byß ich selbs zeyt und weyl haben mag,-ich vernym, das Sebastian Franck ouch Caspar Schwenckfeld, und noch ainer bey im seyen-, das er flyssig um sich sech. Dann es sind leut, die gar klug und gschickt, ouch sonder seltzam grillen und opinion im kopff habend und sich nienen mitt dem predigern betragen könnend..." *Blarer Briefwechsel* 1, p. 428.

Frecht, pastor in Ulm, who wrote to Bucer about the meeting. Frecht remembered Franck from Heidelberg. Even at this early date he was suspicious of Franck and Schwenckfeld.[11] Shortly thereafter Schwenckfeld moved on to Augsburg.

Franck's connections to Ulm came from his soapmaking activities. When he found little market for his soap in Württemberg, he sought a new market in Ulm and its territories. He apparently visited the city during the summer of 1533 on more than one occasion to sell his product, and found a good demand.[12] Thus by fall of 1533 his thoughts turned to Ulm as a more promising residence. He directed a supplication to the mayor and council at Ulm seeking allowance to move within the city's territory, if not to Ulm itself then to Geislingen in Ulm's territory.

Franck's supplication is a document of great interest. He exhibits an ability to endear himself to the secular authorities, perhaps a skill acquired through his hard lesson in Straßburg. Franck had already spoken to the mayor, Jörg Besserer, and Conrad Aitinger, the influential city scribe. These connections gave him the confidence that his plea would not fall on hostile or deaf ears.[13] Franck opens his supplication by telling the council the nature of his connection to Ulm. It is not just his good fortune in the city which directs him to Ulm, states Franck, but also a special love and predilection for the city.[14] He points out to the council that it was not his own will, but that of God which directed him there.[15] Franck emphasizes that he wishes to be of use to the

---

[11] "Sed mihi, quod ingenue dico, et Schwenkfeldii et Franci spiritus suspectus est." *QGT* 8, pp. 202-203; the letter is dated October 30, 1533.

[12] "hab ich es nach verzweifelnen dingen mit Vlm versucht/ ob mich Gott alda wölle segnen vnd bin disen sommer ein mal oder 7 auff die freyen wucken märckt mit saiffen hieher gefaren/ da hett mir got gluck vnd sein segen geben/ das ich mich disen sommer etwas von Vlm hab genärt." "Brief Sebastian Francks an der Burgermaister und Rat der Stadt Ulm." Ulm Archive, Tresor.

[13] "wa eur f. w. weitter etwas fälet, soll es Eur f.w. an herr Jörgen Besserer Burgermaister vnd an herr Conradt Atinger statschreibern erkundigen, mit den ich müntlich geredt hab allerley." Ulm Archive, Tresor.

[14] "Auß diser meiner anligenden not vnd zwfallendem gluck/ auch dz ich ein sondere lieb vnd naigung zw der stat Vlm habe..." Ulm Archive, Tresor.

[15] "weil mir Got ye on mein zuthon den weg hatt zeygt vnd ein thür meiner narung/ on yedermans nachteyl bey ein f.w. auffthon." Ulm Archive, Tresor.

city.[16] Not that he desires to serve in an office, Franck immediately adds, not in these dangerous, confused times. He hopes the council will not hold this against him.

> What I have from the Lord, these things I want to convey in writ-
> ing to the people of God, and not bury; this requires a free man
> who is not bound by any office, so that no one thinks he has want-
> ed to write this or that and sing the song of the one who gave him
> bread.[17]

Franck assures them that his trading in the town will not lead to a rise in prices, but will in fact keep them reasonable.[18] Presumably Franck is here countering objections that might be made by native soap-makers.

The supplication clearly shows Franck's sensitivity to the communal consciousness of the city—thus his emphasis on the providential influence in his choice of Ulm, and his own desire to serve the good of the city. The oblique reference to his literary activity, that he wishes to pass on in writing what he has from God to his people, is indicative of one motivation, perhaps the major, in Franck's move. Ulm has a printing industry. As Hans Hillerbrand has wryly noted,

> the picture of Sebastian Franck pushing his cart with handmade
> soap, trying to convince housewives of the advantages of cleanli-
> ness as being second only to godliness, suggests that this was the
> wrong calling for the man.[19]

Whether Franck took up soapmaking out of a conviction of the virtues of simple labor, or for purely practical reasons, it is hard to imagine this restless person as satisfied by the simple life. One suspects his move to Ulm was not so much a search for a better market, though what he said about Ulm's market may well be true, as a desire for the advantages of a large Imperial city, with the printers and intellectual life that collected around them. Franck's publishing activity of

---

[16] "Beger auch nit müßigs prot essen, sonder zw arbeiten vnd mich mit willen laßen brauchen, warzu ich einen Erbern Rath taugenlich vnd wamit ich gemeiner Statt nutzlich sein verhoff, oder geacht würd." Ulm Archive, Tresor.

[17] "Was ich von hern hab, dz will ich schrifftlich dem volck Gottes mitzu-teylen nit vergraben, diß will aber ein freyen man haben, der mit keinem ampt verstrickt sey, damit nit yemant acht, er habe dise oder jenem zu lieb ge-schrieben, vnd diß lied gesungen, deß prot er esse." Ulm Archive, Tresor.

[18] "Also will ich mit meiner war auch, wills Gott, kein theurung vnd die saiffen in ziemlichen gelt behalten." Ulm Archive, Tresor.

[19] *A Fellowship of Discontent* (New York, 1969), p. 39.

the next year indicates that while he plied the trade of soap-maker he had not given up his literary endeavors. The move to Ulm facilitated this activity.

Franck sent his supplication for residence to Jörg Besserer and the privy council sometime between August 15 and 18, for on August 18 Jörg Besserer sent a letter to his father Bernhard, the most influential politician in Ulm in this period (who was at that time in Augsburg), reporting on Franck's request. He tells of his conversation with Franck on August 15. Franck made a powerful impression on the mayor, and his letter heartily recommends him. Franck had spoken to him "with long, humble, solicitous words," as, he states, his father would see from the contents of the supplication.[20] Jörg Besserer was convinced Franck would make a good citizen and was particularly taken by his statement that he only sought work and not self enrichment.[21] He is aware of Franck's expulsion from Straßburg, but says, because of Franck's outstanding character, he should be accepted until some future incident proves otherwise.[22] Considering the Straßburg magistrates' experience with Franck, Besserer's inclination towards him may seem inexplicable. But the force of Franck's personality, and the persuasiveness of his words were apparently such that the mayor was won over. Besserer's opinion of Franck is solid evidence that Franck's personality did not inevitably lead to the alienation of city magistrates. As we shall see, the sympathies of the Ulm magistrates were in part drawn toward a spiritualist theology such as Franck promoted.

Bernhard Besserer must have been favorably impressed by his son's report, for a short while after Franck moved to Ulm with his wife and two children. Approximately one year later he applied for, and received, citizen status. The entry in the *Bürgerbuch* of Ulm reads,

---

[20] "sich bei mir anzeigt und mir mit langen demütigen und hocherbietlichen worten...fast den Effekt, wie du aus inliegender seiner Supplikation vernehmen wurdest." This letter is preserved only in a copy which is contained in the Georg Veesenmeyersche Briefsammlung in the Ulm archive. These are late eighteenth or early nineteenth century copies. The copy is printed in Julius Endriß, *Sebastian Francks Ulmer Kämpfe* (Ulm, 1935), pp. 34-35; here p. 34.

[21] "der allein Arbeit, keins müßiggangs, Prachts oder Reichtums keinswegs acht oder begehrt..." *Sebastian Francks Ulmer Kämpfe*, p. 34.

[22] "Kann dir dannocht seinthalben zu weiteren Bericht nit bergen daß ihm (wie seinthalben unglimpflich erschollen) die Stadt Straßburg nit anders verboten...Auß dem allem mir je einleucht diser Mann sollt nit hinzuwerfen, sondern zu küntigen Fürfall...bei der Hand zu behalten sein." *Sebastian Francks Ulmer Kämpfe*, p. 34.

Noted on Thursday [actually Wednesday-see the council re-cords[23]] after the Apostles Simon's and Jude's Day [Oct. 28] year 1534; an honorable council has conferred, out of grace, the citizenship rights to Sebastian Franck, on reception of his supplication; thus he is from now on our established citizen, to be taxed by us, serve us, and be prepared and obedient to all other commands, bans, and matters, and as our other citizens, to be harmless. Yet with this condition; where [the city] or the honorable council be troubled by the emperor or if his writings harm the general well being of the city, then he will no longer have his citizenship privileges, and the council is not obligated to deal with him further.[24]

Although Franck was in the good favor of some of the leading magistrates, he was not above suspicion. We have already noted Frecht's initial reaction to Franck. Obviously Franck's troubles in Straßburg were widely known, and the council was not eager to have such an incident repeated. The strictures, though, are political and do not touch theological opinion. Thus Franck might have felt encouraged to publish his theological views. It had not been the theologians in Straßburg who had caused him trouble. Franck must have been aware, though, of the problems Schwenckfeld had encountered, and might have suspected his opinions, too, would come in for close scrutiny by the Ulm pastorate. Never-theless, all reasons for moderation withstanding, during the course of 1534 Franck brought out four books, all under his own name. These lay out his theological views in detail. The *Weltbuch*, published in Tübingen, was his geog-raphy of the world, which was the last section of his *Chronica*, whose printing

---

[23] Alfred Hegler, *Beiträge zur Geschichte der Mystik*, p. 113.

[24] "Nota auf Donnerstag nach Simonis und Juda Apostolarum anno 34 hat ein E. Rat Seb. Francken von Wörd auf sein übergeben Supplikation das Bur-gerrecht aus Gnaden geschenckt, also daß er nun hinfüro unser eingesessener Bürger sein und uns steuren, dienen und aller andrer Gebot, Verbot und Sachen gehorsam und gewärtig sein soll, wie ander unser Burger ungefahr-lichen. Doch mit diesem Anhang: wa er oder ein E. Rat seinthalben von Ro. kay. oder ka. Majestät angefochten wurden oder daß er sich in seinem Schreib-en, daraus gemeiner Stadt Nachteil entstehn, vertiefe, daß er alsdann seines Bürgerrechten nit mehr fähig, sich auch ein E. Rat sein in keinen Weg anzu-nehmen schuldig sein soll." Ulmer Bürgerbuch 1534, #1497; *Sebastian Francks Ulmer Kämpfe*, p. 35. The Ratsprotokol is published in Hegler, *Beiträge*, pp. 113-114, and reads basically the same. The Bürgerbuch goes on to state that Franck's two children, Adam and Abel, do not receive citizenship. Franck's wife, according to the city's custom, would have received citizenship.

the Straßburg city council had forbidden.[25] The so-called *Four Regal Little Books* were published in Ulm, and contained translations of Erasmus' *Encomion Moriae* and Agrippa, as well as two revealing expressions of Franck's own thought.[26] Also published in Ulm was Franck's *Paradoxa*, which ostensibly presented two hundred eight paradoxes drawn from Scripture and other places, and provided him a forum to work out his theology of Word and Spirit.[27] The fourth work was a small tract published in Augsburg on the nature of God.[28] With the exception of the *Weltbuch*, which had been awaiting a publisher, presumably all these works had been written in the period since Franck's completion of the *Chronica*. Franck's residence in Ulm opened up connections to printers there and in Augsburg. These books would not be the immediate cause of Franck's troubles in Ulm, but they provided the pastors of Ulm plenty of ammunition to fire at Franck throughout his later troubled stay there.

Franck's three theological books of 1534 are the most detailed expressions of his spiritualist views, in fact are some of the few works by Franck which have extended passages in his own voice, without compilations of material or translations. We have already discussed those of his contemporaries who were of greatest influence on his thought. Franck, however, explicitly rested his mystical views on two more venerable sources—sources which he refers to and quotes continually throughout his later writings. These are the so-called *Theologia Deutsch* and the sermons of Johannes Tauler. Franck's mysticism is dependent on his reading of these two spiritual masters. The *Theologia Deutsch* is a tract of obscure origins which came to prominence during the Reformation era.[29] Probably Franck encountered this work long before 1534, but it is with

---

[25] *Weltbuch* (Tübingen: Ulrich Morhart d.Ä., 1534).

[26] *Das Theür vnd Künstlich Büchlin Moriae Encomion* (Ulm: Hans Varnier d.Ä., 1534). Each section has its own title. Franck refers to it in his introduction as "Die vier Kronbüchlin" (p. Ai-v), and it is commonly referred to as such in the literature.

[27] *Paradoxa ducenta octoginta* (Ulm: Hans Varnier d.Ä., 1534). I have used the edition (Pforzheim: Georg Rab, 1558), which I have checked against the original.

[28] *Das Gott das ainig ain/ vnd höchstes gut/ sei* (Augsburg: Silvan Otmar, 1534).

[29] See Ozment, *Mysticism and Dissent*, chapter 2, for a history of the influence of the *Theologia Deutsch* in the sixteenth century.

his publications in that year that he first makes heavy reference to the tract. More than any other individual work Franck valued the *Theologia Deutsch*. He praises it highly in his *Paradoxa* and later would attempt to translate it into Latin.[30]

The *Theologia Deutsche* takes its departure from a statement in Paul, "when the perfect comes, the imperfect passes away," to which the author adds "and the divided."[31] This point is explained.

> The perfect is one being, which has grasped and enclosed in itself
> and in its being everything; without and outside this [being] there
> is no true being, and in it all things have their being.[32]

The divided or imperfect has its origin in the perfect, and is that which is called creature or creaturely.[33] All that is divided is not the perfect. The divided is graspable, knowable, and speakable; the perfect is for all creatures ungraspable, unknowable, and inexpressible in the creature as creature.[34] This describes the problem that humans face. They, the creaturely and the divided, are, in their creatureliness, incapable of knowing or grasping the perfect, which is God. Because of their "I-ness" (*icheyt*) and their "selfness" (*selbheyt*) it is not possi-

---

[30] "die alten Lehrer haben leider wenig erkantnuß von Christo gehabt/ Taulerus ist der best vnder ihn/ vnd die Teütsch theologey bezeügt auch ein rechten Christum..." *Paradoxa*, p. aii-v.

[31] "wen das volkomen kumpt, ßo vernichtiget dass unvolkommen unde das geteilte." *Theologia Deutsch*, ed. Hermann Mandel (Liepzig, 1910), p. 7. This is the Luther edition of 1518. Franck most likely used the Worms edition of 1528, which was Ludwig Hätzer's reworking of the Luther edition. See Ozment, *Mysticism and Dissent*, p. 25. For the purposes of this discussion the differences between the two editions are not significant.

[32] "Das volkommen ist eyn weßenn, das yn yhm und yn seynem wesen alles begryffen und beschlossen hatt, und an [ohne] das unnd außwendig dem kein wars weßen ist, unnd yn dem aller ding yr wesen hand." *Theologia Deutsch*, p. 7.

[33] "Aber das geteilte ader das unvolkommen ist das, dass auß dißem volkommen geursprungt ist ader wirt...und das heisset creature." *Theologia Deutsch*, p. 7.

[34] "Die geteiltenn sind begreiffenlich, bekentlich und sprechenlich; das volkumen ist allen creaturen unbegreifflich, unbekentlich und unsprechenlich jnn dem als creature." *Theologia Deutsch*, p. 8.

ble for them to know God.[35] Humans have no true being except in the perfect; the being they seem to have is an accident, and appearance.[36]

> Sin is nothing other than that the creature turns away from the
> unchangeable God and turns toward the changeable; that is that
> they turn from the perfect to the divided and imperfect and most
> of all to their self.[37]

The vital question for the author of the tract, and those who accept his description of the human predicament, is "how may one change this situation and better oneself?"[38]

> In order to do this God took human nature or humanness on himself and was incarnated, and humans became begodded (*vergottet*).
> There occurred the improvement.[39]

The obvious reference here is to Christ's incarnation. But that was not a once-and-for-all-time-effective act. Christ's incarnation is the perfect type of an event which must take place in all humans. God must be made incarnate in each person, and each person must become "begodded."[40] In order for this to occur one must empty oneself of self, and passively suffer God's work and will in oneself.[41] One lives always with sin, with the creaturely, until the death of

---

[35] "von yr icheyt und selbheyt ist es [to know the perfect] yr unmuglich." *Theologia Deutsch*, p. 9.

[36] "hat kein weßen anders dan yn dem volkommen, sunder es ist eynn zufall...und ein schein der nit wesen ist." *Theologia Deutsch*, p. 9-10.

[37] "Sundt sey nit anders dan das sich die creatur abkert von dem unwandelhaftigen got unnd kert sich zu dem wandalbaren, dass ist; das sie sich keret von dem volkommen tzu dem geteilten und unvolkommen und allermeist zu yr selber." *Theologia Deutsch*, p. 10.

[38] "Von wem oder yn wilcher weis geschah die pesserung?" *Theologia Deutsch*, p. 11.

[39] "Darumb nam got menschlich natur oder menscheyt an sich und ward vermenscht, und der mensch ward vergottet. Alda geschah die pesserung." *Theologia Deutsch*, p. 11.

[40] "So soll es geschehen, ßo muß gott auch yn myr vermenscht werden...Das got alle menschen an sich nem, die da sindt, und yn yhn vermenscht wurde und sie yn yhm vergottet, und gescheh es nit yn myr, mein fall und mein abkeren wurd nymer gepessert." *Theologia Deutsch*, p. 11.

[41] "Und yn dißer widerpringung und pesserung kan ich oder mag oder soll nichtz nit dar zu thu, sunder einn ploß lautter leiden, also das gott allein thu

the body.[42] Even in the soul there are two eyes, one which looks to God, the other to the creature and time, and the latter hinders the former, just as the self hinders God's work in man.[43] The world is possessed with the devil, which is all lies, falsehoods, evil and unvirtuousness.[44] Neither learning or reason can resolve this conflict between the outward self and the inward true being which is possessed by God.[45] It is God who is the one who works within the soul and effects its "begodding," and humans must merely suffer this action of God.

> Whoever wishes and supposes himself to be obedient, passive, and subservient to God must and should in all things be passive, obedient, and subservient in a suffering manner and not in an active manner.[46]

---

und werck unnd ich leide yhn und seyn werck und seinen willen." *Theologia Deutsch*, p. 12.

"Ich sprich: der mensch solt also gar an sten und sein, das ist selbheit und icheit, das er sich und das sein als wenig suchte und meynte yn allen dingen, als ob er nit were...'was ist den das, das da ist und davon tzu halten?' Ich sprich: alleyn eins, das man gott nennet." *Theologia Deutsch*, p. 31.

[42] "Aber die clag und der iamer, der umb die sund ist, der sol und muß bleiben pis an den leiblichen tod yn einem vergoten menschen." *Theologia Deutsch*, p. 67.

[43] "Nun hat die geschaffen sele des menschen auch zwey augen. Das eyn ist muglichkeyt zu sehen yn die ewigkeit; das ander, zu sehen yn die tzeit und yn die creaturen...aber diße zwey augen der sele des menschen mügen nit mit eynander yr werck geüben...Und soll das linck aug seyn werck uben nach der außwendigkeyt, das ist die zeit und die creaturen handeln, ßo muß daz recht aug gehindert werden an seiner beschawung." *Theologia Deutsch*, p. 17-18.

[44] "Es ist war yn eyn synne, das alle die werlt besessen und gehafft ist mit dem teufel, das meynet man mit lugen und mit falscheit und ander poßheit und untugent." *Theologia Deutsch*, p. 43.

"Und in disem leben und liecht und seiner liebe ist alles, das dem teufel zu gehort und sein eigen ist..." *Theologia Deutsch*, p. 84.

"Darumb ist der teufel und nature eins." *Theologia Deutsch*, p. 85.

[45] "Niemant gedenck, das er zu disem waren liechte und waren bekentnus kome oder zu Christus leben mit vill fragen oder von horen sagen oder mit leßen oder studieren noch mit großen hochen kunsten und meisterschaft oder mit hocher naturlicher vernunfft." *Theologia Deutsch*, p. 39.

[46] "Und wer got gehorsam, gelassen und untertan sol und wil sein, der muß und sol allein gelassen, gehorsam und untertan sein yn leydender weis und nit yn tunder weis..." *Theologia Deutsch*, p. 43.

The author emphasizes again and again the atemporal, transphysical nature of God, who works in the human's soul only as they empty themselves, and who finds that point in the human soul that is still regenerate.[47] God is the being of all being, and the life of all living things, and they have their being more truly in God than in themselves.[48]

The effect of the *Theologia Deutsch* is to subordinate all physical and historical expressions of God and means of salvation to the direct action of God in the human soul. Christ's significance is as a type—one who was obedient, passive and suffering so that God worked and willed perfectly in him. Taken to its extreme Christ becomes no more than the most exceptional of humans, a conclusion that the *Theologia Deutsch* certainly does not draw. Learning, knowledge, speaking, preaching and all other human, physical means of perpetuating the physical church are devalued in the face of God's filling of the soul of the one who empties out all manifestations of self. This is God's direct work and is above words. Humans must merely suffer, take on Christ's cross, crucify the self so that it may be resurrected in God. The drama of salvation history is set within the divisions of the human being. The *Theologia Deutsch* is more than just congenial to Franck. It is a source for his own ideas and vocabulary—a statement about the action of God in the small regenerate portion of the human soul. Here was one place to which Franck could point, almost without reservation, when asked who before him had believed as he professed.

Another venerable source for Franck's views were the sermons of Johannes Tauler. Franck turns often to the writings of those who went before, both pagan and Christian, but none with greater frequency than Tauler. Tauler was a follower, if not a student, of the more speculative German mystic Johannes Eckhart. Twenty-eight propositions of Eckhart were condemned by John XXII in 1329, "for what can be summed up as a heretical doctrine of creation."[49] As Heiko Oberman notes, the doctrine of creation was in this way

---

[47] "Auch sol man mercken, das gots gebot und sein red und all seyn lere gehort zu dem ynner menschet, wie er mit got vereynet war..." *Theologia Deutsch*, p. 71.

[48] "Wan got ist aller wesenden wesen und aller lebentigen leben...wan alle ding haben jr wesen warlicher in got dan in yn selber." *Theologia Deutsch*, p. 61.

[49] Heiko Oberman, *The Harvest of Medieval Theology* (Cambridge, MA, 1963), p. 326.

effectively safeguarded as the doctrine of redemption was not.[50] One does not find in Tauler a depiction of creation which bypasses or reinterprets the event of the fall as is common in Neo-platonic influenced mysticism, no doubt because of the condemnation of Eckhart. With the doctrine of redemption, though, Tauler moves away from a strictly orthodox interpretation. And it is the question of redemption where Tauler was most instructive for Franck. For Tauler's interpretation of the sinful state of humanity, and the individual's role in reconciliation with God, and the work of God to effect this redemption, all found resonance in Franck's thought.

For Tauler humans exist in a low state as a consequence of the fall.

> Because of the poisoning of the first fall nature has sunk down to the lowest part. Humankind is made and stands between two ends, that is time and eternity. Time should be nothing else to us but a passageway to the end. And eternity should be our dwelling place, our end.

> Because of the natural fall, because of their blindness, poor humankind turns everything into the sickest habit and takes complete rest while still on the way, and forgets his true goal.[51]

"People seek rest in things which appear entirely good," states Tauler:

> When one goes astray in some way, then he goes in a great hurry to the external confession, before he gives humbly to God internal confession of guilt.[52]

Humans, who started as one with God, have fallen from this state, and travel through time, though when they know their true end, they know that this trip's purpose is back toward eternity, which is the original oneness with God. Part of

---

[50] *Harvest of Medieval Theology,* p. 326.

[51] "Kinder, von der vergiftikeit des ersten valles so ist die nature also nidergesunken in das niderste teil. Der mensche ist gemacht und stat enzwischent zwein enden, das ist zit und ewigkeit. Die zit solte númme haben von uns, denne einen durgang zů dem ende. Und ewikeit solte unser wonunge, unser ende sin." *Die Predigten Taulers,* ed. Ferdinand Vetters (Berlin, 1910), p. 202.
  "Nu kert der arme mensche von des natúrlichen valles wegen alles in die krankste site von siner blintheit wegen und nimet alles růwe in dem wege und vergisset sines rechten endes." *Die Predigten Taulers,* p. 202.

[52] "Och sůchet der mensche růwe an gar gut schinenden dingen. Als der mensche im selber iergen engangen ist, so ilt er sere zů der uswendigen bichte, e er Gotte innerlichen bichte mit demůtigem schuldig geben." *Die Predigten Taulers,* p. 203.

the legacy of the fall is that humans lose sight of their end and become caught up in the physical things, which at their best are but an outward depiction of an inward act or truth. How could any outward thing truly capture God, who is above all that we could imagine or recognize?[53]

What is needed is for God to work in us. For this to happen one must empty oneself of all self possession so that God may do his work.[54] How is it, though, that God, who is spirit, can work in humankind, which is flesh? For Tauler it is because humans retain at the base of their being a capacity for, or a tendency toward, God—a divine spark left over from our original state of oneness with God.[55] Whatever true being we have is a part of God's being, for he is the being of all beings.[56] When one prepares oneself by the constant suppression of self and the "I," and holds oneself silent in order to suffer the presence of another being, then God will work within us, speak his word, and we shall hear it, and the two shall become one.[57] Tauler's depiction of this process is carefully modulated to leave room for some mediating function on

---

[53] "Wan Got enist alles des nût das du von im genemmen kanst; er ist über wise, über wesen, über gût, und alles des nût das du von im bekennen oder genemmen kanst." *Die Predigten Taulers*, p. 204.

[54] "wan unser ichtikeit und annemlicheit die hindert Got sines edelen werkes in uns." *Die Predigten Taulers*, p. 205.

[55] "Kinder, da ist der grunt do dis wore bilde der heiligen drivaltikeit inne lit verborgen, und das ist so edel das man dem enkeinen eigenen namen enmag gegeben. Under wilen heisset man es einen boden, under wilen ein dolten der selen. Und als wenig als man Gotte einen eigenen namen mag gegeben, als mag man dem namen gegeben. Und der gesehen mochte wie Got in dem grunde wonet, der wûrde von dem gesichte selig. Die nehe die Got do hat, und die sipschaft, die ist so unsprechlich gros das man nût vil dannan ab getar sprechen noch enkan gesprechen." *Die Predigten Taulers*, p. 262.

[56] "Nu mag der mensche in disen eigenscheften sin gemute erspiegelen in wûrklicher wise, das er an sehe das Got ist ein luter wesen, das aller wesen wesen ist, und doch enist er aller dinge in keines. Alles das ist und das wesen ist und wesen hat und gut ist, da inne ist Got." *Die Predigten Taulers*, p. 277.

[57] "Wan wenne zwei süllent eins werden, so mus sich daz eine halten lidende und daz ander wûrckende." *Die Predigten Taulers*, p. 9.
"Wenne der mensch alsus die stat, den grund bereitete, so ist kein zwifel do an, Got müsse do alzumole erfüllen...Und darumbe soltu swigen: so mag dis wort diser geburt in dich sprechen, und in dir gehört werden." *Die Predigten Taulers*, p. 10.

the part of the church. When he speaks of the reception of the Holy Spirit he delineates three ways in which one is prepared for this reception.

> This seclusion one must have necessarily if one is to receive the Holy Spirit and his gifts; one should think fully on God and seclude himself from all that is not God...And this seclusion and expectation of the Holy Spirit is not the same in all people. Some receive the Holy Spirit in perceptible, figurative ways with the senses. Others receive it much more nobly in the highest reasoning powers, in a reasoned way far above the senses. The third receive it not only in this way, but they receive it in the hidden abyss, in the secret kingdom, in the wondrous ground, where the noble picture of the Holy Trinity lies hidden, which is the most noble part of the soul...And there his gifts will be nobly received according to the godly manner.[58]

Tauler's ideal is that God work directly within the soul, but he concedes the efficacy of the outward means of spiritual enlightenment, by which one assumes he means the outward services and acts of the church. He talks in another place of the shame of the Christians, who, with all their aids, including the sacraments, still do not recognize what they have within them. This is in contrast to Proclus and Plato, who, though heathens, recognized the distinction between the ephemeral outward world and eternity.[59] Though the church puts

---

[58] "Dise abgescheidenheit mus man von not haben, so er den heilgen geist und sine goben entpfohen sol, er sol Got meinen blöslichen und sich abgescheiden von allem dem das Got nút enist. Und dise abgescheidenheit und die wartunge des heiligen geistes die ist ungelich in den luten. Die einen die enpfohent den heiligen geist in sinnelicher biltlicher wisen mit den sinnen. Mer die andern enpfingent in vil edellicher in die öbersten krefte und vernúnftigen krefte in vernúnfitger wisen verre úber die sinne. Die dritten enpfingent in nút alleine in der wise, sunder sú enpfiengent in in das verborgen abgrunde, in daz heimliche rich, in den wunnenclichen grunt, do daz edele bilt der heiligen drivaltikeit verborgen lit, das daz alleredelste der selen ist...Und do werdent sine goben edellichen enpfangen noch göttelicher wisen." *Die Predigten Taulers*, p. 92.

[59] "Disem grunde woren die heiden heimlich und versmochten ze mole zergengkliche ding und giengen disem grunde nach. Aber do kamen die grossen meister als Proculus und Plato und gabent des ein klor underscheit den die dis unterscheit als verre nút vinden enkonden...Kinder, dis kam alles us disem inwendigen grunde: dem lebent si und wartent des. Das ist ein gros laster und schande das wir armen verbliben volk, die cristen sint und als grosse helfe hant, die gnade Gotz und den heiligen globen und das heilig sacrament und als manig grosse helfe, und gont recht umbe als blinde hünr und erkennent unser selbes nút das in uns ist..." *Die Predigten Taulers*, p. 332.

forth worthy pictures of grace received, the real locus of God's activity, for Tauler, is immediately in the ground of the human being. This has the effect of trivializing doctrinal disputes, among other things.[60] Though of the same holy order, Tauler is far from Aquinas in his understanding of the sacraments. Having access to the universal truth which is God directly within oneself greatly qualifies the value of the universal which is made flesh in the sacrament. Tauler qualifies his promotion of the direct experience of God in the ground of being by admitting that it is perhaps very few who can actually experience this, and that even then it is only a glimpse of the loss of self which will be eternity in God.[61] Still, as is the case with Neo-platonic mysticism, the history of God's acts in time, including the incarnation, becomes a type which recurs eternally within the highest part of the human soul.[62] In this way all things outward became penultimate, and the desired knowledge and experience is something beyond knowledge and experience, the sinking into the divine abyss.

This brief depiction of Tauler's mysticism will suffice to explain Franck's attraction to Tauler, and to mark out the differences between the two. It should be emphasized that Tauler remained within the institutional church, and preached submission to its authority, even if his mysticism might have detracted somewhat from the church's claim of mediating grace. Tauler avoided the speculative excesses which were condemned in Eckhart. With Franck any question of remaining a true son of the church had been rendered moot even before he came to his mystical speculations. Being outside the context of the church Franck had no recourse to the outward means of grace which might be a safety net for those not fortunate enough to have success in their spiritual exercises. As we shall see, for Franck there is only one outward world, and the inward Word, and there is no longer any halfway house.

---

[60] "Und dar umbe lossent úwer tispitieren hinan ab sin und gelobet es einvelteklich und lossent úch Gotte. Die phaffen was hant si anders ze tunde? und die enwurden och nie also subtil als ietz in der vernunft. Aber sehent das es in úch geborn werde in dem grunde; nút in vernunftiger wise, sunder in weselicher wise, in der worheit, nút in redende, sunder in wesende." *Die Predigten Taulers*, p. 299.

[61] "waz sú do vint, das ist úber alle sinne, vernunft kan es nút erlangen, nieman mag es begriffen noch verston, es ist ein war fúrsmag des ewigen lebendes." *Die Predigten Taulers*, p. 56.

[62] "Daz wort daz sprichet: ein kint ist uns geborn und ein sun ist uns gegeben; es ist unser und zumole unser eigen und úber alle eigen, er wurt alle zit geborn one underlos in uns." *Die Predigten Taulers*, p. 8.

Franck's publications of 1534 are the fullest statements of his own beliefs. And while the *Theologia Deutsch* and Tauler's sermons are his two major reference points, Franck is not averse to referring to figures whom he had earlier denounced, in order to support his argument.[63] But while Franck's mystical writings resonate with the faith of the Rhenish mysticism exemplified in Tauler and the *Theologia Deutsch*, the possibilities available to Franck for reconciling this mysticism with the world are much different. When judged in comparison to Tauler and the *Theologia Deutsch* Franck's writings seem cold and abstract, devoid of the pastoral concern which animates Tauler's voice in particular. It has been said of the sermons of Tauler and the *Theologia Deutsch* that if you have read one sermon or one chapter you know what the rest will say. This is an exaggeration, but there is a tedious repetition of themes in these works, a trait Franck's *Paradoxa* shares.

The *Paradoxa* is a long, verbose work. Although titled *Two Hundred and Eighty Paradoxes*, the final count comes out to two hundred and ninety-two individual and sets of paradoxical statements. Paradox could take many different and complicated forms in the writings of the Renaissance and Reformation period, providing a myriad of interpretive problems.[64] In the hands of a subtle and ironic craftsman, such as Erasmus in his *Praise of Folly*, the use of paradox could lead the reader into a house of mirrors. Franck is much more direct in his use of paradox, and wishes to teach a principle of interpretation, both for

---

[63] Among others Franck quotes or cites Staupitz, Petrarch, Thomas á Kempis, Aquinas, Bernard of Clairveaux, Pseudo-Dionysus, Boethius, Augustine, Ambrose, Origin, Cyril, Tertullian among Christians, and Seneca, Cicero, Cato, Pythagoras, Plato and Socrates, among the pagans. Though much is made of Franck's praise and use of pagan sources, in practice he is not much different than many humanists and mystics, who lift up those who lived before the time of Christ who seemed to express some moral truth or spiritual insight specific to Christianity. The overwhelming majority of Franck's authoritative references are to Scripture, then to Christian authorities, and lastly to enlightened pagans. It should be noted, too, that Franck does not draw his mystical teaching directly from Eckhart. What Franck knew of Eckhart most likely was drawn from Tauler. There are few references to Eckhart in Franck's writings. Since Eckhart had been condemned by the church in 1329 his books were not readily available. His writings were not rehabilitated in a major way till the nineteenth century. A few of his sermons are appended to a 1521 edition of Tauler's sermons; Joannis Tauleri, *Des heiligen lerers Predig...* (Basel: Adam Petri, 1521). This work was republished in 1522.

[64] See Rosalie Colie, *Paradoxia Epidemica* (Princeton, 1966), especially her introduction.

Scripture and for the world.

> In short, the Pharisees...have put Christ to death with the letter, because he lived and taught against the letter (though not against the spirit [*sinn*]) of the Scripture.[65]

The learned have not understood Scripture or Christ because they have not understood that the Christ who is captured by the letter of the Scripture is the false Christ, the Antichrist, who puts the true, spiritual Christ to death.

> Accordingly, because the letter of Scripture is cloven and not at one with itself, there emerge all sorts of sects.[66]

> Alone the free, non-sectarian, impartial Christendom, that is bound to no thing, but stands free in spirit on God's Word and can be grasped and seen with faith, not with the eyes, is of God. Its godliness is bound neither to a sect, a time, a place, a law, a person nor an element.[67]

Here are the poles of Franck's world view. There are those who stand bound to the letter, seeking to discover the Word of God in the outward form of Scripture, and thus breaking up into sectarian strife, for as Franck knows from Scripture itself, "The Scripture is a book closed with seven seals."[68] Against this are those like Franck himself,[69] who are taught first by the Spirit, apart from all outward things, and read the word, being already instructed by the Word.

---

[65] "Kurtzumb/ mit den buchstaben haben die Phariseer (so disselben volsteckten) Christum zu tod geschlagen/ weil er wider din Buchstaben (aber nit wider denn sinn) der schrifft lehrt und lebt/..." *Paradoxa*, p. Av.

[66] "Dennach weil der buchstab der schrifft gespalten/ vnd mit ihm selbs vneins ist/ kommen alle sect darauß." *Paradoxa*, p. Avii.

[67] " allein das frey/ on sectisch/ vnpartheisch Christenthumb/ das an der ding keins gebunden ist/ sonder frey im Geist auff Gottes wort steht/ vnd mit glauben/ vnd nit mit augen begriffen und gesehen kan werden/ ist auß Gott/ Deren frommkeit weder an Sect/ zeit/ statt/ gesatz/ person/ vnd element gebunden ist." *Paradoxa*, p. Avii.

[68] "Die Schrifft is ein verschlossen Buch mit siben sigil." *Paradoxa*, p. A-v

[69] "In und bey diser bin ich/ zu der sehne ich mich in meinem Geist/ wo sie zerstreüzt vnder den Heiden vnd vnkraut vmbfert/ vnd glaub dise gemeinschafft der heiligen/ kans aber nit zeigen/ bin aber gewiß dz ich in der kirchen bin/ sey wo ich wöl/ such sie derhalb/ wie auch Christum/ weder hie/ noch dort." *Paradoxa*, p. Aviii-v.

These need no sect, baptism, church, or following, but are pious for themselves.[70]

What are the exegetical implications of this split?

> If one only holds in all things the opposite of that which they [the world] speak, believe, do hold, etc., then one is in the right. The truth exists only in wondrous sayings, which the world does not speak, hold, do, or believe. If you hear the mob speak, believe, or hold something, so hold, speak, and believe the opposite, then you will certainly have the Gospel and the Word of God. The right way lies deeply buried. All things are a perverted Silenus,[71] and much different than they seem.[72]

Thus Franck uses paradox. By showing to be true those statements which the world holds to be impossible one gets to the heart of the contradiction of the world and the Spirit, and exposes and explains the truth as far as possible in the world of language and outward words. "God has hidden the unseen, essential in the seen and the figurative," Franck states. One must travel inward, away from the world, and find the treasure hidden in the self. This is not the individual's own nature, but that part of the unseen Spirit of God that lies hidden in the human soul. Then will one see through the outward appearance of the world, to the treasure hidden within. All things exist in this paradox: what appears outwardly is deceptive appearance, which seems true but is not, and what is inward, unseen, and thus seems untrue when compared to outward appearance, is the actual, essential truth.[73]

---

[70] "Ein yeder kan für sich selbs wol frum sein/ wo er ist/ darff nit eben hin und her lauffen/ ein sondere sect/ tauff/ kirchen suchen/ anrichten/ vnd auff ein hauffen sehen/ vnnd seinem anhang zulieb glauben/ from sein/ vnd dienst heüchlen." *Paradoxa*, p. Avii-v.

[71] The tutor and attendant of Bacchus, represented with a bald head, and riding on an ass, usually drunk.

[72] "Halt einer nur in allen dingen/ wie vnd was sie redt/ glaubt/ thut/ helt/ etc. das widerspil/ so hat er das recht. Die warheit seind eytel wunderred/ die die welt nit also helt/ thut/ redt vnd glaubt. Hörestu den Böfel etwas reden/ glauben/ vnd halten/ Halt/ red vnd glaub du das widerspil/ so hastu dz Euangelium/ vnnd Gottes wort warlich. Das recht ligt tieff/ Es ist all ding ein verkerter Silenus/ vnd vil anders/ dann es scheint." *Paradoxa*, p. Bii-v.

[73] "Dann die warheit ist vnsichtbar im gaist/ derhalb one allen schein der welt. Daher hat Christus/ sein wort/ reichthumb/ sig sterck/ Reich/ etc. kein ansehen vor der welt/ Esaie Liii. wie alle Gottes werck. Was aber menschlich/ sichtbar/ vnd weltlich ist/ das wie es allein scheint/ also gilt es auch vor aller welt. Wer nun nicht verfaren wil/ der bleib nit herauß and dem schein/ sonder

Franck's presentation of his paradoxes exhibits no particular progression of themes, not unexpected by one who does not believe that human knowledge is harmonious or symmetrical in the outward word. His discussion circles around on itself, the same themes being discussed from a number of angles. He draws his statements from a variety of sources, though biblical passages and popular sayings are most numerous. Many are most likely direct inventions of Franck, or drawn from mystical writings such as the *Theologia Deutsch*. These statements are often the common assumptions of the spiritualist faith.[74] What emerges is a loosely connected series of theological observations revolving around the spiritualist principles expressed in the introduction.

Franck's discussion of most subjects spills over into each other.[75] Franck starts the *Paradoxa* with statements about God's nature. "God is and effects all in all, with the exception of sin,"[76] is one of his basic principles. "God is alone good, truthful, true, indeed goodness, truth, wisdom, devotion,

---

grab tieff in acker/ vnnd reiß weyt auß der welt in sich selbs/ da wirdt er den vergraben schatz finden. Es hat auch die natur/ das köstlich ist vergraben/ das schlecht an weg gelegt. Also hat Gott das vnsichtbar/ wesentlich/ in das sichtbar figürlich verborgen/ Den rechten menschen/ Gottes wort/ sig/ frid/ leben/ etc. nit für die hund vnd seüw an weg gelegt/ sonder mit eüsserem fleisch/ schein vnd buchstaben bedeckt/ das kein vnbschnitner darüber kan kommen. Ja mühe vnd arbeit kost es/ verleügnung sein selbs/ gelaß vnd haß seiner seel vnnd lebens/ will man disen schatz vnnd Christum finden/ vnnd den Silenum auffgewinnen/ das erschein/ was darinn ist. Wer wil wissen/ was in einem Tempel sey/ muß nicht heraussen bleiben/ vnd allein davon lesen/ vnnd hören sagen/ das ist alles ein tod ding/ sonder dareyn gehen/ vnd selbs erfaren/ vnd besichtigen/ denn lebt erst alles/ vnnd diß im Geist sehen vnnd erfaren/ heißt die Schrifft glauben. Das verstendige vns Gott." *Paradoxa*, p. Biii to Biii-v.

[74] "Das Alt und Neüw Testament ist eins in Geists." *Paradoxa*, p. Niii-v.
"Gott gibt Israel nit gesatz deß lebens." *Paradoxa* p. Oii-v.
"Tempel/ Bilder/ Fest/ Opffer/ vnd Ceremoni/ gehören nit inns neüw Testament." *Paradoxa*, p. Piiii-v.

[75] An attempt will be made here to expose the major themes of Franck's theology as presented by the *Paradoxa*, though the imprecision and inchoate nature of Franck's discussion mean the treatment here will exhibit an order not necessarily found in Franck's own work.

[76] "Gott ist/ vnd wirckt alles in allen/ die sünd außgenommen." *Paradoxa*, p. Bvii.

and love itself,"[77] states Franck. Yet because "no one knows what God is"[78] God's nature is rendered problematic for humans, since all that one could speak or know about God is rendered null and void. "God has no name,"[79] says Franck. "Blessed is the people whose God is the Lord."[80] But Franck also states, "no one knows God as God."[81] How does humankind come to a knowledge of this God, who is the very definition of good? Certainly not by any effort on the individuals part, for, according to Franck, "the fool counts just the same as the wise before God."[82] "We have the same appearance before, [are all] the same corrupt earthen clods, and all by nature children of wrath."[83] God is a neutral God, God of the heathen as well as of the Jews and the Christians,[84] who distinguishes between no outer appearance, but sees all things exactly as they are—corrupted. God is not good or God because he corresponds to some goodness outside himself, but he is that good, and the only thing we know about him is that he is "indeed the contradiction of the human heart."[85] "God is the one thing necessary, out of whom comes all good."[86] And yet he is completely unknown to humans.

Of course human's and the world's ignorance of God is part and parcel of their very being (which is non-being before God). "Mankind, world, flesh,

---

[77] "Gott ist allein gut/ warhaftig/ treüw/ Ja die gute/ warheit/ weißheit/ trew/ vnd lieb selbs." *Paradoxa*, p. Bviii-v.

[78] "Niemandt weiß was Gott ist." *Paradoxa*, Biiii.

[79] "Gott hat keinen nammen." *Paradoxa*, p. Bvii-v.

[80] "Selig ist das volck/ deß der Herr sein Gott ist." *Paradoxa*, p. C-v.

[81] "Gott kennet niemandt/ dann Gott." *Paradoxa*, p. Ciii.

[82] "Es ist eben der Narr wie der weiß vor Gott." *Paradoxa*, p. Nvii.

[83] "Wir seind in gleichem angesehen vor Gott/ ein einiger verderbter batz/ vnnd all von natur kinder deß zorns..." *Paradoxa*, p. Nvii-v.

[84] "Gott ist auch der Heiden Gott." *Paradoxa*, p. Mviii-v.

[85] "ya gerad das widerspil des menschlichen hertzens." *Paradoxa*, p. Qii.

[86] "Eins ist allein von nöten."; "Auß einem alles."; "Es geht alles auß Gott." *Paradoxa*, p. lvi-v. "Nun disem einigen notstück/ darauß das ander alles fleüßt/ gibt die Schrifft vil nammen/ vnd ist doch alles nur eins/ also das allein andere wort sind." *Paradoxa*, p. lvii-v.

and devil are one," states Franck. And moreover, "all humans are godless, blind, foolish, and mendacious."[87] "Satan is the prince, all natural humans are the world..."[88] He explains this further:

> And it is an eternal synecdoche, what is said of one human, and it is true for all. Reason: there is only one evil human, Adam, and in him are all his children. On the other side there is only one pious holy human—Christ—who is a new person born out of God.[89]

Franck sees humans and the world as a type for which Adam is the definition.

> Although mankind is a good creation of God, formed according to his image, he is nevertheless become deformed and wasted through sin.[90]

This deformation of humans and the world is thoroughgoing. "All humans are damned and there is not one who is holy among them."[91] This destruction extends even to the just. "There is not one just person on earth who does right and does not sin."[92]

> For give me any holy person you please, he is pious only according to the Spirit and inner person. He must always deaden his unwilling flesh with force.[93]

---

[87] "Mensch/ Welt/ Fleisch/ vnnd teüffel eins."; "Gottloß/ blindt/ thorecht/ vnnd lugenhafft sind alle menschen." *Paradoxa*, p. Liiii.

[88] "Satan ist der Fürst/ Die Welt/ das sindt alle natürliche menschen." *Paradoxa*, p. Liiii.

[89] "vnnd ist ein ewig Synechdoche/ was von einem menschen wirdt gesagt/ ist von allen war. Vrsach/ Es ist nur ein böser mensch Adam/ vnnd in ihm all sein kinder/ Widerumb/ Nur ein frommer säliger mensch Christus/ vnd neüw mensch auß Gott geboren." *Paradoxa*, p. Lv.

[90] "Darumb ob wol der mensch ein gut gemächt Gottes ist/ nach seinem bild formiert/ so ist er doch also verderbt/ beülend/ vnd vngestalt worden durch die sünd." *Paradoxa*, p. Lv-v.

[91] "Alle menschen seind verdampt/ vnnd keiner selig vnder ihn." *Paradoxa*, p. Lviii.

[92] "Die frummen auch sind nicht frum." *Paradoxa*, p. M.

[93] "Dann gib mir einen Heiligen wie du wilst/ so ist er nur nach dem geist vnnd innern menschen frumm/ sein vnwillig fleisch muß er immerzu mit gwalt abdeüben." *Paradoxa*, p. M-v.

"The best are only half pious,"[94] Franck says.

> We are assembled of flesh and spirit, a wonderful mixture of
> death and life, mortal and immortal, of two entirely contradictory
> natures...[95]

> The true, essential human is inward and unseen...We are each
> first made out of nothing or the dust of the earth, afterwards out
> of God to the image of God; he blew into our visage a living
> breath or spirit, so that we become a living soul.[96]

Franck has not contradicted himself with his depiction of human nature.
One must always keep in mind the two views available to Franck. While humans, as known and defined by themselves—the so-called natural humans—are
equated with the world and called man, what is essential and true in
humans—that is humankind as it could be known by God—is their spirit, which is
good and receptive of God. That the natural human is equated with the physical, fleshly human, created out of the dust, raises questions about God's act of
creation, which Franck does not investigate.[97] What Franck does investigate is
the concept of sin. Sin, by an accident, became transplanted into the essence of

---

[94] "der best/ nur halb frumm ist." *Paradoxa*, p. M-v.

[95] "Wir sindt vom fleisch vnnd geist zusamen gesetzt/ ein wunderbarlich
mixtur von tod vnd leben/ tödtlich vnd vntödtlich/ von zweyen gar wider-
wertigen naturen." *Paradoxa*, p. Miii.

[96] "Der recht wesentlich mensch ist inner vnd vnsichtbar/ wie anderswo/
Christianus inconspicuus homo/ gehöret/ Wir sind ye ein mal auß nit oder
staub/ von der erden gemacht/ nachmals auß Gott/ zu dem bild Gottes/ der
bließ in vnser angesicht einen lebendigen athem/ oder geist/ das wir wurden
ein lebendige seel." *Paradoxa*, p. Miii.

[97] Franck does state in his *Von dem Bawm des wissens guts vnd böses*, which
makes up part of the "Vier Krönbuchlein", "Der mensch war gleichwol gut
gemacht/ doch nit aus Gott/ sonder aus nicht/ Darumb naiget er sich alzeit
immer zu wider ab/ zu seinem nicht vnd eitelkeit. Welchs Nicht/ ich die Sünd/
Teüffel/ Tod/ vnd Hell/ mit dem Alten Vätern/ fürnemlich mit Taulero/ nen.
Und disz ist villeicht der inwonend Teüffel gewesen/ in Adam vnd auch in
Lucifer." *Das Theür vnd Künstlich Buchlin*, p. i ii-v. Here is an elaboration of
the advent of sin, but it is not a theme Franck expands on further. It is a good
example of how Franck stops before he involves himself in the true theological
paradoxes.

humans, not because God put it there.[98] Franck wishes no confusion on this point—God is not the cause of sin. Rather, humankind turned God about, using the will, that power which comes from God, against him.[99] Adam turned from God and ate the fruit of the tree of knowledge. This act is endlessly repeated in humans, so that they know now according to the flesh. Humans want to be God themselves.[100] It is from this point that Franck can launch his many and extended attacks on human arts.[101] It is with this eating that humans have fallen into the state of non-being described above.

There is a perspective in which sin and evil is from God and serves his ends. Sometimes God withdraws himself so that men—David and Paul are Franck's examples— who have become proud and secure in their flesh find themselves as their sin moves them to repentance.[102] As defined by humans, evil, that is, suffering, pain, etc., is often God's punishment for sin, to turn them away from self and back to God. As Franck puts it, "the more evil the person, the better the luck," or more graphically, "the devil shits only on the great

---

[98] "Nun wirdt die sünd (ob sie wol ein accidens oder zufal ist) also in die natur vnnd wesen deß menschen versetzt/ das der von natur nicht wert wirt genennt/ Ephes. ii. per Alleosim/ oder Methonimiam/ wie auch das fleisch bös wirdt genennt/ so es doch ein gut creatur Gottes ist/ vnd allein das accidens/ der angenommen affect deß fleischs (so yetzt fleisch wirdt genennt) bös ist/ vnd die sünd eygentlich zu reden/ wider das fleisch vnnd die natur ist/ wie Augustin..." *Paradoxa*, p. svii-v.

[99] "Wie kan dann nun Gott der sünd ein vrsach seyn/ wie sie böß vnd sünd ist? Wir verkeren Gott in vns selbs/ stälen ihm den freyen/ gemeinen willen/ den wir mit ihm gemein solten haben/ vnd eignen vns zu/ Ja ziehen Gottes krafft/ wie die spinnen/ auß der güten blumen gifft/ lincks in vns/ vnd geben dann erst vil ihm die schuld/ daß er diß vnd nicht anderß in vns hab wöllen wircken/ welches die höhest vnnd letst gottslesterung ist/ auß Gott ein teüffel vnd sünder machen." *Paradoxa*, p. Hiv to Hiv-v.

[100] For Franck's extended commentary on the tree of good and evil and the eating of the fruit see the section of the "Vier Krönbuchlein" cited in footnote 97.

[101] "In vil weißheit ist vil vnmuts/ vnd welcher vil erfert/ muß vil leyden."; "Der vil sucht/ dem gehet vil ab/ vnd der vil begärt/ dem mangelt vil."; "Der vil fragt/ geht vil irr."; "Dem ist wol der nichts weiß." *Paradoxa*, p. k.

[102] "Durch die sünd erlöst Gott offt von Sünden." *Paradoxa*, p. Hvi-v.

crowd."[103] Franck's point is that worldly success turns one from God as one
becomes enamored with the physical.

> Therefore he [God] is also near when he is far, and much nearer
> than when he seems near, when everything goes well according to
> the flesh (which is the luck of the godless, who have no distant
> God, but a near one).[104]

God's way is the way of the cross, which Christ with his outward life modeled
for us.

Christ, of course, is the one who reconciles humans to God. For Franck
Christ is both God and human. Franck emphasizes the two aspects and puts
what he considers the proper value on them.

> Christ is according to the flesh only an image and expression of
> God, according to the Spirit however, and the Godhead [he is] the
> Word and God himself.[105]

On account of our weakness God took on flesh to show outwardly what was
known only inwardly in the Old Testament. But "Christ is yesterday, today and
in eternity."[106] Christ is God's Word, which is eternal, and was known by the
fathers of old.[107] Through this humans become capable of receiving God.[108]
"But in us is the Word, the image of God,"[109] asserts Franck. "And it is

---

[103] "Ye böser mensch ye besser glück."; "Der teüffel scheißt nur auff den
grossen hauffen." *Paradoxa*, p. J-v.

[104] "Darumb ist er auch ferr/ nahend/ vnd vil näher/ dann so er nahendt
scheint/ so es vns nach dem fleisch (welchs glück der gottlosen ist/ die kein
Gott ferr/ sonder nahendt haben) wol gehet..." *Paradoxa*, p. Jiii-v.

[105] "Also ist Christus nach dem fleisch nur ein bild vnnd außdruck Gottes/
Heb. 1. Nach dem Geist aber vnnd Gottheit/ das wort vnd Gott selbs/ Johann
1." *Paradoxa*, p. Rvii.

[106] "Christus ist gestern/ heut/ vnd in ewigkeit." *Paradoxa*, p. Rviii-v.

[107] "Darumb welche im alten gelassen/ dem wort haben ohren geben/ vnd
gehört/ was Gott in ihn red/ die haben Christum gehört/ vnnd mit dem Abraham den tag deß Herren gesehen." *Paradoxa*, p. S.

[108] "Darvmb dann der mensch auch zum bild Gottes erschaffen/ vnnd in
Christo außgemacht wirt/ das ist/ Gott hat seiner weißheit/ art/ vnd wäsens
ein muster/ zundel/ gespür/ liecht/ vnd bild/ in deß menschen hertz gelegt..."
Paradoxa, p. Sii-v.

[109] "Sonder in vns ist das wort/ das bild Gottes." *Paradoxa*, p. Siii.

Christ, whom the Holy Spirit has formed in us."[110]   In us is something of the Word, which is Christ, through which we can be remade in the image of God. Thus there occurs in us those things that occurred outwardly.

> What occurs is, is never, but becomes again. Therefore the whole Bible again and again is repeated, and goes into an essence; Adam's fall, the tree of knowledge, repentance, death, life, suffering, the resurrection of Christ...[111]

This drama, however, is inward. Thus the outward revelation of Christ is subordinated to the inward revelation. Franck can speak in the traditional language of the church concerning sacraments, crucifixion, feast days, etc., although he is referring only to a spiritual act. Christ is not to remain an outward image, but must live, suffer, die, and be resurrected within us. We must feed on Christ.

> Accordingly the flesh of Christ is called a food of the soul, which is a wondrous saying, that flesh should feed the spirit. That occurs in this way: if I view Christ with spiritual eyes and not as the pharisees only from outside, and know him in spirit, what God has intended with him, indeed in him, how he has courted us, served us, chosen us, and wanted to draw us to himself, then he would come into the flesh and begod (*vergottet*) us.[112]

This is a typical piece of Franckian exegesis; he consistently allegorizes so that outward acts of God, practices of the church, dogmatic teachings, and the sacraments become metaphors for depicting an inward way of coming to a knowledge of God. Though one assumes Franck is trying to describe his own inward experience, it is this very way of understanding all of reality, Franck's description of the spiritual significance of the flesh of Christ, etc., which becomes the endpoint of his theological program. There is no meaningful outward sign or act which is of any real use in receiving the flesh of Christ. All things stand in spirit.

---

[110] "Welches ist Christus/ den der Heilig Geist in vns formiert." *Paradoxa*, p. Siii-v.

[111] "Was gewesen ist/ ist nimmer/ wirt aber wider. Darumb muß die gantz Bibel für vnd für widerholt/ vnd in einem wesen gehn/ Adams fall/ der baum erkanntnuß/ die Buß/ Item der tod/ leben/ leiden/ vrständ Christi..." *Paradoxa*, p. Sv.

[112] "Demnach wirdt das fleisch Christi ein speiß der seel genennet/ das wunderbarlich ist zusagen/ das ein fleisch den Geist sol speisen. Das geschihet aber also/ wenn ich Christum mit Geistlichen augen/ vnnd nicht wie die Phariseer allein von aussen/ ansihe vnd erkenn ihn im Geist/ was Gott mit/ ja in ihm gemeint hab/ wie er vns damit hoffiert/ gedienet/ gemeint/ gewölt/ vnnd zu ihm ziehen hab wöllen/ vnnd darumb inns fleisch krochen/ das er vns vergöttet..." *Paradoxa*, p. Tv-v.

Christ's life, death and resurrection are meaningful only as far as they are grasped spiritually.

With Christ we are near the center of Franck's theology. As we have seen, Christ is used to express the inward spark, or Word, or image of God which is laid in the ground of the human being. He is that spirit which comes into the soul to enliven it. Christ can be both that which is within us and that which fills us, because he himself had two aspects to his being, as he was both God and human. This is where Franck's Trinitarian language becomes muddy. Franck had previously stated his sympathies for Servetus, and it is doubtful he worried too much about the orthodox Trinitarian formulae. With Christ Franck introduces the center of his theology, the Word of God. Christ is the Word of God, but since the physical Christ is but an image or manifestation of this Word, the Word itself takes on a more primary significance than any outward knowledge of Christ.

> God's Word abides forever; all things are and are still becoming today through the Word; there is only one Word of God; God still speaks today his Word, which creates all things.[113]

> This, I say, is God's Word, that has always been in God, and always will be. Consequently, everything which is outward and temporal, which began in time, such as circumcision, etc., in the New Testament baptism, the keys, the bread of God, even Christ himself according to the flesh are not God's Word, but only a shadow and a figure of the same (just as all outward things are of this type, only to indicate, to figure and to introduce in the truth, which is spirit and life and not the letter or outward ceremony.)[114]

The Word is God's absolute power, which teaches immediately, directly, without any means. "God does and teaches all things in the blink of an eye,"[115]

---

[113] "Gottes wort bleibt ewiglich."; "Alle ding seind vnd werden noch heut durchs wort gemacht."; "Es ist nur ein Gottes wort."; "Gott spricht noch heüt sein wort/ das alle ding erschafft." *Paradoxa*, p. Jviii-v.

[114] "Diß sprich ich/ ist Gottes wort/ das allweg in Gott gewesen/ vnd seyn wirt. Derhalb alles was eüsserlich ist vnnd zeytlich/ mit der zeyt angfangen/ als Beschneydung im Neüwen der Tauff/ Schlüssel/ deß herenbrot/ auch Christus selbs nach den fleisch/ sind nit gottes wort/ sondern allein ein schatt vnnd figur desselben (wie aller eüsserlichen ding art/ nur zu deüten/ figurieren/ eynzuleiten in die warheit/ welche geist vnd leben/ vnd kein buchstab oder eüsserlich ceremonien ist)." *Paradoxa*, p. K.

[115] "Gott thut vnnd lehrt alle ding in einem augenblick." *Paradoxa*, p. Jiiii.

Franck states.

> Rapidly runs his Word. Whoever discerns it itself experiences what occurs and enlightens them in the blink of an eye, about which they have to speak and write an entire day.[116]

> He teaches us more in the wink of an eye, than all outward words, sermons, and Scripture [from now] until the judgment day.[117]

Outward forms are denigrated from being useful images of inward truths to weak images preventing one from grasping more fully inwardly that which God would teach.

This is so because of the relation of the outward to the inward. In fact outward things distract from the inward reception of the Word. To be a self-possessed self is to be captured by the outward flesh and the outward world.

> Whoever stands as a simple unformed chaos stands under the Word, empty of all things; out of them God's Word (which can never let nothing remain nothing, and vice versa can never make something out of something) must certainly create something.[118]

Far from being an aid in the process of "begodding," outward forms, by being outward, frustrate the work of God's Word. For human will has two choices, to be passive (*gelassen*) and suffer God's Word to work, or to take the things of the world and the self, and take the devil for God.[119]

When Franck turns then to analyze the work of God in history, the ways in which he has revealed himself in outward things, he finds little of value.

---

[116] "Geschwind laufft sein wort/ Wer sein selbs war nimpt/ der empfindt diß/ das ihm offt in einem augenblick eynleücht vnnd zufelt/ davon er einen gantzen tag zu reden vnnd schreiben hat." *Paradoxa*, p. Jiiii-v.

[117] "der vns in einem augenblick mehr lehrt/ dann all eüsserlich wort/ Predig/ vnd schrifft/ biß an Jungsten tag." *Paradoxa*, p. Jv.

[118] "Wer nun als ein ledig/ vngeformet Chaos vnder disem wort stehet/ aller ding nicht/ auß dem muß Gottes wort (das nicht nit nicht kan lassen seyn/ wie widerumb auß etwas nicht etwas machen) gewiß etwas erschaffen." *Paradoxa*, p. Kii-v.

[119] "allein der erschaffen mensch ist seines willens/ zwischen tod vnd leben/ vnder Gott gestelt/ zu wollen vnd wöllen (aber nit zu wircken) frey gesetzt/ das er sich vnder Got geb/ oder den Teüffel zum Herren annemme." *Paradoxa*, p. Eviii-v.

Under paradox 86, "God gives Israel no law of life,"[120] Franck shows how
the Israelites saw what the heathens had and wanted the same. Franck asks:

> What has God, who is spirit, intended with this child's play and
> fantasy, that he goes about in Israel with such peculiar clothing,
> gestures, arks, sacrifices, and tabernacle?

It is just as if God wanted to let the child play with the rattle or the puppet,
until he could bring them along further.[121] The history of the church is like
that of the Jews, and God would have them lay aside their ceremonies and all.
Everything is now to be understood according to the Spirit and Truth.[122]
What God reveals outwardly is done only for the sake of human weakness. But
we are forbidden to return to these weak figures and elements.[123]

> Christendom exists only in spiritual divine services: namely in
> purity of heart, innocent life, good conscience and uncolored love,
> in the baptism and the circumcision done without hands and abso-
> lutely not in ceremonies or anything outward.[124]

Franck states that he could prove his point more forcefully if he had not taken

---

[120] "Gott gibt Israel nit gesatz deß Lebens." *Paradoxa*, p. Oii-v.

[121] "Was hat doch nun Gott/ der ein Geist ist/ mit diesem fleischlichen
Gotts dienst/ eüsserlichen ceremonien/ vnd mit disem kindswercks vnnd fan-
tasey/ gemeint/ das er mit so seltzamer kleidung/ geberd/ Arch/ opffer/ Tab-
ernackel in Israel vmbgehet. Es fraget Gott glatt nicht darnach/ Israel sahe der
gleichen von den Heiden/ vnd wolt es nur haben/ da wolt Gott dem kind das
schlötterlin lassen/ vnnd mit ihnen der Docken spilen/ biß er sie weyter
brecht." *Paradoxa*, p. Oiii.

[122] "vnd im Neüwen alles einkert/ vnd auff sein weiß/ nach art deß Testa-
ments/ geistlich vnnd warheit/ ein geistlich Reich/ Priesterthumb/ gottsdienst/
Tauff/ Himmelbrot/ des geists/ feür/ vnd warheit." *Paradoxa*, p. Pii.

[123] "Welches alles innß alt Testamentisch gehört/ damit sie ye Mosen wid-
eräffern/ oder ein figur verlassen/ vnd ein andere an die statt verordnen/ vnnd
also von einer figur in die andere faren/ oder gleichsam als der warheit vnd
freyheit verdrüssig/ von dem wein wieder zum zeiger/ von Neüwen wider inns
Alt/ vom lebendigen menschen Christo/ wider zu seinem bild lauffen/ Welches
vns Paulus so hoch verbeüt/ Galat. v. vi. Vnd vns in der warheit vnnd geist
bestendig heißt leben/ das wir nit zurück wider gehen/ zu den schwachen figur-
en/ Elementen..." *Paradoxa*, p. Piii-v to Piiii.

[124] "das Christenthum in eyteln geistlichen Gottesdienst/ nemlich in reinig-
keit deß hertzens/ vnschuldigem leben/ in der lieb von reinem hertzen/ gutem
gewissen/ vnd vngeferbter lieb stehet/ in der Tauff vnd Beschneydung on hend/
vnd gar nicht in Ceremonien/ oder ichtes eüsserlichs." *Paradoxa*, p. Piiii.

the paradox form, and could show the example of history.[125] We have already seen in the *Chronica* how Franck enumerated the stark absence of God's Word in the outward course of things. The primacy of the inner Word is finally absolute, drawing all that is outward into it, and appropriating everything outward for an inward truth revealed to those who have foresworn the letter for the spirit. The true understanding of all things comes only to those who can read them correctly, who have experienced within themselves the action of God who inflames the spark of the soul. Those who have experienced this have a privileged position from which they view the world. The authority of the learned, the consecrated, and those who inhabit church offices is of little consequence to one who has been taught directly by God, who teaches more in a wink of an eye than everything outward would ever be capable of. With the *Paradoxa* Franck has switched the poles of discussion. Those who are considered learned by the world are the true blind, those who are considered holy are the most impious.

What Franck has done is appropriate the hidden God (*Deus absconditus, verborgener Gott*).[126] This is in starkest contrast to Luther, who considered the hidden God to be God in his wrath, unapproachable by humans, known only by the masks in which he is revealed in history. It is God as he is revealed in Christ in the Scriptures who is the merciful one. Luther's paradoxes are truly paradoxical, as the wrathful God who has created some to damnation is revealed as loving and merciful in Christ.[127] Franck has made the hidden God the one who is revealed, and the paradox of Luther, so irreconcilable in the human mind, is dissolved into the paradox of Franck, that God is a hidden God, which contradicts conventional understanding, but is easily grasped through the inner Word. His polarization resolves the paradox, rather than leaving it beyond human comprehension, and thus truly paradoxical. His own knowledge

---

[125] "Diß wölt ich wol nach leng mit vilen exempeln vnd Historien außfüren/ wenn ich mir nicht hett fürgenommen kurtze Paradoxa vnd Symbola zu schreiben/ vnd auff alle ding nur mit einem finger deüten/ vnd mit willen mehr den gedancken zulassen/ dann auszusprechen. Es muß je dem verkerten vnd vnreinen alles verkert vnnd vnrein seyn/ nicht allein gelt/ gut/ sünd/ finsternuß/ das böß/ weyb/ kind/ etc. sonder auch Gott/ die Heilige Schrifft/ Christus/ sein wort/ das liecht/ leben/ gut/ vnd alles." *Paradoxa*, p. giiii-v.

[126] "Gott ist ein verborgner Gott." *Paradoxa*, p. Kiii-v.

[127] On *Deus absconditus* in Luther's thought see Brian Gerrish, "'To the Unknown God'," in *The Old Protestantism and the New* (Chicago, 1982), pp. 131-149, 334-345. See especially footnote 9, p. 335, which lists the extensive literature on this topic.

contradicts the knowledge of the world, which knows only the outward image, while he has had revealed to him the inward truth.

Franck's *Paradoxa* was an offense to the authority of the church. He was claiming a direct access to the Word of God, bypassing all conventional means, such as Scripture as understood by the learned, sermons, sacraments, songs,, prayers, etc. Those who administered and taught in the church, particularly in the fledgling order which was emerging from the reform efforts in Ulm, would perceive Franck's writings as a threat and a challenge. On the other hand those who administered the temporal realm would not be quite so unsympathetic to the man who was ejected from one city for disruptive writings and who would cause great consternation among their own clergy.

Although Franck was apparently aware of Erasmus' role in his expulsion from Straßburg, nevertheless in 1534 he brought out a German translation of the *Encomion Moriae*, which was bound together with other works to form a compendium Franck referred to as the "four regal little books."[128]   Franck bound his translation of the *Moria* with the other works because, as he explained:

> they all four have one argument and goal, namely, that the entire world's course, essence, piety, and wisdom is nothing but vanity, foolishness, sin, a fable, and an abomination before God...Therefore these books mock all human wisdom and piety, and insist on the rebirth, that one must dismiss human wit, artifice, etc., extract it, destroy it, be translated in Christ, rest in God's Word...[129]

---

[128] The other contents are: *Von der Haylobßigkaitt vnd vngewißhait aller Menschlichen Künst vnd weyßhait*, a partial translation of Agrippa of Nettesheim's *De incertitudine et vanitate scientiarum declamatio inuectiva* (Cologne: Melchior Novesianus, 1531), to which is also attached *Ein Lob des Esels*, a translation of chapter 13 of the *De incertitudine*, "Ad Encomium assini digressio": a work of Franck's, *Von dem bawm deß wißens Gutz vnd böß*: and another work of Franck's, *Encomion: Ein Lob des Thorechten Göttlichen Worts*. The whole work, because of Franck's interliniary commentary plus his own chapters, works as a personal observation on the divide between world and spirit so prominent in the *Paradoxa*.

[129] "weil sie ia alle viere/ ains Arguments vnd zwecks sindt/ Nämlich/ das der gantzen welt lauff/ wesen/ frumkait/ vnd weyßhait/ nichts dann ain Vanite/ thorhait/ sünd/ fabel/ vnd greüel sei vor gott.   Darmub spotten dise Büchlin aller menschlichen weyßhait vnd frummkait/ vnd dringen all auff die wider geburt/ das man menschlicher witz/ kunst/ etc. müß vrlaub geben/ außziehen/ verneüt/ vnd in Christum vbersetzt/ in gottes wort ruen..." *Das theür vnd künstlich Büchlin*, p. A-v.

Franck here intends to bring together disparate material to make his point about the absolute dissimilarity between the world's knowledge and the true spiritual knowledge. Franck's efforts at coordinating his own voice, Agrippa's, and Erasmus' exemplifies the distance between his own mind and Erasmus', and demonstrates Franck's tendency to flatten other thinkers to conform to the dualism of his own thought.

This is not to say that Franck's translation of Erasmus is deliberately misleading. It is a straightforward, if uninspired, rendering of the text, devoid of the elaborations which sometime mark his translation work. The translation, however, is marred by many errors, and much of the delicate humor of the original is lost.[130] There is ample evidence that Franck, while confessing to be an ardent admirer and follower of Erasmus, drew a different meaning from Erasmus' text than the great humanist might have desired. Erasmus' reaction to Franck's *Chronica* was something more than bad temper of old age provoked by the endangerment of courtly favors. Franck misappropriated Erasmus' work to the service of his own spiritual beliefs. In Franck's view *The Praise of Folly*, a classical declamation with playful use of irony and light tone mixed with passages of bitter sarcasm and a positive spiritual vision, is clearly promoting his own message of the uselessness of human knowledge and the need for the infusion of the divine Word. Erasmus' vision, though, of the spiritual ecstasy is not the Neo-platonic "Word" mysticism of Franck, being much more directly related to the Greek sources through the church fathers.[131] Still there was much in the *Moria* that was serviceable for Franck's purposes, when selectively read.

One passage better than any other demonstrates Franck's misapprehension of Erasmus' meaning. This is the section where Folly speaks of emotion and reason, how emotion belongs to folly, and is avoided by the wise who are ruled by reason.[132] Folly states:

> That is why the Stoics segregate all passions from the wise man,
> as if they were diseases. But in fact these emotions not only act

---

[130] See the comments of Rudolf Kommoß, *Sebastian Franck und Erasmus von Rotterdam*, pp. 29-30.

[131] See M.A. Screech, *Ecstasy and the Praise of Folly* (London, 1980) for a nuanced discussion of this aspect of Erasmus' thought. On Erasmus and the influence of Pseudo-Dionysus see pp. 20-21.

[132] "Jam primum illud in confesso est, affectus omnes ad Stultitiam pertinere. Quandoquidem hac nota a stulto sapientem discernunt, quod illum affectus, hunc ratio temperat." Desiderius Erasmus, *Opera Omnia*, vol. 4 (Leiden, 1703), pp. 429-430.

as guides to those hastening towards the haven of wisdom, but also wherever virtue is put into practice they are always present to act as spurs and goads as incentives towards success. Yet this is hotly denied by that doubled-dyed Stoic Seneca who strips his wise man of every emotion. In doing so he leaves nothing at all of the man, and has to ʻfabricateʼ in his place a new sort of god who never was and never will be in existence anywhere. Indeed, if I may be frank, what he created was a kind of marble statue of a man, devoid of sense and any sort of human feeling.[133]

Franck translates this passage faithfully, but his editing reveals his misreading of the text. Franck breaks off after the sentence concerning the "double-dyed Stoic Seneca," and comments on the passage:

The Peripatetics think the emotions and desires are given by nature and poured into us, that we be led through them to virtue and be inflamed. Cicero is also of this opinion...However Seneca, a Stoic, is adamantly opposed, takes away all emotions from the wise, and this opinion is in accord with our faith of the Holy Scriptures. For we must excise all emotion, and be reborn, which Seneca also, as through a fog, has seen, and has better expressed than our scholastic theologians have done these many years. For all our emotions and desires are bad, and are true spurs and goads to all evil, Gen. 6, 8, Matth 15.[134]

---

[133] "Eoque Stoici perturbationes omnes ceu morbos a sapiente semovent, verum affectus isti non solum paedogogorum vice funguntur ad sapientiae portum properantibus, verum etiam in omni virtutis funtione, ceu calcaria stimilique quidam adesse solent, velut ad bene agendum exhortatores. Quamquam hic fortiter reclamat bis Stoicus Seneca, qui prorsum omnen affectum adimit sapienti. Verum cum id facit, jam ne hominem quidem relinquit, sed novum potius Deum quemdam δημιουργος, qui nusquam nec exstitit umquam, nec exstabit: imo ut apertius dicam, marmoreum hominis similacrum constituit, stupidum, et ab omni prorsus humano sensu alienum." Erasmus, *Opera Omnia* 4, p. 430. English translation, *Praise of Folly*, trans. Betty Radice (London, 1971), pp. 105-106.

[134] "Peripatetici mainen die Affect vnd anmut seien von der natur darzu geben vnd in vns gossen/ das wir durch dise zu der tugent werden gelait vnd entzündt/ In der mainung ist auch Cicero/...Aber Seneca ein Stoicus/ ist hart darwider/ entzeücht alle Affect dem Weysen/ vnd die mainung ist vnserm glauben von der Hailigen schrifft gemäß/ Dann wir müssen alle Affect außziehen/ vnnd neu geborn werden/ welchs auch Seneca als durch ain nebel hat gesehen/ vnd baß troffen/ dann vil iar vnser Schul Theologen/ Dann all vnser Affect vnd begird sindt arg/ vnd sind die rechten spieß vnd sporn zu allem vbel/ Gene. 6. 8. Matthei. 15..." *Das theür und künstlich Büchlin*, p. Giiii to Giiii-v.

Franck then continues with the text of the *Moria*. In the original text clearly a criticism of Seneca is intended ("he leaves nothing at all of the man" etc.), but Franck sets in the comment, "picture and image (counterfeit, contrafactur) of a wise man."[135] He thus tries to separate the ensuing criticism from the preceding mention of Seneca, maintaining him as the source of true wisdom. Whether the point of this passage simply escaped Franck, or he willfully reinterpreted it is difficult to say.

Erasmus was, in this passage, engaging in a very subtle play of meanings. It is sometimes difficult to read Folly correctly, since she is, after all, foolish. But of course she speaks often as a rebuke to the wise. Here she is making the telling point that the Stoics are so wise that they have developed an ideal which can accommodate no living person. Folly states,

> Well, if that's what they like they can enjoy their wise man, love him without a rival, live with him in Plato's Republic or in the kingdom of ideas, if they prefer, or else in the gardens of Tantlus.[136]

This passage can turn around on Erasmus himself, normally an admirer of Seneca. No doubt Franck was aware of Erasmus' normally positive evaluation of Seneca and would not accept a negative meaning as Erasmus' intention. For whatever reason, Franck's own comments turn the passage around to conform to his own view, praising Seneca, as he attempts to deflect any criticism onto the wise. Franck gives a straightforward translation of the passage, but his interpretation mangles the meaning. Perhaps he should have paid closer attention to Folly's message. The dogged linear progression of his own mind sacrificed a nuanced depiction of human personality and its motives for stark black and white renderings. Placed beside the enigmatic Erasmus, Franck seems a bit simple and naive. Franck's two other major interjections into the Erasmian text read very explicit interpretations into the complicated meanings of Erasmus. The aim is always theological and anthropological, to set up the distinction

---

[135] "Bild vnd contrafactur aines weysen." *Das theŭr und künstlich Büchlin*, pp. Giiii.

[136] "Proinde, si libet, ipsi suo sapiente fruantur, citraque rivalem ament licet, cumque eo vel in civitate Platonis, vel si malint, in idearum regione, vel in Tantaliis inhabitent hortis." Erasmus, *Opera Omnia*, p. 430. *Praise of Folly*, p. 106.

between the inner true meaning of God's Word and the corrupt outer world.[137]

It is of note that Franck bound together his translation of Erasmus with that of Agrippa, believing the two to be complementary of each other and to Franck's own works. In Agrippa's *De incertitudine* Franck found a work much more serviceable to his own purposes. In this denunciation of human artifice Franck encountered a polemic against human learning which could easily match his own. Many passages distinguish vain human learning from those arts which are taught directly by God. The many years in which the world existed without the written word, and the many changes in ancient tongues, are brought forward to demonstrate the evanescence of outward learning.[138] Franck chooses his passages carefully (for only a small percentage of the work is included), and they very effectively promote his own polemic against vain learning. Agrippa and Franck share many common influences, and it is not surprising Franck can extract from *De incertitudine* such telling quotes. Neo-platonism, particularly Pseudo-Dionysus, exercised a decided influence on them both.[139] They shared a bleak pessimism about the learning of the day, and resorted to secret founts of knowledge to gain access to divine revelation which bypassed the orthodox mediators. Here the similarity ends, as Franck cleaves to the invisible inward Word, while Agrippa had resort to the occult practices and esoteric knowledge of his day, a sort of learning in which Franck exhibits no interest. Franck found much in Agrippa's violent polemic congenial, but his mind did not travel the

---

[137] See *Das theür und künstlich Büchlin*, P. Biii-v and following for two pages of Franck's comments. This is his longest interjection. The passage concerning Silenus, pp. Gii to Gii-v, also turns Erasmus' meaning towards Franck's. Also pp. Giii to Giii-v have another comment by Franck interpreting the text toward a clearer inward/outward distinction. See also the comments of Barbara Könneker, *Wesen und Wandlung der Narrenidee im Zeitalter des Humanismus* (Wiesbaden, 1966), pp. 327-328, footnote 104. The article by Günter Hess, "Kommentarstruktur und Leser. Das 'Lob der Torheit' des Erasmus von Rotterdam, kommentiert von Gerardus Listrius und Sebastian Franck," *Der Kommentar in der Renaissance*, eds. August Buck and Otto Herding (Boppard, 1975), pp. 141-165, compares the different readerships and results of these two commentaries, Listrius learned exercise and Franck's attempt at popularization.

[138] *Das theür und künstlich Büchlin*, p. Xii and following.

[139] See Charles Nauert Jr., *Agrippa and the Crisis of Renaissance Thought* (Urbana, Ill., 1965), especially chapter 6.

same unusual path. His own position was little indebted to Agrippa.[140]

The *Four Regal Little Books* provide a illuminating example of Franck's reading habits and use of texts. Though Erasmus, Agrippa, and Franck himself represent no real common front, in Franck's eyes their common denigration of human learning can point to only one real answer, Franck's own spiritualist faith. All writings that point to this faith become witnesses to this truth. With outward words and learning this negative campaign to prove the vanity of learning is perhaps the best that can be done in service of the divine truth. That Erasmus felt no sympathy for Franck, or that Agrippa plumbed the depths of occult practice in search of knowledge, is either ignored or overlooked by Franck. His own writings in this compendium are an extension of themes already developed in the *Paradoxa* concerning human knowledge. Though there is a gap between Erasmus' wit and Franck's earnestness, this compendium actually demonstrates well the Renaissance polemic against human knowledge, as well as Franck's appropriation of that theme. It is one of the most interesting, and most overlooked, of Franck's works.

Franck's writings of the early Ulm period demonstrate not so much his own disregard for the dangers of heterodoxy as the state of flux in which doctrine stood. In Franck's own mind his efforts could be portrayed as an attempt at the further reform of the church, although this very attempt was not very well reconciled with his views on the possibility of reform in the outer world. Still, Franck did not work to conceal his authorship, or clandestinely circulate his writings, because he did not consider himself to be in violation of any standard of orthodoxy which necessarily would determine the reaction toward his book. In this belief he was only partially correct.

---

[140] Paola Zambelli, "Magic and Radical Reformation in Agrippa of Nettesheim," *Journal of the Warburg and Courtauld Institute* 39 (1976), pp. 69-103, is far off the mark in the assertion that "Franck's writings owed as much to Agrippa's inspiration as to Erasmus's," or that "when he was censored at Ulm by the Lutheran authorities, the ideas he derived from Agrippa were frequently attacked" (p. 102). Erasmus was seminal in the formation of Franck's ideas and is constantly referred to in his works, however mistakenly. Aside from this partial translation of *De incertitudine* and a few quotes in the *Chronica* there is little evidence of Agrippan influence. What is depicted as Agrippa's ideas came to Franck through other spiritualist and mystic writings, not from Agrippa.

CHAPTER FOUR: FRANCK'S STRUGGLES IN ULM

The reaction in Ulm to Franck's works was neither so immediate nor so unambiguous as with the *Chronica* in Straßburg. Franck had not expressed himself on temporal authority in his 1534 works as he had in the *Chronica*. On the other hand, his writings were theologically unorthodox, when measured against the nascent theologies of the reform, and challenged the authority of all temporal church structures. These writings would associate his name with Schwenckfeld, a figure considered suspect by many of the main reformers in Southwestern Germany.

As noted earlier, Martin Frecht, chief pastor in Ulm, was suspicious of Franck from the beginning. Frecht corresponded with Bucer,[1] and it is possible Bucer colored Frecht's attitude toward Franck, as the Straßburg reformer had developed an increasingly negative opinion of Franck. Originally quite mild in his expressions toward Franck, Bucer came to see him as an enemy of the church, so much so that by the time of the publication of his *Dialogi* in May of 1535 he felt it necessary to devote a number of pages refuting Franck and warning against his writings. It appears Bucer perused Franck's *Chronica* and *Paradoxa* carefully and did not like what he found there. It would have been surprising if a leader of the church did not find Franck's views completely untenable. This was both Frecht's and Bucer's reaction, and thus they sought ways to force Franck's departure from Ulm.[2] Although it is not clear whether Frecht expressly asked Bucer to write Melanchthon for help with the situation, this is what Bucer did.[3] Melanchthon then obligingly informed Philip of Hesse of the problem. His description of the peril represented by Franck must have been compelling, for soon after Philip sent off a letter to the city council of Ulm,

---

[1] For an overview of the extent of this correspondence see J.V. Pollet, O.P., *Martin Bucer: Etudes sur la correspondance*, vol. II (Paris, 1962), chapter 7, "Bucer et Frecht," pp. 197-220.

[2] The degree of Frecht's opposition to Franck and the favor Franck had found with the Besserers can be ascertained from a letter from Frecht to A. Blarer dated Nov. 4, 1534, where he complains bitterly about the situation. *Blarer Briefwechsel* vol. 1, pp. 595-596.

[3] This exchange can be traced through references in the following letters: Frecht to Bucer, Jan. 12, 1535, *QGT* 8, p.414; Bucer to A. Blarer, July 7, 1535, *Blarer Briefwechsel*, vol. 1, p. 710; Melanchthon to Frecht, Nov. 18, 1535, *Corpus Reformatorum*, vol. 2, p. 823. See also Georg Veesenmeyer, *Collectaneen von Melanchthons Verhältnissen in welchen er mit Ulmern stand* (Ulm, 1797).

warning them in no uncertain terms against Franck. In the letter dated December 31, 1534, the Landgrave states,

> It has been brought to our attention that a certain person, Sebastian Franck by name, is said to be permitted residence by you, and has in speech and writing let go out many improper things, especially against authority, such that one may recognize and take him openly for a troublemaker and Anabaptist. Therefore, meaning well, we have not wanted to fail to make you cognizant of that which has come to us, so that you expel this man from you and thus no suspicion or rebuke grow on his account, not only that the papists might be set against you, but also others.[4]

He ends by again assuring them of his good intentions, which, with his veiled reference to the bad will of "others," might reasonably be in doubt.

As with the Straßburg incident, the charges brought by Philip against Franck deal with disruption of order and not with any specific doctrinal deviance. Franck is a disrupter and Anabaptist (to sixteenth-century authorities the two were synonymous), though the warning concerns not so much a threat to Ulm's internal peace, but what the opinion of outsiders might be. No doubt for Philip, who had been trying to consolidate a united evangelical front against the threat of the Emperor, any potential for disruption of the harmony of the evangelical estates was serious business. His own treatment of the Anabaptists was in fact the most generous of any prince,[5] but the displeasure of three prominent reformers must have warned him of potential splits in the ranks over Franck. Philip knew little enough of Franck, but his very note bore witness to the Ulm authorities of the truth of his claim; Franck was gaining for Ulm unwanted notoriety.

Franck, in apparent ignorance of the fate about to befall him, was developing plans to get back into the printing business. He had made contacts in Augsburg from his previous publishing activity. In 1534 Silvan Otmar of Augsburg had published one of his tracts. Franck also had connections to Heinrich

---

[4] "Uns wirdet angezaigt, daz sich ainer, gnant Sebastian Franck, bey euch halten und mancherley ungeschickte dinge, in reden und schriften, insonderhait wieder die oberkait, ausgehen lassen soll, also, dasz man ine offentlich fur ainer aufrurischen und widerteufer, erkennen und vernemen möge. Derhalben so haben wir guter wolmeynunge nit untherlassen wollen, euch solchs also, wie es an uns gelangt ist, zu erkennen zu geben, damit ir denselben man von euch weysen und seinethalben in kainen verdacht und verweys wachsen und nit allein die papisten, sonder auch andere euch zuwider machen möget." Hegler, *Beiträge*, p. 114.

[5] See F.H. Littell, *Landgraf Philipp und die Toleranz* (Bad Nauheim, 1957).

Steiner and Philip Ulhart.[6] In Augsburg he met Jörg Regel, also from Donau-wörth,[7] a man sympathetic to Franck's spiritualist views, though more inclined toward Anabaptism than Franck. Through Regel Franck also met, and favor-ably impressed, Bonificius Wolfhart, pastor in Augsburg.[8] On January 21, 1535, both men wrote Bernhard Besserer and Daniel Schleicher on behalf of Franck. Regel praised Franck, and put forward a plan to set him up as a printer. Ulm should allow Franck some space for his trade, Regel was ready to loan Franck 100 guldin, and a Jew, who was known in Augsburg, and who had a set of He-brew type, would move to Ulm to help Franck publish Hebrew texts. This, Regel suspected, would be so lucrative that a 100 guldin profit a year could be made on it alone, outside of any German books printed. Wolfhart's letter fol-lowed the same lines as Regel's.[9] Here was expressed Franck's great desire, and perhaps the time had seemed ripe to work his way back into the printing trade. But with Philip's recent letter, Franck would have been better served if he still were identified with the less problematic trade of soap-making. Franck soon would find himself concerned with more than plans for a new trade.

The Landgrave's letter had the effect desired by Frecht, Bucer and Mel-anchthon. On January 25, 1535, the council recorded its decision.

> Concerning the letter of my grace Landgrave Philip of Hesse, that Sebastian Franck in his writings is considered by many to be dis-ruptive and an Anabaptist, and desires to be rid of him—it is de-cided, that my graces Mr. Mayor and the privy council of five be sent to him, and should tell him to change his residency and to

---

[6] Steiner printed three different editions of *Von dem grewlichen laster der trunckenhait.* See Kaczerowsky, pp. 27-34. He also printed two editions of Franck's *Cronica...der Türckey*, Kaczerowsky, pp. 41-43. Silvan Otmar published *Das gott das ainig/ ain/ vnd höchstes gut*, Kaczerowsky, p. 83. Ulhart, known for his Anabaptist sympathies, later published a number of works by Franck, as well as collaborated with him on publications. See Kaczerowsky, pp. 8, 93-95, 114; also Karl Schottenloher, *Philipp Ulhart* (Munich, 1921).

[7] On Regel's unusual life see Maria Zelzer, *Geschichte der Stadt Donau-wörth*, vol. 1 (Donauwörth, 1958), pp. 146-153.

[8] On Wolfhart see Karl Wolfart, "Zur Biographie des M. Bonificius Wolf-hart," *Beiträge zur bayerischen Kirchengeschichte* 7 (1901), pp. 167-180.

[9] These letters are printed in Julius Endriß, *Sebastian Francks Ulmer Kämpfe*, pp. 36-39.

remove himself within a month.[10]
Philip's letter struck a nerve among the council members, who were deeply
concerned about the safety of the city and their ability to protect its interests
outside the walls. If this were the only concern of those who ruled Ulm, Franck
would have been sent packing post haste. In fact this was just the beginning of
a protracted struggle which revealed many of the fissures in Ulm's ruling order
which gave the control of religion in the city its deeply ambiguous character.

Though today Ulm is a city of at most middling size and significance, the
cathedral that towers over it bespeaks a past when Ulm was one of the richest,
most populous, and important cities of the Holy Roman Empire.[11] It ruled
over a territory of about 830 square kilometers,[12] larger than all but Nuremberg's among Imperial cities, and had a population of around 20,000 residents,
a size achieved by only a few other cities in the Empire.[13] It was the most
important city in the Swabian circle of Imperial cities, and until the 1530's, one
of the leading cities in the Swabian League.[14] The pressures of holding onto
its territory meant that political decisions of the authorities in Ulm were heavily
influenced by what can anachronistically be called foreign policy. Concerns
about Imperial politics deflected the course and content of religious policy.[15]

---

[10] "Uf schreiben meins genedigen lantgraf Philipsen zu Hesse, dasz sich
Sebastian Franck in seinem schreyben also halte, dasz er bei menigklich fur
ufrurisch und ainen widerteufer geacht, mit begern, sich sein zu entschlahen - ist
entschloszen, dasz main gunstiger herr burgermaister und die funf ine be-
schicken und im sagen sollen, sein an wesen hier zuverkern und sich in monats
frist hinweg ziehen..." Hegler, *Beiträge*, pp. 114-115.

[11] A piece of doggerel which was common up to the time of the Thirty
Years War ran, "Straßburger Geschütz/ Nürnberger Witz/ Venediger Macht/
Augsburger Pracht/ Ulmer Geld/ bezwingt die ganze Welt." Quoted in Kon-
rad Lübke, "Die Verfassung der freien Reichstadt Ulm am Ende des alten
Reiches" (Dissertation, Tübingen, 1955), p. 2.

[12] Eugen Trostel, *Das Kirchengut im Ulmer Territorium* (Ulm, 1976), p. 15,
footnote 2.

[13] *Cambridge Economic History*, vol 4 (Cambridge, 1967), p. 82.

[14] On Ulm's situation among the Swabian circle see Herbert Jäger, *Reichsstadt und schwäbischer Kreis* (Göppingen, 1975).

[15] Georg Schmidt, *Der Städtetag in der Reichsverfassung. Eine Untersuchung
zur korportiven Politik der Freien- und Reichsstädte in der ersten hälfte des 16.
Jahrhunderts* (Wiesbaden, 1984), provides a study of Imperial politics of the

The nature of Ulm's polity also affected the behavior of the mayor and the councils. Ulm had what is generally called a guild constitution, the councils having a large guild representation. Pressure from the larger populace thus had a greater influence in shaping the council policy concerning reform than in a patrician dominated council such as Nuremberg's.[16] All these factors had an obvious influence on Ulm's course of reform.

Perhaps the most famous figure in Ulm's reform was the Franciscan preacher Johann Eberlin von Günzberg, one of the earliest publicists of Luther's criticisms of the church and reform ideas.[17] Eberlin left the city in the summer of 1521, though, and the reform ideas were given voice by a number of lesser known followers of the new teachings. Ulm would not have a dominating figure such as Bucer, Brenz, or Blarer to push forward reform. This gave the secular authorities somewhat more initiative in shaping its course, especially since in Bernhard Besserer, many times mayor of Ulm in this period, the city possessed a politician of great skill and subtlety. The real impetus for reform came from the populace at large. The council felt it could not suppress

---

cities. His study portrays the influence of religious politics as secondary in the cities' behavior as against the other important concerns of the day. His study deals only briefly, though, with the period after 1530. This is in contrast to the picture painted by Martin Brecht, "Die gemeinsame Politik der Reichsstädte und die Reformation," *Zeitschrift der Savigny-Stiftung für Rechtsgeschichte, kanonistische Abteilung* 63 (1977), pp. 180-263, who emphasizes the extent to which the cities' political behavior vis á vis the Emperor was influenced by specific concerns about the reform of religion. As we shall see, the case of Ulm might provide support for both positions.

[16] See the interesting study of H.R. Schmidt, *Reichsstädte, Reich und Reformation: korporative Religionspolitik 1521-1529/30* (Stuttgart, 1986), particularly his chart of city constitutions, p. 21, and the chart of how various groups and individuals influenced reform, p. 16. Unfortunately his study does not extend beyond 1530. As we shall have opportunity to note later, Eberhard Naujok's study, *Obrigkeitsgedanke, Zunftverfassung und Reformation: Studien zur Verfassungsgeschichte von Ulm, Esslingen und Schwäbisch Gmünd* (Stuttgart, 1958), traces the change in the understanding of the *Obrigkeit* in which the citizen becomes the object of ruling force, a move away from the guild rule ideal.

[17] These and other details of the early voices of reform in Ulm can be found in C. Theodor Keim, *Die Reformation der Reichsstadt Ulm* (Stuttgart, 1851), section 2.

the calls for change without risking disruption.[18] Their response was ambivalent. In 1524 they called the evangelical preacher Konrad Sam. His sermons
proved to be popular events, eventually being given in the great cathedral itself,
but at the same time there was no action by the council to restrict the mass.
The council allowed both the evangelical and Roman clerics to preach anything
they could draw from Scripture, a reflection of their very careful approach to
reform.[19] Their overriding concern was that nothing which might be proclaimed or practiced in the church detract from their status as *Obrigkeit*. The
Peasant's War served only to reinforce this careful stance. Though the city
authorities were more sympathetic to the common man's claims than most, they
had no inclination to involve the city on their side in the struggle.[20] Konrad
Sam was in correspondence with Luther from early on and received from him
his writings.[21] With the outbreak of the eucharistic controversy, Sam, and apparently a greater part of the citizenry who had sympathies one way or the
other, took their stand with the Zwinglian teaching. In 1526 an edited version
of a Sam sermon—*A report for the common man, whether the body of Jesus Christ
is to be sought and honored in heaven at the right hand of God, or on earth essentially in the bread*—was published in Ulm. Both Zwingli and Oecolampadius
wrote to congratulate Sam on this statement.[22] Sam was an unapologetic supporter of Zwingli and, unlike Bucer and Capito, did not try to mediate between
the two positions. In his catechism of 1529 he provides, in question and answer
form, a thorough refutation of Luther's position.[23] All this set him at odds
with followers of Luther's teachings. The Zwinglian teaching would exercise an

---

[18] Martin Brecht, "Ulm und die deutsche Reformation," *Ulm und Oberschwaben* 42/43 (1978), pp. 96-110; p. 98.

[19] Keim, pp. 98-99.

[20] Hans Greiner, "Ulm und Umgebung im Bauernkrieg," *Ulm und Oberschwaben* 16 (1909), pp. 1-68.

[21] Keim, p. 87.

[22] Keim, p. 124. Huldrich Zwingli, *Werke*, vol. 8, #499.

[23] This catechism is reprinted in *Die evangelischen Katechismusversuche vor
Luthers Enchiridion*, vol. 3, ed. Ferdinand Cohrs (Berlin, 1901), pp. 75-128. See
especially p. 126 and following. See also the article by Johannes Haller, "Die
Ulmer Katechismusliteratur vom 16. bis 18. Jahrhundert," *Blätter für württembergische Kirchengeschichte* 9 (1905), pp. 42-69, 124-142. The first section deals
with Sam's catechism.

influence in Ulm long after the death of Sam, and cause certain problems for those who followed in his office, especially for Frecht.

The Diet of Augsburg and the events surrounding it reveal the tensions involved in Ulm's religious/political situation. Early in 1529 the permissive decree of the first Diet of Speyer was ended by the second Diet in this city, where it was resolved that the Edict of Worms should be enforced. There were to be no more innovations or secularizations. Catholic practice was to be tolerated, and Anabaptism and Sacramentarianism were to be suppressed. In response six Lutheran princes and fourteen south German cities, including, in an act of uncharacteristic decisiveness, Ulm, offered a protest, declaring their right to answer to God alone in matters pertaining to salvation.[24] In response to the precarious situation in which the evangelical estates found themselves, Philip of Hesse attempted the reconciliation of the parties divided over the Eucharist, in order to provide a united front to the Emperor. Bernhard Besserer of Ulm aided in this by attempting to mediate between the southern German and Swiss territories and Nuremberg. Ultimately Philip's attempt failed, and Besserer's actions ended up angering the Swiss, while drawing Ulm no closer to Nuremberg or the north German princes.[25] The effect of all this was to set Ulm in opposition to the will of the Emperor, while creating no strong alliance with the other protesting estates.

Though not officially "reformed," Ulm could not be set by the authorities in obedience to the Speyer decree, for in general the sentiment of the citizenry was with the reform party. Still, in the period up to the end of the Diet of Augsburg, the council would try to convince the Emperor of their conformity to his dictates. As Sam wrote Bucer, "They [the council] have decided in this time that nothing may be renewed in the church."[26] The Emperor exercised particular leverage by threatening to take away Ulm's authority over the city of Heidenheim and its territories and give it to the Wittelsbach princes. These rich territories were recently acquired by Ulm, and the council was most anxious

---

[24] Lewis W. Spitz, *The Protestant Reformation 1517-1559* (New York, 1986), pp. 114, 161.

[25] Heinrich Walther, "Bernhard Besserer und die Politik der Reichsstadt Ulm während der Reformationszeit," *Ulm und Oberschwaben* 27 (1930), pp. 1-69; pp. 27-29.

[26] Quoted in Hermann Steck, "Die Reichsstadt Ulm und der Augsburger Reichstag im Jahre 1530" (Dissertation, Tübingen, 1927), p. 15.

to retain them.[27]   When push came to shove at the Diet of Augsburg, Ulm futilely attempted to maintain a neutral position. The city did not wish to sign the *Augustana* because of its sacramental teaching, and it avoided being brought into the *Tetrapolitana* (the confession of Straßburg, Constance, Memmingen, and Lindau) in order to maintain its position of neutrality. In the end the city gave over no real confession.[28]   They maintained they supported any religious decision of a Christian council which rested on Holy Scripture.[29]   This was not what the Emperor sought. Perhaps if Bernhard Besserer had remained healthy some middle ground might have been found, but towards the end of the Diet he fell ill. At this point the Emperor directly threatened to take away Heidenheim if the city did not enforce the decision at Speyer. Faced with this prospect, the decision was brought to a vote of the guilds, and, with a certain amount of management, the Speyer decree was overwhelmingly rejected.[30]   This popular decision was presented to the Emperor in the softest terms possible. Though displeased the Emperor did not take away Heidenheim, nor had he apparently ever intended to.[31]   As this episode demonstrates, while sentiment for reform in Ulm was strong enough to require some sort of accommodation by the authorities in outside politics, it did not dictate a decisive political course. Other considerations affected these decisions, particularly concern over the position of the city in relation to the Empire, and the security of Ulm's territory. Ulm's territories were particularly vulnerable to the aspirations of neighboring princes, and in fact with the restoration of Ulrich in Württemberg, Ulm was forced to give control of Heidenheim into his hands.

With the vote of the guilds the council finally moved officially to set through the reform of the city. In April of 1531 the council took the first step. They contacted the city councils of Straßburg, Basel, and Constance in order to acquire the aid of the reformers in these cities for the reformation of Ulm's church order. It was felt, especially by Bernhard Besserer, that if Ulm's reform

---

[27] Steck, pp. 18-38.

[28] Steck, pp. 69-70.

[29] Steck, p. 44.

[30] Julius Endriß, *Die Ulmer Abstimmungslisten vom November* 1530 (Ulm, 1930).

[31] Steck, pp. 86 and following.

was to achieve its aim, outside help was necessary.[32] In its initial period the sentiment of those behind the reform was solidly Zwinglian, and this action expresses this solidarity. The importance of Ulm to other southern German and Swiss cities was expressed in the personalities who were dispatched to aid the reform—Bucer from Straßburg, Oecolampadius from Basel, and Ambrosius Blarer from Constance. With the aid of these three, against Bernhard Besser-er's cautions to go slowly, the council went ahead with a thoroughgoing reform of church practice, both in Ulm and its territories. The church order which was finally adopted and announced to the Emperor and other territories was most heavily influenced by Bucer. Consequently it avoided all the sharp edges of Zwingli's teachings while retaining a marked Zwinglian emphasis in its state-ment on the sacraments (baptism and Eucharist).[33] The order would have been even more markedly Zwinglian had the reformers had their way. But on the exercise of the ban and institution of sumptuary laws the council proved resistant, for, as in Straßburg, they did not wish to give up the right to oversee the functions of the church. The minsters were allowed verbal admonition of the errant, but the legislation of morals was retained by the council, much to the dismay of the pastors.[34] The actions of the council here were fully in line with its behavior prior to the reform, when caution regarding change bespoke both worries about its effect on outward relations and the possibility that through the popularly supported push for the christening of institutions and social relations a regiment of powerful priests might obtain a sort of Savon-arolan authority in the city.[35] The councils' ideas of authoritarian rule clashed

---

[32] Julius Endriß, *Das Ulmer Reformationsjahr in seiner entscheidenen Vor-gänge* (Ulm, 1931), p. 15.

[33] Keim, p. 247. On Bucer's role in the Ulm church order see two articles by Ernest-Wilhelm Kohls, "Ein Abschnitt aus Martin Bucers Entwurf für die Ulmer Kirchenordnung vom Jahre 1531," *Blätter für württembergische Kirchen-geschichte* 60/61 (1960/61), pp. 177-213, and especially "Martin Bucers Anteil und Anliegen bei der Abfassung der Ulmer Kirchenordnung im Jahre 1531," *Zeitschrift für evangelisches Kirchenrecht* 15 (1970), pp. 333-360. The *Ordnung*, including the apology (*Gemein Außschreiben*) is published in Martin Bucer, *Deutsche Schriften*, vol 4 (Gütersloh, 1975), pp. 183-305. See also Gustav An-rich, "Die Ulmer Kirchenordnung von 1531," *Blätter für württembergische Kirch-engeschichte* 35 (1931), pp. 95-107.

[34] Paul Hofer, "Die Reformation im Ulmer Landgebiet - religiöse, wirt-schaftliche und soziale Aspekte" (Dissertation, Tübingen, 1977), p. 89.

[35] E. Naujoks, *Obrigkeitsgedanke*, p. 56.

with the ideal of the use of ban by a priesthood of believers.[36] The Ulm
church ordinance attested both to popular religious sentiment in its sacramental
teachings, and the sentiment of those who ruled, in its exclusion of a provision
for the ban.

Of course the council was not monolithic in its sentiment. Unfortunately,
for the most part any variation in opinion among the council members has not
been recorded for posterity. In the instructions for Ulm's representatives to a
Diet in Memmingen an interesting voice of dissent is recorded. When the topic
of baptism was raised it was discussed how soon after birth the child should be
baptized. They agreed that the next sermon after the birth was to be recommended for baptism into the Christian community. Hans Muller, head of the
guild of goldsmiths, however, wished to know why baptism had to be bound to
a place or time since it was an outward thing. Parents should be allowed to
baptize their own child one, three, four, five days, one or more years afterwards,
in their own house or wherever they desired, by themselves or by others, according to the words of Christ. It is an outward thing, Muller stated, and thus no
piety is in the act.[37] When the subject of the Eucharist was raised, the council
as a whole had nothing to say. Muller again gave his own view, that in accordance to 1 Corinthians 4, each should take his own wine and bread, for if a
pastor or minister is appointed to do it every day, things will be directed back
toward the old papistry.[38] The council's collective opinion of their colleague's

---

[36] E. Naujoks, *Obrigkeitsgedanke*, pp. 76-77.

[37] "Tauff. Von dem dess tauffs halben gestallt, wissen meine Herrn, noch
zuweiln, annderst nit zurech, dann das sy jne dasselb, gefallen lassen, doch den
gestallt (die weil jnn des predicanten rattschlag, kain zeitt, jnn der die new
geporn kindlin, vor den Cristenlichen gemain, getaufft werden sollen, bestympt)
das davon zurechen were, Das ain jedes New geporns kind, die nechste predig,
nach seiner gepurt vor der Cristenlichen gemaind geteufft, vnd alls pald, dem
volck, ain ermanung von Tauff gethan werden sollen.

Vermaint aber Hanns Muller Zunfftmaister, dieweil der tauff nun ain
eusserlich ding, so sey nit von noten, den an ain statt oder vff ain zeit zubinden,
derhalben woll er ainen jeden zulassen, seine kinder jn ainen tag, dreyen, viern,
funffen, in ainem monat, in ainem oder mer jarn, in seinem hauß oder wo jne
verlust, durch sich selbst oder ander, nach den worten christi, jnn namen gott
des vatters, Sons, vnd hailigen gaists, zutauffen, Dann so es nun ain eusserlich
ding, so sey oder stee kain seligkait darinnen." Ulm Archive, vol. 8983/I, pp.
134 to 134-v.

[38] "Nachtmal. So haben meine Herrn, in haltung deß nachtmals diser zait,
sonder enderung zuthun auch nit gewist, Dann das Hanns Muller zunfftmaister,

views can be gathered by the notes in the margin of both passages which state "do not read."[39]

The above incident is illustrative of both the presence of dissenting opinions even among the city council members, and also the council's interest in the question of baptism. The council in general avoided formulations for disputed doctrinal questions. Usually they sought to avoid firm statements which represented the unity of the church, being aware of the conflict of opinion. When the pastors wished to nail the binding articles of belief to the door of the Cathedral, they were checked by religious overseers appointed by the council.[40] The council members have been depicted as Erasmian in their resistance to an independent ruling dogma, seeing it as merely a means to aid the moral life.[41] The purpose of baptism was to introduce the child into the Christian community, and the meaningful question was when that should occur. There were numerous good, non-dogmatic reasons why the council might prefer infant baptism. More importantly all the evangelical estates accepted infant baptism: only the discredited Anabaptists promoted adult baptism. Also infant baptism effectively produced a consecrated community from birth forward. Thus while Hans Muller may have considered baptism adiaphora, few other council members considered this a respectable position, even if they were not always of one mind with their pastors. In addition the council feared the dispersion of its own authority among the common citizens.

The council faced the problem of dealing with those who did not wish to participate in a church that was not made up of visible Christians who confessed their faith through adult baptism. Ulm had a relatively small Anabaptist move-

---

vermaint, kainen pfarrer oder diener in dem selben, Es sey in verkundung gottlichs worts, oder raichung weins vnd prots, sonder das in haltung deß nachtmals, ainer der darzu verordenet leren, vnnd dann ain jeder Christ, vom wort gottes, Es sey in psalmen, oder andern leern, wie der hailig sanct Paulus, zu den Corinthiern in den erste am xiii schreipt, das, das Cristenlich vnnd gut sey Rech vnnd leeren, Auch deß herin wein vnd prot, selbst messen vnnd nemen mog, Dann wo pfarrer oder diener in denselben bestimpt, so wurde es sich von tag zu tag imer dahin gerichten, Ettlicher massen, widerumben in das allt bapstumb ein zutretten." Ulm Archive, vol. 8983/I, p. 134-v.

[39] "Liß nit." In both places the section on Muller is indicated by lines. Ulm Archive, vol. 8983/I, pp. 134-134-v.

[40] Naujoks, *Obrigkeitsgedanke*, p. 84.

[41] Naujoks, *Obrigkeitsgedanke*, p. 85.

ment within its walls and territory when compared to cities of approximately its own size, such as Straßburg and Augsburg.[42] The first recorded activity is in 1527. In March of 1528 the council inquired of Straßburg and Nuremberg how they had responded to the Anabaptists. Nuremberg sent back a published instruction and warning for the Anabaptists. Since Ulm had no one official church form at that point, the Nuremberg teaching on baptism was no solution to the problem. The mayor and council did, in the same year, issue a call against the Anabaptists, in response to the Emperor's mandate of 1528. It called upon the Anabaptists to be obedient in all ways, especially regarding rebaptism.[43] This, needless to say, did not stop Anabaptist activity in the city. Between 1530 and 1532 numerous reports of Anabaptists show up in the records. In February 1531 the council called on Konrad Sam to present his suggestions for dealing with the increasing numbers of Anabaptists who were trickling into the city.[44] These suggestions were adopted almost without revision by the council. Those who were outsiders (*frembd widerteuffer*) were to be expelled from the city and territory without a hearing.[45] Those who were residents, though not citizens (*beiwoner*) should be questioned, and if they confessed Anabaptism, also be expelled. If those who had been expelled returned, they could

---

[42] Claus-Peter Clasen, *The Anabaptists in south and central Germany* (Ann Arbor, University Microfilms, 1978) has published lists of the names of Anabaptists as recorded by the various localities which tried to control their activity. A rough comparison of numbers can be gained by these lists. Augsburg takes up six pages (pp. 99-104), Straßburg three pages (pp. 93-96), and Ulm only one page (p. 115). Four large volumes of documents have been published from Straßburg concerning that city's religious dissenters. By contrast documentation from Ulm is relatively modest, the larger part devoted to the struggles of the pastors with the council over Schwenckfeld and Franck.

[43] "Ruff wieder die wiedertauffer." Ulm Archive, vol. 1753, p. 1.

[44] "Nachdem die sect den Widertauffer hie vasst zunempt meret, vnd sich frembd, nit geuarlich lissten, in die statt drynngen vnd vnderscheuffen, haben mein gunstig gepietend herren, Burgermaister vnnd gehaimen Ains Ersamen Raths predicanten Conrat Somen beschickt den in seinem gut beduncken, gehört, der hat vast die meinung gerath wie meine herren entschlossen haben vnd nachvolgt." Ulm Archive, vol. 8983/I, p. 128. There are two other versions of this contained in the archive, vol. A 1753, p. 2; and vol. A 1208/II, pp. 682 and following. The three are virtually identical.

[45] "Das dennach all frembd widerteuffer, so hie erfarn, on ainich verhör, der statt vnd ains Erbern Raths herrschafft verwisen werden." Ulm Archive, vol. 8983/I, p. 128.

be flogged as an example.[46] If, however, a citizen displayed this tendency, the pastors and learned were to be sent for, the citizen was to be questioned, and with all possible diligence, through the Holy Scriptures, be turned away from his errors. Even if he did not mend his ways, still, if he conducted himself well and did not attempt to draw others into his sect, he was to be endured for a time. If then he would not be instructed from Scripture, he should be expelled from the city. At any time in the future should he walk away from this misguided sect then he should be pardoned.[47] That Anabaptism was perceived by the council as a threat to its authority is reflected in the oath suggested for those expelled Anabaptists who would regain admittance to the city. They were above all to swear obedience to the mayor and the council as well as renounce their sectarian ways.[48]

This became the basis for dealing with Anabaptism in Ulm. Soon thereafter, the expulsions began from the city. In the next two years over twenty

---

[46] "Item so dann hieig Beywoner dem widertauff anhengig erfarn,, die sollten beschickt vnd ir halltung gehört werden, vnd sie den widertauff bekannt, auch dermassen, mit vnd gegen in gehandlt werden, wie vor laut...So sich aber vber sollich verweisen, wider entringen vnd das verpott nit meiden, sonder vffsetziger weise, in die statt oder herrschafft geen vnd anhang machen wollten, so sollen dieselb alsdann (andern zu exempel) mit Ruten vssgestrichen werden." Ulm Archive, vol. 8983/I, pp. 128-128-v.

[47] "Wo aber Burger dem widertauff verwandt oder dem selben naigig hie weren, dieselben sollten alssdann fur die predicant vnd gelerten beschickt, in bei sein der herren so ain Rath darzu ordnen möcht verhört vnd möglicher vleiss angekert werden, mit hailiger gottlicher schrifft von irem irren zuweisen, Sover sie sich dann beicht vnd bekeren leissen hett sein weg, wo nit so sy dann allain dem tauff anhangen, vnd sonst wie ander Burger alle beschwerd tragen, sich Burgerlich hallten, Niemant zu Inen ziehen, oder vff ir sect weisen wöllten, weren sie auch doch allso zugedulden, sich in ainem monat dem nechsten von irem furnemen zuweisen so sie sich dann mit göttlich hailliger schrifft, nit weissen lassen, sollten sie der statt auch verwisen werden, Doch aber allso wann sie furan vber kurzen oder lang zeit komen, sich ains bessern vnderweisen lassen, vnd von diser verfuerisch sect abtretten werden, das man sie dann wider begnaden solle." Ulm Archive, vol. 8983/I pp. 128-v to 129.

[48] "Aid dern so wider einkomen. ir werdt schweren der sect des verfuerischen widertauffs gantz abzutretten, mit denen so derselben verwant sein khain gemainschafft haben, noch die behausen beherbergen, noch vndertzuschlaiffen, alle beswerden wie annder gehorsam Burger, leiden, tragen, vnd furnemblich ainem Burgermaister vnd Rat in allen auffrechten Redlichen sachen, wie jn dann alle jar auff sannt Jeorigen tag, schweren werdt gehorsam zusein, alls getrewlichen vnd ungevarlichen." Ulm Archive, vol. A 1753, p. 3-v.

expulsions from Ulm and its territory are recorded.[49] One particular recorded instance of Anabaptist opinion demonstrates why both the council and the pastors could find a common enemy in the Anabaptists and their supposed subversive influence. The report on one Matheus Strizell (or Sturizell) tells of the attempt to import a tract from Augsburg to Ulm and to distribute it surreptitiously through local sympathizers.[50] The booklet itself[51] is a perfect example of what the council repeatedly refers to as obstinate (*halsstarrig*) sectarianism. It was titled *A new dialogue, question and answer between a pastor and a baptist concerning preaching, eucharist, baptism and true Christian community, delightful to read.*[52] This was an Anabaptist recruitment tract, as the dialogue is written to show the pastors positions to be shot through with errors. In the end the pastor must admit the force of the Anabaptist's arguments and concede that to become a Christian, he must conform his life to the apostolic model presented by the Anabaptists. The main charge made against the pastor is that he serves in a church which baptizes babies who do not know what baptism signifies, and administers the Eucharist to all regardless of moral standing, a consequence of not practicing discipline and exercising the ban in his so-called church.[53] The

---

[49] Following the document in footnote 49 is recorded this statement: "Auff dise hevorgeschriben ordnung, vnnd ains Erbern Ratts beuelch gmess, haben mein gunstig gepiettend herrn, Burgermaister vnnd die funff, all widertauffer beschickt, von denen auff gelegt, wie die ordnung vermag." Ulm Archive, vol. A 1753, p. 4. Following this are listed all the acts of the council from 1531 and 1532 expelling individual Anabaptists, pp. 4 to 7-v, after which follows an alphabetical register recording their names. No acts of the council after 1532 are recorded. Other reports of Anabaptist activity from 1531 are recorded in Ulm Archive, volume A 1208/A, pp. 686-689.

[50] Ulm Archive, vol. A 1208/I p. 697.

[51] The booklet is bound in the vol. A 1208/I next to the account of Matheus Strizell, pp. 691-696.

[52] *Ein new gesprech/ frag vnnd antwort zwischen ainem Predicanten vnd ainem Tauffer/ von wegen deß predigen/ Abendmals/ Tauffs vnd recht Christlicher gmain/ hübsch zulesen.* No printer, printing date, or location is given though it is said to come from Augsburg. The initials F.H. are printed by the title, but no name of the author is given.

[53] "Nun antwurt ich/ von wegen das wir nit an dein predig gen/ noch das Obentmal mit dir vnd den deinen halten/ ist diß die vrsach/ du predigest vnd lerest/ man sol Gottes vnd Christi gebot vnd willen halten/ vnd du bist der erst der sie vbertrit/ als mit dem kindertauff..." Ulm Archive, vol. A 1208/I, p. 692.

pastor has submitted the church to the worldly authorities, though he knows they do not do what is right, thus the blind lead him to destruction.[54] These charges must have been doubly infuriating for the pastors, who indeed had tried to institute discipline and the ban, only to have their efforts frustrated by the council. The tract touched a real sore point, and coupled this with a rather simplistic promotion of adult baptism as scripturally authorized, and a charge of false piety against the pastors. Of course, for the temporal authorities Anabaptism was the ultimate attempt to wrest oversight of the church from them by setting up a church whose disciplinary function was its political structure, and thus was completely removed from any control by "worldly" institutions. The threat was not to be countenanced.[55] Thus Sam's suggestions found acceptance by the mayor and council.

The measures taken against Anabaptism must have proved effective, for

---

"Item du heltest nit Christliche Ordenung inn deiner gemain/ weder brüderliche straff/ hand/ ein oder außschliessung/ Auch kain vnderschait noch absonderung/ brichest dy brot mit jederman." Ulm Archive, vol A 1208/I, p. 693.

"du soltest solcher an dem Abendmal erfarn/ da jederman bei einander were/ alda je kainer mit lasterhefftigen das brot der gemeynschafft brechen sol..." Ulm Archive, vol. A 1208/I, p. 694-v.

[54] "Müssen dann die weltlichen Oberen vnd richter dein lere richten? Ich mainte/ es solten deine schäffel/ oder zuhorer richten nach dem wort Pauli." Ulm Archive, vol. A 1208/I, p. 693.

"weil du erkennst die kindertauff nit auß Got sein/ warumb schweigstu deß inn deiner predig/ machest dich vnschuldigs bluts teilhaftig/ vnd sagst nit der Oberkait mit Petro das sie selbs richt.." Ulm Archive, vol. A 1208/I, p. 694.

"Das nimm zu gutem an lieber freundt/ laß dir die sach zu herzen gen/ forcht Gott/ vnnd thu buß/ greiffs predigen anderst an/ oder ste gar dauon/ das bit ich dich/ odder es wurde inn dieser weiß Obrigkait/ hiert vnd heerdt/ blinde vnd blinden fürer mit einander verderben." Ulm Archive, vol A 1208/I, p. 694-v.

[55] As an interesting sidelight to the behavior of the *Obrigkeit* is their attitude toward undesirable elements in the population and their use of expulsion, which is discussed by Eberhard Naujoks, "Ulms Sozialpolitik im 16. Jahrhundert," *Ulm und Oberschwaben* 33 (1953),pp. 88-98. There is a relationship between reform and the development of a social politics which went against early capitalism. It was marked by the combatting of interest taking, and the setting up of poor relief. The authorities had, since the 1490's, increasingly made it more difficult for outsiders to gain residence in Ulm, a policy checked during the early years after the reform, but taken up again after 1537.

after 1532 there is no recorded Anabaptist activity again until 1537. The next attempt at expulsion for religious heterodoxy was aimed at Franck.[56]

The program adopted by the authorities for dealing with Anabaptism is important for understanding Franck's own problems in Ulm. It shows an instance in which the city authorities, both secular and spiritual, agreed on the subversive nature of a particular religious heterodoxy. These guidelines informed the action that was taken against Franck. The pastors viewed Franck in the same light as they viewed the Anabaptists, as a religious heretic whose teachings detracted from the right formation and authority of the church, a misleader of the people. The secular authorities, however, did not all see Franck in this light.

Two personalities played a large role in the events that revolved around Franck in Ulm, and represent the differing views of clergy and council, the leading politician of the city, Bernhard Besserer, and the head pastor Martin Frecht. Besserer was the dominant character in both Ulm's political life and the legislation of religion. Besserer was mayor in Ulm starting in 1514/15 and then every third year till 1538/39.[57] Besserer used the independence in foreign policy given the mayor and the privy council (*fünf geheimen*) to put his own stamp on the politics of the city.[58] Besserer not only occupied the office of mayor many times, but served as Ulm's representative at the Diets of Worms and Augsburg, among others.[59] By the 1530's the city would make no significant decision without consulting Besserer. With the lack of any reformer of the stature of Bucer, Zwingli, or even Ambrosius Blarer, Besserer, who had begun

---

[56] It is unlikely that apathy is the cause of the lack of Anabaptist expulsions. In 1533 the Nuremberg city council wrote the privy council of Ulm expressing fear about the Anabaptists and their potential to stir up the peasants, as occurred in 1525; Ludwigsburg Staatsarchiv, B207, Bü 69, p. 43. In 1535, at the request of the privy council in Biberach, the council in Ulm sent suggestions for dealing with the Anabaptists; Ludwigsburg Staatsarchiv, B207, Bü 69, pp. 44-45. Also the events in Münster could not but have set the council even more adamantly against Anabaptism.

[57] Karl Rabus, "Der Ulmer Burgermeister bis 1548" (Dissertation, Tübingen, 1952), p. 248. One could only be mayor every third year, although Besserer rotated to the office of *Alt-Burgermeister* and head of the privy council in the intervening two years.

[58] Heinrich Walther, "Bernhard Besserer," p. 6.

[59] Heinrich Walther, "Bernhard Besserer," pp. 13, 29.

to play a serious role in religious affairs in the 1520's,[60] was able to exert a good deal of influence on religious policy. Besserer's sympathies lay with the new evangelical faith, though, he did not share many of the theological principles of the reformers. He shied away from binding piety to outward forms or the letter; and he constantly had before his eyes the political consequences which were bound up with the new religion. He often checked the attempts of the clergy to push forward with reform when he saw that it compromised the political interests of the city.[61] As the Imperial city required peace for its trade and industry, Besserer strove at most points to achieve unity in religious as well as worldly affairs.[62] In the last years of his life (1537-1539) he exchanged letters with Philip of Hesse, and it is clear from these, though he had been affected by the teachings of Luther and especially Zwingli, he tended toward a Schwenckfeldian sort of piety, with its accents on the inwardly grasped faith and the pious life over and against any outward ceremony.[63] We have seen that Besserer's initial reaction to Franck was positive. Other important figures in Ulm shared Besserer's religious sentiments. We have already heard from Jörg Besserer, his son. In addition Conrad Aitinger, the city scribe from 1520 to 1540, played a very important role in practical politics, and was Besserer's right hand man. His son Sebastian, also a clerk, was a sympathizer of Schwenckfeld's.[64] Among the temporal authorities of Ulm there was some sympathy for views which would not be sanctioned by the pastorate.

Martin Frecht, on the other hand, worked long and hard for the institution of visible reforms in the church, including its order, discipline, and the definition of orthodox standards.[65] He battled doggedly for the elimination of

---

[60] Heinrich Walther, "Bernhard Besserer," p. 13.

[61] Heinrich Walther, "Bernhard Besserer," p.41.

[62] Heinrich Walther, "Bernhard Besserer," p.42.

[63] Heinrich Walther, "Bernhard Besserer," pp. 46-48. These letters are in part published by Walther, pp. 64-69.

[64] Heinrich Walther, "Bernhard Besserer," pp. 4, 55. Also R. Emmet McLaughlin, *Caspar Schwenckfeld*, pp. 172, 192, 198, 221.

[65] The literature on Frecht is thin, but see G. Bossert, "Martin Frecht," *Realenzyklopädie für protestantische Theologie und Kirche*, vol. 6 (Leipzig, 1899), pp. 241-244, and more recently two articles by Werner-Ulrich Deetjen, "Licentiat Martin Frecht, Professor and Prädikant (1499-1556)," *Die Einführung der Reformation in Ulm*, eds. Hans Eugen Specker and Gebhard Weig (Ulm, 1981),

sectarian and competing voices in the church. As we have seen, the city council and Konrad Sam had vigorously pursued the Anabaptists in 1531 and 1532. When Frecht came to the leadership of the church with the death of Sam in 1533, the Anabaptist threat was apparently eliminated from the city. His main battle would be against two individuals, Schwenckfeld and Franck.

Frecht has received a very bad press from the biographers of Franck and Schwenckfeld. He has been depicted as "a censor of sanctimonious impatience and personal hatefulness against those who struggle honorably for existence and freedom of belief," as "the eternal petty bourgeois," and as a "fanatic."[66] There has been little effort to understand the motivations behind his actions. In his favor Frecht was a somewhat gifted pastor and scholar. He was a native of Ulm, and studied in Heidelberg with, among others, Franck. He developed at that time a circle of friends with humanistic interests. Sometime before 1529 he achieved the degree of licentiate of Theology. He took up the Zwinglian position in the Eucharistic controversy, although he regretted the divisions caused by this strife. From early on he was in correspondence with Bucer, Melanchthon, Oecolampadius, Blarer, and Vadian.[67] He published very little but was widely respected by these other reformers.[68] He was called to Ulm in 1531 to be "Reader of Holy Scripture," the title he retained until 1548. In Ulm Frecht was placed in a very difficult position. Sharing with Bucer a vision of reform, he encountered a city council which was unwilling to concede any authority to those entrusted with leading the church. Frecht, de facto leader of the spiritual authorities in the city and recognized as such, carried no official title. With the death of Sam, Frecht took on the responsibilities of the former head pastor,

---

pp. 269-321, and "Martin Frecht," *Theologische Realenzyklopädie*, vol. 11 (Berlin/New York, 1983), pp. 482-484.

[66] Teufel, *"Landräumig"*, p. 56, and Peuckert, p. 281. Teufel, whose analysis constantly reverts to envy and mean-spiritedness to explain the various attempts to silence Franck, states, "Man darf vielleicht neben den Glaubensfanatismus als zweites Motiv bei Frecht eine gewisse Eifersucht auf Franck als Geschichtsschreiber vermuten" (p. 56).

[67] To name only those in whose printed edition of letters Frecht's letters show up with frequency. See Deetjen, "Licentiat Martin Frecht," p. 319, for unpublished sources for Frecht's letters.

[68] See the works listed in Deetjen's article in the *Theologische Realenzyklopädie*, pp. 483-484.

though the city council at first looked elsewhere for a new minister.[69] Eventually the council appointed him as Sam's successor. Since the council allowed to him only the power of the word to pursue order and orthodox uniformity in the church, that is what Frecht used, both on the populace and the council. His stubborn persistence and occasional shrillness are in part a result of the limited tools available to him and his frustration at their ineffectiveness, especially with the council. Frecht, too, was extremely wary of unseen subverters of the church. In a note to the council advising them of the dangers of Anabaptism and the activities of the sect which had come to his ears, he warns that the real danger is not the Anabaptist that one sees, but those who sneak around and are subtle and secret. Because of these one should be diligent and vigilant, for only a little yeast leavens the whole loaf, and only a small unobserved spark makes a great fire.[70] This is a good example of the paranoia which afflicted Frecht in his relations with those who held what he saw as heretical views. His experience at Ulm would demonstrate to him the pernicious effect two lone individuals could have on the city council itself, frustrating his vision of church reform, two men Frecht was convinced were destroyers of the church in disguise.

Franck's expulsion from Ulm did not remain long in effect. On January 29 the council recorded another order, to investigate the matter further by assigning the mayor and the five privy council members to the case.[71] This

---

[69] See Keim, pp. 313-314.

[70] "Was der Teuffer halb, meinen gunstigen herrn Den fünff anzuzaigen seyn.

Dweil zü unsern gfarlich Zeytten, zwayerlay Teüffer sich von Gmainer Evangelischer hauszhaltung Gottes abschwaiff machen, Erstlich die Gruben offenlich Teüffer, Darnach die sübteilen vnd heimlich Teuffer, die meins erachtens schedlicher dann die ersten seynd dweil je der feünd so tuckisch vnd heimlicher weyss, ainer nachstelt schedlichter ist denn der abgesagt vnd offenlich feind, ist deszhalb dester vleissiger vnd achtsamer auff der selbig züsehen...ein wenig sauerlings verseweret den gantz Taig, so gibts die erfarung, ein veracht vnd versaümpt klein füncklin liechts, macht ein gross feuer vnd Brünst..." Ulm Archive A 1208/I, p. 684. The piece is undated but is bound with other material from 1531-1532. See also his letter to A. Blarer dated April 5, 1534, in which he talks of Schwenckfeld as one who presents a false face. *Blarer Briefwechsel*, vol. 1, pp. 482-483.

[71] See Hegler, *Beiträge*, p. 115. Hegler notes that the *Schulpfleger* is also assigned to investigate the case. What he does not note is that in the original this is crossed out. The *Schulpfleger* was a committee appointed to oversee education, and was headed by Frecht.

was done in response to a no-longer extant supplication from Franck. Legally not even an Anabaptist who was a citizen could be expelled so arbitrarily, without a hearing. What exactly was done is not recorded, but their investigation left the council of two minds. On March 3 two decisions concerning Franck were recorded. The first allows him to retain his citizenship, but forbids him to publish or write, especially in Ulm. This, however, is crossed out and the next entry records the order that he leave the city by June 24th. The council does allow a refund of his taxes.[72] Franck was not discouraged from pursuing the matter. On March 7th, Frecht wrote to Ambrosius Blarer, telling him of the winning letters Franck had written to Frecht. These were carried over by Franck's pregnant wife and twin boys. Frecht was not particularly moved, claiming it was not in his power to decide the matter.[73] No doubt he was satisfied with the outcome. But Franck did not limit his efforts to Frecht. Some time between May 3rd and June 11th he presented the council with a second supplication. He called on the council,

> especially that one does not treat me poorly, but as with everyone, justice be administered, and I not be expelled unheard, which is against the general order, custom, and law of this praiseworthy city. (For what happens to me today, tomorrow may happen to someone else.)[74]

Franck's lifelong residency in Imperial cities shows in his Ulm appeals, with their canny use of themes central to the constitutional orders of these cities. Though decidedly not a politician, Franck did instinctively draw upon the language of rule in these cities when appealing to the council members. He was aware of Ulm's laws governing Anabaptism, for he demanded the same rights to a hearing.[75] Franck was most distressed over the charge of Anabaptism which

---

[72] Hegler, *Beiträge*, p. 115.

[73] "Nunc Francus scriptis blandissimis me convenit omnia se facturum pollicens, quia ipse velim; mittit gravidam uxorum et gemilliparam cum liberis ad me, quasi in mea sit manu eum vel pelere vel retinere in urbe." *Blarer Briefwechsel*, vol. 1, p. 668.

[74] "Namlich dasz man mich armen, wie yederman bey der gerechtigkait handhab und nit wider gemeine ordnung prauch und recht diser löblichen stat onverhört ausztrieb (dan was heut an mir ist, möcht morgen an ainem andern sein.)" Hegler, *Beiträge*, p. 116.

[75] "Wie man doch ye vnd allwegen von alter bisher teufer, juden, hayden und allerlay rottengayster zu verhär hat komen laszen, so will ich mich vohr raths, schriftlich oder mundtlich auf all wider mich eingelegt articul dermasz

had been lodged against him. He advised the council that he was the exact opposite of an Anabaptist, having never sought division or sect.[76] No doubt the events then taking place in Münster make the charge of Anabaptism that much more alarming for Franck, for he remarked, "soon they will perhaps also call me a Münsterite."[77] He also spent much energy disputing the charge that he injured the majesty of the Emperor and that he was a rebel. He was convinced that anyone who read his book with understanding must perceive his effort as one of impartiality, a member of no party.[78] It is a tribute to the purity and sincerity of Franck's unconventional vision that he simply could not understand why his books provoked such reaction. One might think that his own vision of the world as turned about would force him to recognize that his books were doomed to condemnation. But, though Franck diagnosed this condition, he must have had faith in his own eloquence to provide the cure, for his response retained a vigorous, if wounded, tone, and never betrayed any resignation. Nevertheless he did, in his second supplication, concede to lay down the pen if the council so desired, since now he had another avenue to support himself and his family which would bring great honor to the city—printing.[79] Franck asked for a two year probationary period, and if he were a detriment to the honor of the city, then the judgment of the council would stand.[80] As he

---

verantwurten, dasz man mein unschuld greifen musz." Hegler, *Beiträge*, p.116.

[76] "wie mich villeicht etlich mit onwarhait abmalen...ein ketzer und teufer usz mir machen willen, denen ich doch mein tag nie angehangen bin, sonder das widerspil...Hab mir auch kainerlay sect und zertrenung nie gefallen lassen." Hegler, *Beiträge*, p. 117.

[77] "Werden mich villeicht bald Münsterisch nehnnen." Hegler, *Beiträge*, p. 117.

[78] "wie ein ieder herzhaftiger verstendigen der mein pucher liset, mich onparteisch urteiln muß..." Hegler, *Beiträge*, p. 118.

[79] "Bin auch ganz und mer dann froo, das ich die feder (dieweil mir gott ein ander thur, mein und meiner kind nahrung zu uberkomen ufgethan) hinlegen soll und will vermittelst der hulf gottes und fromber leut hie in E F W stat mit derselben begunstiger ein stattliche namhaftige truckerei...dadurch mein, meiner kind und gemeiner stat Ulm nutzen, nahmen ehr und wolfart kommen und erwachsen soll." Hegler, *Beiträge*, p. 119.

[80] "mit mir doch nur ein oder zwey jar versuchen und zusegen; wa ich denn in diser zeit der stat Ulm kein ehr einleg, sonder nachtilig pin, und das, so mich mein widersächer beschuldigen, ewer E F W wahr sein befynden: so besteh es

had done with Frecht, Franck wished to make sure the council was aware of his family situation and the consequences his expulsion would have on his pregnant wife and children. Franck states in his conclusion,

> Concerning all this I leave it to your honors to decide the trou-
> ble, need, poverty, and misery which your honors expulsion of me,
> my wife, and children, though innocent, from domestic honor to
> the beggar's staff, indeed even to death. For should the council
> then withdraw citizenship and without a decree expel me out of
> their city and territory, I could never again appear anywhere,
> would become a stateless person and an outlaw, having [to suffer]
> for the rest of my life, and in all places, not one but many
> deaths.[81]

Franck is convinced that if he were expelled from Ulm no other place would then allow him entrance. He can only envision ruin for himself and his family and civic death.

Fortunately for Franck his supplication at least had the effect of prolonging the process against him. On June 11th the council agreed to hear his case when the mayor was present. Franck's supporter Jörg Regel wrote the council, informing it of his loan to Franck, which he specifies as 700 guldin.[82] The decision the council finally handed down was to explore the matter further. Especially the two books he had recently published in Ulm were to be searched, and if passages were found which were detrimental to the council or the community, Franck was to give a clarification and account of this. At that point a further decision would be rendered.[83]

---

bey ewer E F W urteil, die ich auch hiemit roborirt und bekröftigt haben will." Hegler, *Beiträge*, p. 119.

[81] "Uber das alles gib ich auch ewer E F W zu erwegen die ergernusz, noth, armut und elend, darein ewer E F W mich, mein weib und kinder onschuldiglich von heuszlichen ehrn an pettelstab ja bisz in tod verwisz; dan sollte mich ewer E F W also bürgerlich tödten und one ein abschid ausz irer statt und land verweisen, wurde ich niendert mer einkomen könden, were gleich damit landröumig und geächt, muszt all tag nit ain sonder vilmal sterben..." Hegler, *Beiträge*, p. 120.

[82] Hegler, *Beiträge*, p. 121-122.

[83] "ist entschloszen, in der handlung zu verordnen, sich in seinem schriften und buchern und sonderlich in den zwey buchern, so er hie auszgen lassen hat, mit grund und vleis zu ersehen und zu erkundigen, und warinnen er gefelt, misz oder das geschryben oder auszgen lassen het, das ainem ersamen rat oder gmeiner stat nachtailig were, dasselb aingentlich auszzuziehen, es Francken zu

This was Frecht's opportunity to convey to the council his objections to Franck's publications, particularly concerning the *Paradoxa*. This he did in two statements, one under his own name, and one as the head of the school committee. Both pieces express the same concerns. Under his own name Frecht allows himself some bitter, ironic stabs at Franck.

> Everything is likewise laid in the inward, and not so much on the outward teaching and writing. However, these scribes nonetheless destroy much paper, as a fair reader and judge can indeed ascertain. In addition they use much teaching and writing in order to bring their opinion to the people, just as it is suspected that they wish to rule alone in the church. But nonetheless one is supposed to sing and speak much about spirit and inward teaching and preaching, and what is taught and written outwardly is supposed to be only a witness.[84]

Frecht suspected Franck of motives other than impartiality. The committee on schools makes the same charges against Franck, although in more measured tones. The members begin by quoting the eighth article adopted by both sides at the Marburg colloquy:

> that, to speak properly, the Holy Spirit gives to no one such faith or his gifts without a preceding sermon, spoken word or Gospel, but works through and with such spoken words, and creates faith wherever and in whomever he will.[85]

They then point out a pair of statements from the *Paradoxa*—#163, all tongues and art are impure for the godless, and #226, the world's belief is an impure belief—where Franck, using the same Scripture as the above quote from the

---

uberantwurten und sein antwurt darauf und wie er das erclern und ausfuren wölt zu hören und dahn seinthalben verner zu entschliessen." Hegler, *Beiträge*, p. 123.

[84] "es sey gleich alles an dem innerlichen gelegen und nit so vil an dem eüsserlichen leren und schreiben. Aber nichts destominder verderbent dise scribanten vil papeyr, wie ein billicher leser und richter wol kan urtailen. Zůdem so brauchen sy so vil lerens und schreibens, damit sy iere opinion in die leut bringen, als eben die so bey inen verdacht, als wöllen sy allein in der kirchen regenten seyn. Aber nichts destominder musz man vil von gaist und innerlicher lerer und predigern singen und sagen, und was eusserlich geschriben und geleeret wirt, musz nůr ein zeügnüsz seyn." Hegler, *Beiträge*, p. 127.

[85] "das der hailig gaist ordentlich zů reden nyemants solchen glauben oder sine gabe gibt on vorgeend predig oder mündlich wort oder evangelion etc., sonder durch und mit solchem müntlicher wort wirckt er und schafft den glaüben wo und in welchen er will." Hegler, *Beiträge*, p. 123, 130.

articles of the Marburg colloquy (Romans 10), makes the opposite point, i.e. only the inner Word serves to create faith. This is the first point they wish clarified.[86] The second is related to the first, that "the Scripture is not for teaching, but only to be read as a witness."[87] This they associate with corner preachers, and the names Denck and Hätzer in particular, using Franck's own *Chronica* to substantiate the charge. They then cite again chapter and verse from the *Paradoxa*.[88] They try to anticipate Franck's objections—that he was only comparing the inner to the outer word, that they are like gold and silver—and then state that Franck's writings suggest,

> that not much is allowed to the outward word, Scripture, and sentence. Should not that also at least be declared and clarified, since unfortunately it is apparent that for many spirits more is seen in the inner word, visions, and dreams, even revelations, that in the outer word.[89]

The school committee is eager to have Franck clarify his meaning, since they are certain he will implicate himself with the other "spirits," and here they mean everyone from Müntzer to the Münsterites, who also see the church only realized within. They call for Franck to draw up a confession of his beliefs as the estates did at Augsburg.[90]

They are careful to point out, for the sake of the council, that the *Para-*

---

[86] Hegler, *Beiträge*, p. 130. Two works published in 1535 contain introductions by Franck, and are duly noted by the school committee as further evidence against him. These are both the work of Valentin Krautwald, Schwenckfeld's dedicated ally; *Von der gnaden Gottes* (Ulm: Hans Varnier, 1535) and *Epistola ministri cuiusdam verbi* (Ulm: Hans Varnier, 1535). For the first work see *Corpus Schwenckfeldianorum*, vol. 3, pp. 68 and following, for the second *Corpus Schwenckfeldianorum*, vol 6, pp. 193 and following.

[87] "die gschrift sey nit zur leer, sonder allein zür zeugnusz zu lesen." Hegler, *Beiträge*, p. 131.

[88] Hegler, *Beiträge*, p. 131.

[89] "Darausz dann leichtlich genommen, das am eüsserlichen wort, gschrift und gsatz nit so vil gelegen sey. Solte nur das nit auch wol declariert und erclärt werden, dweil laider vor augen, dasz von vilen gaistern mehr auf das innerlich wort, gesichten und treum, auch offenbarungen gesehen wiert, dann aüf das eusserlich wort." Hegler, *Beiträge*, p. 133.

[90] "Nit mehr möcht man von Franck begern, denn das er sich vlisse, zu schreiben und zu halten, wie die Säxische und der andern protestierenden ständen confession vermag." Hegler, *Beiträge*, p. 134.

doxa was banned in Saxony, Hesse, and Straßburg, that Nicholas von Amsdorff of Magdeburg, a close associate of Luther, had written against it.[91] Not only does Franck's presence threaten the reputation of the city, but also its good order. What is Franck's intention? Though he says he wishes to set up no new church, he states that the Lutheran or Zwinglian churches are illegitimate. The committee suspects that he and Schwenckfeld are in league to institute their own church.[92] The point out:

> With this [Franck's teachings] in the place of the outward office of preacher there would come over time nothing but spiritual speculation on the inner word, visions, and revelations, as one unfortunately sees in the Münster case.[93]

By demeaning things outward Franck threatens the social order. They reach the center of their case against him when they bring forward paradox 44, "the mas-

---

[91] "Allein zeigen wier hie in der gemein an, was in seinen biechern, so hie furnemlich trückt sein worden, den einfaltigen und auch erbawten im wort gottes, die in Sachszen, Hessen, und Straszburg, wie wir vernommen, seine paradoxa verboten haben, ergernusz und anstosz bringen mage." Hegler, *Beiträge*, p. 134.

"Wier wöllen aber hie auch erzelen, wie kürtz verschinen zeyt ein evangelischer predicant Nicolaus Ambsdorffius, prediger zu Magdenburg, im latein ein tractetlein hat lassen auszgon, darin er den Francken mit namen nennet und im genugsam anzaigt, dasz er Franck nit recht schreib und halt vom buchstaben und gaist." Hegler, *Beiträge*, p. 135.

The tract referred to is *Contra Zwinglianos et Anabaptistas themata* (Erfurt, 1534) in which Franck is named and grouped with the Zwinglians. This piece could only make the pastors in Ulm more anxious to distance the city from Franck, since Amsdorf is saying that Franck and the south German and Swiss theologians are in the same camp; the Straßburg theologians are named specifically.

[92] "Do musz jetzund in den Luterischen und Zwinglischen kirchen, wie man sagt, noch kein rechter beruf, dienst, predigampt, hauszhaltung und anrichtung der h. sacramenten seyn. Man wartet aber darauf, wenn das ministerium spiritus, das recht ampt des h. gaists, wiert angon und villeicht ausz der Schleszischen und Fränckischen kirchen kommen, wiewol Franck in der vorred der paradoxen sich hoch verdingt, er warte auf kein newe kirchen. Aber die zwey obgemalten biechlin hie zu Ulm getruckt zaigen anderst an." Hegler, *Beiträge*, p. 136.

[93] "Damit wurde mit der zeit an stadt des eusserlichen predigersampt nichts dann geistlichen speculierungen von innerlichen wort, von gsicht und offenbarung kommen, wie man laider jetz sicht in der Müntzerische sach." Hegler, *Beiträge*, p. 136.

ter (understand God) teaches more in the wink of an eye, in a shout, more than all outer words, preachings, and Scripture until the Judgment Day." The report states:

> It is true that for God *potentia absoluta*, through his wholly perfect omnipotence, anything is possible. He can and may, as it is said, make an axe under a bench crow. However one should speak *de potentia dei ordinata*, of God's ordained power, as he has used it in his words and works, that he, as the oft stated article indicates, gives his grace through the means of his words and sacraments, servants chosen by him. He had, before the law [was given] dealt by the spoken word with the fathers. From heaven Christ converted Paul with his spoken word.[94]

They conclude by listing the specific points they want Franck to clarify.[95] The argument they present against him is not exclusively based on theological concerns, but on the belief that Franck's deviations from certain points concerning the outward rule of the church, upon which both the Zwinglian and Lutheran parties were able to agree, threaten the reputation and order of the city. Franck can be put in the same category as Denck, Hätzer, and all the other spiritualists (*gaisters*), whose fruits are seen in the incidents at Münster. As the committee saw it, Franck undermined the order of the church and the city by placing God's revelation outside any of the means ordained by Him, be they Scripture, sermons, sacraments, etc. The rule of the visionaries would be chaos. Franck was faced with the challenge not so much of winning a theological debate but of convincing the council that in his books he taught a faith congenial to order and community as found in Ulm.

Toward this end Franck drafted and presented to the council his declaration, a document of considerable length. Faced with expulsion he responded with a statement that defended his understanding of the inner and outer words, while asserting his vision as the one most conducive to ecclesiastical and civic

---

[94] "der maister (verstand gott) leeret uns in ainem augenblick, in einem hui mehr dann all eusserlich wort, predig und schrift bisz an jungsten tag. War ist es, das gott, potentia absolúta durch sein stracke volkommene almechtigkeit alle ding muglich seyn. Er kan und mag, wie man spricht, ein axt under dem banck machen krähen. Aber man soll de potentia dei ordinata, von gottes ordentlicher macht röden, wie er die in seinem wort und wircken bräucht hat, das er wie der oftgemalt artickel vermag, sein genad dürch das mittel seins worts und sacramenten dienen gibt, so von im erwelet seyen. Er hat mit dem mündlichen wort auch mit den vätern vorm gsatz gehandlet. Christus hat von himmel mit seinen muntlichen wort Paulum beköret." Hegler, *Beiträge*, p. 137.

[95] Hegler, *Beiträge*, p. 137-138.

harmony. He clarifies some points, obscures others, and protests his love and devotion to the city of Ulm. He begins by addressing what was for Frecht and the city reformers perhaps the most problematic of his doctrines—that Scripture is not the Word of God. He starts by appealing to common sense and to Luther. "When one sees a picture of something, he states, one quite properly says, 'that is St. Peter, that is the Emperor,' thus a person should not rebuke someone who speaks like wise: Scripture is the Word of God."[96] Yet without the Spirit Scripture remains like a picture, soulless. He cites Luther as someone who promotes this view. "Thus Luther states in a sermon that Scripture is not Christ, but the swaddling clothes and manger of Christ in which Christ lies wrapped."[97] Franck's use of Luther in his declaration is a strategic ploy to find his allies at the center of the enemy camp. Franck cannot have hoped to head off Frecht by allowing Scripture to be called the Word of God as a linguistic convention, while maintaining that:

> the word became flesh, but not the Scripture. Indeed it cannot be God or God's Word, which is God himself, because, like other creatures, it has a beginning and an end, but God and his Word are eternal, almighty, God himself without beginning or end.[98]

It did serve to muddy the waters with the council, even though Franck was quoting verbatim from his previous writings. The preachers, who were aware of the distinction between God as being and the Scripture as revelation of that being, would not be satisfied until Franck gave an account of an outer word which could be used to order the church. But Franck could hope that his distinction might strike home with the council when stated so reasonably and with such an august witness as Luther.

Franck defined next "the distinction of the outer and inner word, man,

---

[96] "Doch mag auch die schrifft gottes wort genent werden, wie ein bild ein mensch. Wie man nun mit niemant zancken soll, der glaich auf ein bild zeigt und sagt: das ist S. Peter, das ist der kaiser, also soll man die nit tadlen, die gleich sprechen: die schrift ist gottes wort." Hegler, *Beiträge*, pp. 140-141.

[97] "Daher nent Lutherus in einer predig die schrift nit Christum, sonder die windel und kripp Christi, darin Christus eingewickelt lige." Hegler, *Beiträge* , p. 141.

[98] "dz wort ist flaisch worden, aber nit die schrift. Item durch desz hern wort ist himel und erd erschaften, aber nit durch die schrift. Ey so kan sy ye nit got oder gotzwort sein, dz gott selbs ist, weil sy wie ein ander creatur anfang und end hat, gott aber und sein wort ewig, almechtig, gott selbs on end und anfang." Hegler, *Beiträge*, p. 142.

both testaments, and their servants, calling and authority."[99]   Here again he
conceded nothing to the school committee, but proceeded to divide the inner
Word from the outer and define the former as primary. "This true inner living
Word," says Franck,

> is God's power, the Word of grace and life, through which God
> has created all things and still daily speaks, creates, carries, nour-
> ishes, contains, enlightens, teaches, and makes living and holy.[100]

Franck brought forward a host of witnesses for this position, including Luther
and Tauler, the *Theologia Deutsch* and Staupitz.[101] He then compared this to
the outer word, stating,

> Just as the outer, visible person is only a figure and picture of the
> true inner person, so the outer word is to the inner; and as much
> as the inner person, who is conceived and born through the seed
> of the inner Word of God (which comes from God by means of
> the Holy Spirit) surpasses the outer man, John 1, 1 Peter 1, so
> also the inner Word surpasses the outer; [the relationship is] like
> that between a shadow and the actual thing...flesh and spirit.
> Outer things are fleshly and evanescent, subject to vanity: they
> often pass away emptily. The Word of God, which proceeds from
> his mouth without any mediating force, can never pass away emp-
> tily...But the outer things which have a beginning must someday
> come to an end.[102]

At this point Franck cited an interesting authority to support his point, namely
Schwenckfeld. The school committee had attempted to link these two names,
and here Franck obliges them. In his printed works Franck mentioned

---

[99] "Von dem unterschaid desz eussern und innern worts, menschens, beder
testament, und deren diener, beruf und ampt." Hegler, *Beiträge*, p. 144.

[100] "Disz war inner lebending wort ist gottes kraft, das wort der gnad und
lebens, got selbs, der recht war Christus und das einen mittel, dardurch gott all
ding erschaffen hat und noch teglich spricht, erschaft, tregt, närt, erhelt, erleucht, lert, lebendig und selig macht." Hegler, *Beiträge*, p. 145.

[101] Hegler, *Beiträge*, p. 146.

[102] "Wie nun der euszer biltlich mensch nur ein figur und bilt ist desz waren
innern menschens, also dz euszer wort desz innern, und wie vil der inner
mensch durch den somen desz lebendigen wort gottes ausz got vom h. geist
empfangen und geporn, Joan. I; I Peter 1, den euszern ubertrift, also dz inner
wort dz euszer, wie schatt und ding, flaisch und gaist. Dz eusser ist flaisch
verrucklich, der eytelkeit underworfen, dz oft ler abgeet, so gottes wort, so on
mittel ausz seinem mund geet, nymmer leer abgeen kan,...so dz euszer ange-
fangen aufhören müsz." Hegler, *Beiträge*, p. 146.

Schwenckfeld only once, and then in a somewhat uncomplimentary fashion, and yet here put him forward as an authority. Franck was obviously aware of Schwenckfeld's following among some of the council.

Having separated the inner and the outer words, Franck went on to discuss the implications of this position.

> God maintains order and measure, creating not inner through outer, but like through like. Thus he teaches, punishes, enlightens, or blinds us, inwardly through an equally inner teaching, punishment, light, or turning of his countenance from our soul: outwardly through outward war, hunger, pestilence, tyranny, light, etc.[103]

The only outward teaching Franck seems to allow is the sort that causes suffering and turns the person inward. The outer office of the preacher is superfluous for any of those things with which it is charged, nor does it serve any mediating function. "One should not seize God's domain,"[104] Franck asserts. With Franck's conception there can be no reformation by legislation, none of what Zwingli and Bucer had sought to institute in their respective cities, and which other cities, such as Ulm, had imitated. Franck did, however, have a vision of Christian community.

> In this I have considered and regarded no other community necessary than a voluntarily subservient heart and hand, prepared, opened, and offered to all true members of Christ. I also regarded only that community to be Christian wherein with no coercion, from love [given] freely, two or three lay together their goods and blessings and have them in common when in need, like a sort of community coffer, as according to St. James or as is witnessed in Jerusalem, where expenditures were made from a common purse. This should not be a necessity or a rule for others, in order that some will act out of freely given love and Christian freedom, where there is a need but not out of necessity.[105]

---

[103] "Gott helt ordnung und masz, schaft nicht inner durch dz euszer, sonder gleichs durch gleichs. Also lert, straft, erleucht, oder plent er uns innerlich durch gleich innerlich ler, straf, liecht oder abkere seins angesichts unser seel: euszerlich durch euszerlich krieg, hunger, pestilenz, tyrannei, leicht, etc." Hegler, *Beiträge*, p. 154.

[104] "soll...got nit in sein gebiet greifen..." Hegler, *Beiträge*, p. 150.

[105] "Dahin hab ich gesehen, und achte auch kein ander gmeinschaft nötig, dann ein freywilligs dienstpares hertz und hand, allen rechten glidern Christi berait, offen und angeboten. Ich acht auch kein andere gmainschaft christenlich, es geschehe dann on notzwang ausz freyer lieb, dz etwa 2 oder 3 ir gut und

Franck shared his voluntary communal vision with the Anabaptists, though not their separatism. Therefore he left free the formation of this community and did not make it subject to the coercion of either a temporal or spiritual sword.

One of Franck's greatest concerns was the sectarian situation of outward Christendom, and he gave a suggestion to the council concerning the concord and unity of the church. This was not merely a ploy to convince the council of the benign nature of Franck's own views, but also a sincere attempt to conceive of a society which retained order but left free the spiritual realm. Franck begins:

> ...peace and concord should be in God, that is, according to the will of God and the light of his Spirit and Word, directed by the good conscience into God, and not following the world's course in the flesh, which unifies people in sin, in their designs for trouble, and in a false, pseudo-religion.[106]

Franck did not conceive of unity as being able to exist outwardly, even where it appeared to exist.

> Christ said that he left his peace for his followers, which surpasses all understanding and which survives in the middle of strife, just as life survives in death and all things survive in their contradiction.[107]

Franck had made the unity of Christ's church invisible. He continues:

> Therefore, it seems to me it is a fleshly enthusiasm...when some...are eager to make peace with everyone, indeed with the whole world, or that man has the hope and takes on the task of making the whole world Christian,... bringing and forcing all humans under one roof, in the one pen of Christian faith, for faith is

---

segen in nöten zu hauf legen und gmein haben, wie etwa ein bursch, so gen S. Jacob oder gen Hierusalem zeucht, ausz einem seckel zeren. Disz soll aber den andern kein not oder regel seyn, dz etlich ausz freyer lieb und christenlicher freyheit in der not one not thond." Hegler, *Beiträge*, p. 170.

[106] "Doch soll...frid und concordi im hern seyn, dz ist nach dem willen gottes, nach dem liecht seins geists und worts mit gutem gwiszen in got gericht und nicht nach der welte lauf oder im fleisch, dz man einig sey in sunden, fürnemen zu argem, in falscher vermainter religion." Hegler, *Beiträge*, p. 170.

[107] "Drum spricht Christus, dz er den seinen sein frid lasze, der alle sinn ubertrifft, und mitten im unfrid besteet, wie dz leben im tod und alle ding in seinem widerspil..." Hegler, *Beiträge*, p. 171.

not for everyone, 2 Thess. 3...[108]

The freedom of which Franck speaks is inward, directed toward faith. Outwardly the temporal authorities rule.

> Concerning all this it seems to me that concord is much better served when one leaves free each person's conscience and belief before God. Everyone believes in having his bread and cheese and does not want it any other way. If someone were to strike out prematurely and provoke those authorities instituted by God with pen, mouth or fist, then watch him. See out of what spirit, conviction and calling he acts, whether something should not happen to him, whether God might want him fended off through the authorities, so that he is taught silence, and his untimely exercise is forced back home. For God does not want rabble-rousing and sectarianism.[109]

If someone is punished by the authorities for such actions, Franck states:

> It seems to me he suffers because of his own guilt, who, not being called and running ahead of God, confesses the truth even before the hounds and sows...It is often godly to take up the fine pearls of God's word and conceal them, Matth. 7.[110]

Franck made certain the council members understand the implications of his views for his own behavior. Franck confides:

> Indeed, when the mob runs after me and cries about reverence, I would rather flee than stand before them or start something sepa-

---

[108] "Derhalb dunckt mich disz ein flaischlich eyfer,...dz etlich...gern frid mit yederman, ja mit der gantzen welt machen wolten, oder dz man wolt hoffen und sich understen, die gantz welt christen zemachen...und alle menschen in ein stal und pferich desz christenlichen glaubens zu pringen und nöten, weil der glaub nit yedermans ding ist, 2 Thess. 3..." Hegler, *Beiträge*, p. 171.

[109] "Hierum gedeuckt mich, dz die concordi vil basz bestend wan man einem yeden sein gwiszen und glauben vor got frey liesz. Es glaubet gleich einer an kesz und prot, wolt er nit anders. Wird aber ein yeder vor der zeit ongereimpt ausz brechen und dem von got verordeneten gwalt ins schwert fallen, mit seiner feder, mund oder faust, der sehe drum auf, ausz wz geist, trib und beruf ers thu, ob im nit eben recht geschehe, und got in also durch den gwalt wölle weren und lernen schweigen ia sein onzeitigen auszlauf wider haim zurucktreiben. Dan gott will auch nit rottierung und absonderung." Hegler, *Beiträge*, p. 171-172.

[110] "dann auch die meins gedanckens umb schuld leiden, die onberuft und vor got laufende vor den hunden und sewen auch die warhait bekennen...Es ist oft ein gotseligkeit, dz fein perlin gottes wort aufheben und verhelen." Hegler, *Beiträge*, p. 172.

> rate with them. I have no commission from God to gather togeth-
> er his dispersed Israel and to start a new church, but would rather
> die than have myself understood in such a way, having hated all
> my days great rabbles and societies.[111]

Franck goes on to say:

> we should pray for the rulers and ordained powers, that God give
> them understanding and wisdom, that their service and office
> serve the Kingdom of God, that is, that they see and take care to
> maintain and protect the good outward peace and unity for the
> sake of our outward humanity, so that even if the spiritual person
> does not desire to be harmonized, yet by necessity the outward
> peace will be maintained, good laws and order will be made to
> fend off the outward evil of humans, a good constitution will be
> maintained, and the common good... will be promoted.[112]

Franck was able to follow this up by quoting from Erasmus, that faith stands
more in living than in confession of articles.[113] Franck's separation of the inner Word from the outer had its corresponding political teaching. The best that
can be expected is that the authorities maintain a modicum of order and attempt to promote the common good. All outward things must order themselves
under this force, and since no force should or could extend into matters spiritual, any sort of outward organized religion is rendered illegitimate. Though
Franck was not so explicit, the pastors of Ulm as well as the sectarians were
guilty of throwing pearls before swine, serving without a calling, and of trying to
institute a false unity. Franck is routinely cited as an early exponent of religious

---

[111] "ja wann mir der bofel nachlief und vor andacht wainet, ich wolt im ee
entlaufen, dann vorsteen, oder etwz sonders, mit im anfahen. Ich hab von got,
sein zerstrewt Israel einzusamlen und ein new kirchen anzurichten, kein befelch,
wolt ee sterben, dann mich sollichs understeen, hab auch all mein tag grosz
rotten und geselschaft gehaszt." Hegler, *Beiträge*, p. 172.

[112] "dz wir bitten für alle oberkait und sein verordneten gwalt, dz in got geb
verstand und weiszheit, dz ir dienst und ampt auch zum reich gottes diene, dz
ist, dz sy auf unseren euszeren menschen zu schutz der guten euszerlich frid und
einigkeit zu erhalten, sehen und sorg tragen, auf dz, ob gleich die gemuter nit
zusammen wöllen, doch ausz not euszerlicher frid werde gehalten, gute gsatz
und ordnung machen desz euszern menschens boszhait zu weren, gut pollicey zu
erhalten, gmainen nutz...zu fürdern." Hegler, *Beiträge*, p. 173.

[113] "Etwa stand der glaub mer im leben, dann im bekantnus der articul."
Hegler, *Beiträge*, p. 175.

tolerance,[114] but when forced to express his views before those who rule, and thus forced to deal with the exigencies of rulership, Franck's is more a tolerance of silence that of practice.

Authority was perhaps the most vexing problem for the reformers, and most cleaved in one way or another to an existing political authority in order to protect and promote the reforms of the church.[115] Though they professed obedience to the duly instituted authorities, in practice they were often led into an adversarial relationship with them over the authority of the ministers to conduct the reform of morals, or to suppress heterodoxy. This is particularly true of the southern German cities, as we have seen. The effect of establishing the outward "reformed" church was to set up a body of pastors whose interests often conflicted with those of the secular rulers. The pastors had no actual enforcement authority, except to the extent they could persuade the temporal authorities to act, temporal authorities they were dependent upon to fend off both internal and external foes. Franck had benefitted from this situation, and now he proposed to the council a solution to it. Let each retain his own faith, which was to be tested in his outward behavior, and do away with divisive confessions and practices. The council should enforce order, prevent all sectarian activity, and be the one source of moral authority with the ability to punish. The true church being inward, it should be forced to remain inward. There was no chance the council would actually do what Franck suggested, but that does not mean some would not have a certain sympathy for his vision. Franck's views, as he himself asserted, were not a threat to the temporal rulers but conceded to them far more practical authority than the reformers. Bernhard Besserer's own views bore similarities to Franck's. Although highly unconventional, Franck's argument for unity was not without appeal for a city council not always of one mind with its pastorate.

Franck's declaration to the council is a highly effective piece of writing,

---

[114] See, for example, *Religiöse Toleranz: Dokumente zur Geschichte einer Förderung*, ed. Hans Guggisberg (Stuttgart, 1984), pp. 80-86, for a selection of documents from Franck; also Lotte Blaschke, "Der Toleranzgedanke bei Sebastian Franck," *Blätter für deutsche Philosophie* 2 (1928/29), pp. 40-56; and Meinulf Barbers, *Toleranz bei Sebastian Franck* (Bonn, 1964).

[115] For Luther, for example, this situation was less than the ideal, and existed only because of the period of need in which the church found itself. See Lewis S. Spitz, "Luther's Ecclesiology and his Concept of the Prince as *Notbischof*," *Church History* 22 (1953), pp. 113-141. The practical consequence was to make the church dependent on the secular sword for its governance.

marshalling authorities from Luther to Schwenckfeld to defend his mystical theology, and extending this theology onto the field of political authority to prove himself a loyal servant of the council. He played on the council member's own theological sympathies and the tensions with the pastors. Despite its repetitiousness, one can imagine some of the council being favorably impressed by Franck's plea.

As one might well expect, Frecht was not placated by Franck's clarification. He complained in a letter that it was dark and slippery, itself needing a clarification.[116] Thus he devised a plan to pin Franck down once and for all. Taking a ten-point confession devised by Bucer for Augsburg, the school committee proposed that Franck subscribe to its tenets. The articles confessed the orthodox form of the Trinity, Christ's two natures, crucifixion and resurrection, original sin, reconciliation through Christ, the outward word and sacraments, etc. It particularly emphasized the outward means by which belief is transmitted.[117] In addition, Franck was to recant those parts of his writings where he was at variance with the ten articles.[118] The committee emphasized that this action would prove Franck's dedication to the community of God.

With this, Frecht had backed Franck into a corner. To make this confession would cause Franck to contradict his most closely held tenets. In an attempt to ward off this fate Franck addressed another plea to the council. In it he protests that his earlier declaration seemed to him, and to all those to whom he had showed it, a good clarification. He is willing, in order to set the council's mind at rest, to promise not to publish anything written by himself, and to clear anything he might publish with the committee appointed by the council. Further he will write nothing against the belief and religion of the city or its preachers and teachers, but hold himself in conformity to the common religion and order of the city, "as also I have done up till now."[119] He asks only that they not force him to take a special oath, which would constrain his conscience, but he be allowed, as his fellow citizens are, to have a free unimprisoned con-

---

[116] Julius Endriß, *Sebastian Francks Ulmer Kämpfe*, p. 19.

[117] Hegler, *Beiträge*, p. 182.

[118] "Was nur in meinen schriften im truck auszgangen solchen artickeln entgegen und zuwider wäre, will ich sollichs hiemit revociert, widerrieft und gäntzlich widersprochen haben." Hegler, *Beiträge*, p. 184.

[119] "Wie auch biszher gethon." Hegler, *Beiträge*, p. 185.

science. Faith should not be captured in words.[120] He ends with a reminder to the council of his wife and children and what it would mean for them if the family were expelled from the city in the winter.

The council, however, was not ready to settle the matter. On October 26, 1535, having heard from the members appointed to investigate the case, and then from Martin Frecht, the council once again directed Franck to clarify himself on those points with which the school committee was still dissatisfied.[121] It is possible Franck would have eventually been forced either to subscribe to the confession or leave the city but for the intervention of Bernhard Besserer. On October 26, Besserer sent his thoughts on the case to the council. As has been previously indicated, Besserer was the most influential individual in the city, and was at this time serving again as mayor. He defends Franck from the attempt to force his subscription to the articles of confession. The council has never committed itself to these articles, Besserer notes, but only to a Christian reform and order for its church. This is what should be observed, according to Besserer, and not points which please Bucer. This leads Besserer to observe, in somewhat caustic tones, that allowing the preachers to follow their whims could be detrimental to the council as well as the learned, and lead to a situation of servitude.[122] Besserer firmly rejects Frecht's suggestion. He goes on to list a number of points to which Franck should accede, most of which Franck had already conceded. Besserer does draw out a number of complaints concerning Franck's writings on authority, on his depiction of Ulm falling from Zwinglianism to Lutheranism (the council, according to Besserer, should be held as Christian), and other objectionable points from his histories. This, and not doctrinal formulations, is what bothers Besserer. He is willing to allow Franck to stay in the city if he will concede these points. The council followed on November 5 with a decision to allow Franck to stay, but under the following condition:

that he shall in no way allow something to come out or be pub-

---

[120] Hegler, *Beiträge*, pp. 185-186.

[121] Hegler, *Beiträge*, p. 187.

[122] "Es prechte auch ainem erbern rat ain verklainerung und möchte usz sollicher der gelerten underziehung, wo denen yetzt das, dann morgen ain anders, gewilfart und gestempft wurd, was sy furtruogen und jedesmals furnemen, die vorig der gaistlichen zwingsale ervolgen, das man im nicht mindere, als in vorgeschwepte dienstparkait entlich keme, und muszt man denselben in irem furschneiden allweg zuhörn und recht lassen." Hegler, *Beiträge*, p. 188.

lished and write absolutely nothing without the special foreknow-
ledge and will of the honorable council and its appointed school
committee.[123]

He was also to clarify his past writings without the help of the council. The
matter was left here. If Franck clarified himself further, the documents have
not survived. It is possible Frecht, with other matters pressing on him, did not
pursue the matter in the face of Bernhard Besserer's support for Franck, and
the council let sleeping dogs lie. The matter slumbered for a number of years.

Although earlier biographers of Franck have seen the Ulm struggles as a
galling instance of persecution and clerical intolerance, in fact he was treated
according to the laws governing religious heterodoxy in the city, and came out
of it much better than many an Anabaptist. Franck's publications, particularly
the *Paradoxa*, had infuriated Frecht and the pastorate in Ulm, and had led them
to associate his name with Hätzer and Denck. Franck's denigration of the
visible church not surprisingly caused Frecht to desire Franck's departure from
the city. It was one thing to hold such views privately, but Franck published,
and in the vernacular. What was objected to was not Franck's mysticism, but
the extreme conclusions he drew from it.[124] Franck had made extreme statements concerning temporal rulership, so when a case needed to be generated
against him for the eyes of Philip of Hesse, the task was not difficult. By the
standards of the day Philip was tolerant, but a careful selection of Franck's
writings could have made him appear a relative of the Münster radicals.
Philip's letter was a powerful motivation for the council to rid itself of Franck.
It is a tribute to Franck's skill in pleading his case that he eventually retained
his citizenship. In the face of the evidence he was able to fashion himself con-
vincingly as a loyal *Bürger* and argue the faith of the unencumbered indwelling
Word as the most congenial for a Christian magistracy. Judging from many of
the council members' attraction to Schwenckfeld, Franck's argument had a
resonance with them. Yet he did not have the pedigree of Schwenckfeld, and

---

[123] "Item dasz er on sunder vorwissen und willen ains ersamen rats und
seiner verordneten schulpfleger hinfuro gar nichts schreiben, trucken oder auss-
gan lassen soll in kainen weg." Hegler, *Beiträge*, p. 190.

[124] Teufel misses the point when he accuses Frecht of objecting to a mysticism which was drawn from Tauler and the *Theologia Deutsch*, and was so beloved by the young Luther. Neither Tauler, the *Theologia Deutsch*, nor Luther
drew the extreme anti-clerical conclusions Franck did, and in any case Luther
came to be extremely suspicious of such mysticism. See Teufel, *"Landräumig"*,
p. 73.

his writings in the *Chronica* on authority did not speak well for him. Even the sympathetic Besserer wanted these passages clarified. In essence the council ruled that as long as Franck's views did not work to the detriment of public order, and he showed at least pro forma adherence to the Christian order of the city, he was welcome. Ulm's laws concerning Anabaptism worked the same way, and this was the limit of tolerance in Ulm, as in most of Early Modern Europe. Very few cities, perhaps none, would have offered a more tolerant decision. And since Franck had been denounced by a figure as influential as Philip of Hesse, it is doubtful he would have been allowed to stay but for the tension between the pastorate and the council. To allow Franck's presence in the city served to underscore the council's authority.

One reason Franck was to enjoy a period of peace was the attention attracted by Schwenckfeld. Schwenckfeld had reached an understanding with Bucer, Ambrosius Blarer, and Frecht in May of 1535 at what was called the Tübingen Colloquy. The agreement to which they came was essentially not to disagree, at least not in public. Schwenckfeld was not to disturb or chide the practices of the churches and the pastors were to refrain from attacking Schwenckfeld as an opponent of truth. No agreement on doctrine was achieved.[125] This agreement did not sit well with Frecht.[126] He had expressed the opinion that Franck represented more of a threat to the church than did Schwenckfeld.[127] As events unfolded, Frecht came to see Schwenckfeld as the real thorn in his side. Much of this change of perspective comes with Frecht's participation in the Wittenberg Concord.

Ulm had joined the Schmalkaldic League in 1532, and by 1535/36 its ultimate political fate rested with this alliance. The Swabian League was no longer a viable body through which the political interests of a Protestant Ulm could be promoted. In terms of religious sympathies Zwingli's teaching continued to exercise influence in the city. On the one hand the strife between the Swiss, South German cities, and the Wittenberg camp had disturbed Protestant alliance making since 1529. The Marburg Colloquy was unsuccessful in achiev-

---

[125] The text is in *Corpus Schwenckfeldianorum*, vol. 5, pp. 326-342, esp. pp. 341-342.

[126] See his letter to A. Blarer dated July 28, 1535, *Blarer Briefwechsel*, vol. 1, p. 727.

[127] See his letter to Bullinger of Oct. 14, 1535 in Johann Konrad Füssli, ed. *Epistolae ab ecclesiae helveticae reformatoribus vel ad eos scriptae* (Zurich, 1742), p. 167.

ing a conciliation between the two Eucharistic views. By 1534/35, however, Bucer was working hard to reconcile the Eucharistic views of the South German theologians with those of Luther. His efforts achieved a good deal of success. Ulm theologians participated in this, as reflected in Luther's letter of October 5, 1535.[128] Eventually a meeting was arranged in Wittenberg, between May 22 and 29, 1536, of the most prominent Wittenberg theologians, headed by Luther, and theologians from a number of South German cities, headed by Bucer and including Frecht. The statement agreed to on the Eucharist circumvents previously problematic areas dealing with the actual presence, agrees in rejecting transubstantiation, and leaves open a final formulation in order to consult with other preachers and the authorities. The desire to settle the matter was agreed upon.[129]

Frecht, who would best be labelled a Bucerian,[130] was himself most concerned about bringing a common theological front to the Protestant movement. The objective of the Wittenberg Concord had not been to capitulate to the Wittenberg theologians, but on his return Frecht was coldly received by the populace and the council, particularly by the Besserers.[131] The city, on the whole, still held to a Zwinglian position and the Concord was seen as a betrayal of the city's church order.[132] Frecht himself continued his efforts to achieve a formulation of the Eucharist which would be satisfactory as an evangelical state-

---

[128] *Luthers Werke; Briefwechsel*, vol. 7, p. 296.

[129] For the text see *Luthers Werke: Briefwechsel*, vol. 12, #4261, Beilage I, pp. 200-212, esp. pp. 206-207.

[130] Frecht is frequently depicted as "Lutheran" in contrast to Konrad Sam's staunch Zwinglian sympathies. Ozment titles a section of his chapter on Franck in *Mysticism and Dissent* "Parlay with the Lutherans in Ulm," p. 151. Also Teufel, *"Landräumig"*, p. 56, refers to Frecht as part of the Lutheran pastorate. The literature on Franck uses this adjective for Frecht frequently. In fact his closest correspondent and confidant is Bucer, then Ambrosius Blarer. He had little contact with Luther himself, and only limited contact with Melanchthon. His own desire was to conciliate the split between Wittenberg and Zurich. See the comments of W.-U. Delius, "Licentiat Martin Frecht," pp. 299 and following.

[131] See Frecht's letter to A. Blarer of July 19, 1536, *Blarer Briefwechsel*, vol. 1, p. 809.

[132] See Delius, "Licentiat M. Frecht," pp. 300-301; also Ernst Bizer, *Studien zur Geschichte des Abendmahlsstreits im 16. Jahrhundert* (2nd edition, Darmstadt, 1962), pp. 133-134.

ment of belief. On August 31 he wrote a five-point statement on the Eucharist which had been agreed upon by the pastors of Ulm and Memmingen. It asserts the presence of Christ's body and blood in the bread and the wine, which becomes the food of the soul when received in faith, though the bread and wine are only simple bread and wine.[133] This statement does not make the bread and wine representational, or give the Eucharist merely a memorial significance, yet it also does not assert the actual presence regardless of the spiritual condition of the one who receives it. It is neither explicitly Zwinglian nor Lutheran, and it bespeaks Frecht's mediating efforts. It was Frecht's own efforts which involved Ulm in such a statement as the Concord, and the above statement. By all reports the populace favored an unambiguous Zwinglian understanding, as did the council, although the latter may have been just as pleased to allow the practice to remain vaguely defined.

Schwenckfeld, too, was a critic of the Wittenberg Concord, or at least so Frecht believed. Some thought that the resistance to the Concord was partly the result of Schwenckfeld's efforts.[134] Never shy in the face of criticism, Schwenckfeld, as a result, requested a hearing in order to defend himself. This was granted and he was heard on November 3, 1536 by five councilmen, including Jörg Besserer. Frecht appeared contra Schwenckfeld, who protested his innocence of all sect building, Anabaptism, and any sort of rabble rousing. He claimed he strove only after the true inner faith, and that he had abided by the Tübingen Accord.[135] Frecht charged Schwenckfeld with attacking the Wittenberg Concord,[136] a charge Schwenckfeld denied. In the end, the hearing was a success for Schwenckfeld, as the only action taken was that the five council members charged both sides to abide by the agreement of Tübingen, and to approach each other in a friendly manner when they had something against the other.[137] This was the best Schwenckfeld could have expected from the hearing. For Frecht it was a rebuke. Bernhard Besserer already had Schwenckfeld staying as a guest at his house, and now Frecht's concerns about the undermining of the Wittenberg Concord were turned aside by the council. This could

---

[133] See Ulm Archive, vol. A [9000], p. 141 and following.

[134] See *Corpus Schwenckfeldianorum*, vol. 5, pp. 532-533, for cites to various correspondence accusing Schwenckfeld of resistance to the Wittenberg Concord.

[135] *Corpus Schwenckfeldianorum*, vol. 5, pp. 534-537.

[136] *Corpus Schwenckfeldianorum*, vol. 5, pp. 539-540.

[137] *Corpus Schwenckfeldianorum*, vol. 5, p. 544.

only reinforce Frecht's feelings of frustration concerning his authority to control teaching in the city. He and the council did not have the same concerns, and the council retained all coercive authority. Frecht could only use words and the prestige of his office, a prestige that seemed to suffer in 1536.

Another incident which must have proved aggravating for Frecht that same year was the re-publication of Konrad Sam's catechism.[138] As already noted, the catechism contained an unequivocal statement of Zwingli's Eucharistic views, emphasizing the memorial and spiritual aspects of the feast. Frecht's recent efforts had not necessarily contradicted Sam, but they were in a different spirit, as he had tried to reformulate the statement in a manner closer and less offensive to the Lutherans at Wittenberg. Whoever re-edited and published the catechism was no friend of Frecht and the Wittenberg Concord. While there is no incontrovertible evidence, it has been plausibly suggested that Franck himself did it, a return in kind to Frecht who had created so may problems for Franck.[139] If this were the case it could only have infuriated Frecht. In any event, after 1536 Frecht's voice changed tone, and where previously he had attacked Franck's dangerous publications he now also attacked Franck's person. Time would show that he was looking for an opportunity to reopen the case against Franck and have him expelled from the city.

Under these conditions it would have been wise for Franck to have held to the strictest reading of the council's edict and have published nothing of his own, anywhere, without the approval of the Ulm censor. He apparently supported himself as a printer in Ulm, and most of the items he published were innocuous enough. Still, even in his minor items, he could not refrain from a

---

[138] See footnote #23 for the original publication.

[139] See Walther Köhler, "Zur Frage nach dem Herausgeber des Ulmer Katechismus von 1536," *Blätter für württembergische Kirchengeschichte* 10 (1906), p. 188. The catechism itself was published under the title *Cathechismus/ oder christenlicher Kinder bericht/...kurtzlich gestelt vnd etwas gebessert/ zu Ulm in der Pfarr geprediget* (Ulm, Hans Varnier, 1536). It is unthinkable the pastors would have re-edited this, thereby undermining their own work at Wittenberg. Franck published his works with Varnier at this time. Köhler cites a passage from the later hearings against Franck (Hegler, *Beiträge*, p. 205) where unnamed publications (*scholastica*) which belonged in the school and which were published behind the back of the school committee are ascribed to Franck. The catechism fits that description well.

few interpolated comments.[140] Not all Franck's publications were minor. One of his largest was a new edition of the *Chronica*, which contained two major changes related to Franck's difficulties.[141] In his introduction to the "Chronicle of the Emperors" Franck adds an apology for the earlier introduction which had raised such objections. His apology contains two parts. First he admonishes all to strict obedience to the authorities and protests that he never meant to injure the person of the present Emperor.[142] Yet he undermines his statement by following it up with numerous additions that are unflattering to the

---

[140] For example Franck reports, in his apology to the council on the occasion of his second expulsion proceedings, that he published "ain almanach, ain bawrenkalender, meiner herrn pfennig, etlich recept und ain tafel in die schul." Hegler, *Beiträge*, p. 192. No examples of these writings have survived except *Des Grossen Nothelffers vnnd Weltheiligen Sant Gelts/ oder s. Pfennigs Lobgesang* (Ulm: Sebastian Franck, 1537), a small satirical poem composed by Franck. Also from this period is *Wie man beten und psallieren soll* (Ulm: Sebastian Franck, 1537), a fairly typical piece of Franckian spiritualism, though constructed around advice on how to sing from the heart; a translation of a Sebastian Münster work titled *Sechshundert Dreyzehen Gebot und Verbot der Juden* (Ulm: Sebastian Franck, 1537) to which Franck interpolated his own comments, mostly having to do with the legalism of the Jews and the letter of the law compared to the spirit (see pp. Aii to Aiiii-v or pp. Jiii to Jiiii-v). Franck aided in the publication of two psalters, *Der Ganze Psalter* (Ulm: Sebastian Franck, and Augsburg: Philipp Ulhart, 1537) which contains *Wie man beten...* as a foreword; plus *Der New gesang psalter* (Ulm: Sebastian Franck, and Augsburg: Philipp Ulhart, 1538), which contains a psalm from Franck's pen. Though these pieces were fairly minor, most would be objected to later because of Franck's habit of interpolating his own comments into the text.

Franck was not oblivious to the danger his writings posed to him, as shown by his two pseudonymous publications of this period; Friedrich Wernstreyt, *Das Kriegbüchlin des frides* (Augsburg: Heinrich Steiner, 1539), and Felix Frei, *Was gesagt sei: Der Glaub thuts alles* (Tübingen: Ulrich Morhart d.Ä, 1539) and (Augsburg: Philipp Ulhart, 1539) (it is not clear which printing is prior). The latter book is Franck's own phrasing of the Reformation principle of "justification by faith alone" made suitable for one who believes in the inward Word. The former is Franck's anti-war tract, with extensive quotes drawn from Erasmus. Being anonymous these books do not figure into the struggles Franck experienced in this period.

[141] *Chronica* (Ulm: Hans Varnier, 1536). In addition many details are added to the first section of the *Chronica*, of little interest for the themes here discussed.

[142] *Chronica* (Ulm, 1536), p. Biiii-v.

emperors.[143] He then prints unchanged his original offending introduction. The overall effect was an amplification of the original introduction. This is a prime example of Franck's near inability to modify his public statements for the sake of political expediency or self-preservation. The second change to the *Chronica*, however, shows he was not completely incapable of modifying his works. He excised the portion of the original which described Ulm and Augsburg as going over to Lutheranism.[144] The repudiation of this statement had been a condition of his continued residency in the city. It is surprising that Ulm allowed the publication of this work which had caused such controversy in its first edition. No immediate cry, though, was raised against its appearance. The city was not so generous with Franck's three major original works of this period, *Die Guldin Arch, Das verbütschierte Buch* and the *Germaniae Chronicon.*[145] Franck was forced to publish these in Augsburg and Frankfurt.

Die Guldin Arch was a large book, over 250 folio leaves, in which, as Franck described it:

> the Holy Scripture and all the kernels of the writings of the best, most distinguished, exceptional, prophetic and apostolic, venerable teachers and fathers of the church are found, also the enlightened

---

[143] *Chronica* (Ulm, 1536), p. Bv and following.

[144] *Chronica* (Straßburg, 1531), p. FFiiii.

[145] *Die Guldin Arch* (Augsburg: Heinrich Steiner, 1538). *Das verbütschiert mit siben sigeln verschlossen Büch* (Augsburg: Heinrich Steiner, 1539). *Germaniae Chronicon* (Frankfurt a.M.: Christian Egenolff, 1538). Franck was denied permission to print these books in Ulm and thus they appeared in Augsburg and Frankfurt. See Hegler, *Beiträge*, pp. 198, 200. He was also denied permission to print a few other books.

Franck's third large work of this period, *Germaniae Chronicon*, will not be discussed as it was only peripherally involved in the controversy surrounding him. It is nonetheless a very interesting work, another compilation of Franck's from other historians, interspersed with his own observations. It exemplifies his feelings of native pride in Germany and his love of German lore. Franck's sources for this work have been investigated by Willi Prenzel, *Kritische Untersuchung und Würdigung von Sebastian Francks Chronicon Germaniae* (Marburg, 1908). Philip Kintner, "Studies in the Historical Writings of Sebastian Franck" (Dissertation, Yale, 1958), pp. 80-82, notes that Franck uses natural law to analyze the world and its governance, his prime example being the *Germaniae Chronicon*. This represents something of a departure for Franck and can be explained by his experience in Ulm where he was forced to come to grips with some explanation for worldly rule.

heathen and philosophers.[146]
No doubt when presenting this to the censor, Franck protested that this was not his own work but a collection of the best from the past. It is in fact made up overwhelmingly of quotations from Scripture, with numerous witnesses from the church and a few enlightened heathen. Franck appended his usual introduction and interspersed his own comments between various quotations. The overall effect is not greatly different from the *Paradoxa*, and he shows again his remarkable innocence and persistence in even presenting it to the censors, which included the school committee.

His introduction contains a denunciation of the learned, "councils of the devil."[147] Franck intends his book to be a witness to the Scripture alone, and from there to point the reader to God, "the true single author."[148] Franck wishes to let Scripture interpret Scripture, so that the book could called a forest of Scripture, and could be used as a concordance.[149] "Since now this book," he states, "is not mine, but is from the Holy Scripture and the old teachers and fathers of the church, I hope that because of this, it will be pleasing to you."[150] He emphasizes the spiritual interpretation over the literal, using a figurative interpretation of Christ as the ark of the covenant to exemplify his point.[151] He ends his introduction with a long bewailing of the theology of the day, the theologians' efforts to answer, measure and define everything, leav-

---

[146] "Die Guldin Arch/ Darinn die Heilige schrifft vnd alls der Kern bester/ fürnembster/ außerlesener/ Prophetischer vnd Apostolischer/ alter Lehrer vnd Vätter der kirchen/ sprüch/ gefunden werden/ Auch der erleuchten Heyden vnd Philosophen." *Die Guldin Arch* (Bern: Benedickt Ulmann, 1569), p. i. All quotes from this edition were checked against the original.

[147] *Die Guldin Arch*, p. ii.

[148] "Ich diese mein Arch...allein als ein zeiger/ einweisung vnnd einleitung in die schrifft/ wöllen fürstellen/ damit jedermann von mir vnd allen Menschen auff die Schrifft/ vnd von der Schrifft...auff Gott den rechten einigen Dichter...gewiesen werden." *Die Guldin Arch*, p. ii.

[149] "Ja laß die Schrifft sich selbst außlegen/ Derhalb mag diß mein arbeit für einen Walde der Schrifft/ oder für ein Concordantz brauchen." *Die Guldin Arch*, p. ii-v.

[150] "Weil nun diß Buch nicht mein/ sonder der H. Schrifft vnd alten Lehrern vnd Vättern der ersten Kirchen ist/ hoff ich es werden dir doch von desen wegen/ deß es ist/ angenem werden..." *Die Guldin Arch*, p. iii.

[151] *Die Guldin Arch*, p. iiii.

ing no room for the Holy Spirit, and leading one to think, claims Franck, that they alone have gobbled it up.[152]

The main body of the work is organized under numerous headings dealing with the nature of God, Christ, the Spirit, salvation, and so on. The theology is familiar from the *Paradoxa*, though certain sections, for example the one on free will, are among the clearest in Franck's work.[153] Of note also is the prominence of Augustine in his quotations from the fathers, mentioned almost as frequently as Tauler or the *Theologia Deutsch*. Cicero and Seneca stand out among the heathen witnesses. *Die Guldin Arch* is an extension of the views put forward in the *Paradoxa*.

Complementary to *Die Guldin Arch* is *Das verbütschierte Buch*. Franck apparently composed them at the same time, though *Das verbütschierte Buch* was not published until 1539. It is even larger than *Die Guldin Arch*, running 430 folio leaves. This is Franck's instruction book on how to read the Scripture, or, as he put it, how to open the seven seals with which the Scripture is closed. In his introduction he explains how Scripture was made a closed book so that pearls would not be thrown to the swine. One must first turn to God to receive the spiritual eyes which will allow one to look into Scripture. God spoke in parables, allegories, etc., so that he would speak only to his own, just as Pythagoras to his disciples.[154] Much of what he says here repeats what he said already in other works.

For the body of the book Franck takes up the method for which Hans Denck had been condemned, that of posing contradictory statements of Scripture side by side. This serves a number of purposes. For those who are proud, it confounds their understanding and throws them back on God. For those whose faith is strong, it tests their faith. It also allows Franck to demonstrate the various ways in which the contradictions can be solved, for the most part by spiritualizing the reading just as he did so often in the *Paradoxa*. Franck can thus prove that he is impartial to both sides of the conflicting Scriptures, for he accepts both, just as he is impartial to the various factions of Christendom. All can be solved by looking away from the letter to the spiritual truth which con-

---

[152] "Unser theologi lassen aber yetzt kein raum dem H. Geist/ sonder messen vnnd deffinieren alle ding bey eim eß/ wie/ wo/ wer/ wie viel/ was/ warumb/ etc...gleich als haben sie allein dem Heyligen Geist gefressen." *Die Guldin Arch*, p. vi.

[153] On free will see *Die Guldin Arch*, pp. Vvi and following.

[154] *Das verbütschierte...Buch*, p. b-v.

tains both sides.[155]

Das verbütschierte Buch is in some ways a very mundane book. Many of the Scripture/counter-Scripture divisions are highly artificial, providing easy fodder for Franck's spiritualizing interpretations. Sometimes when Franck does not like either of the striving propositions he writes a third. A few of the collections of striving Scriptures are genuinely interesting, and Franck does not always solve the tension between the pairs, such as the section on authority.[156] But there is a certain tedious predictability about the whole effort. His collection of Scripture quotations is massive, such that the entire text of the Bible could nearly be reconstituted from this book alone. The book does contain Franck's most appealing statement of tolerance based on the universality of God.[157]

Franck states in *Das verbütschierte Buch* that in *Die Guldin Arch* he gives witness of his faith and in this book he tests it.[158] Together the two books represent a very extensive restatement by Franck of his faith. Though he tried to cast the books as compendia of other's writings, and as building up the faith of Christendom, he cannot resist the opportunity to denounce the learned and the theologians or to attack the vanity of the outward world. He does not denigrate the teaching and preaching functions of the pastorate, but those familiar with his writings would know exactly what implications were involved with Franck's position. Predictably Franck's activities did not escape the keen eyes of Ulm's pastorate.

As early as June 6, 1537 the preachers were complaining to the *Religionsamt* about Franck's publishing activity, and it was resolved to warn him not to write from his own head.[159] Soon after the publication of *Die Guldin Arch* in March of 1538, Martin Frecht reported to the appearance of this book "full of

---

[155] Among other passages see *Das verbütschierte...Buch*, p. biii.

[156] *Das verbütschierte...Buch*, pp. cvi-v and following.

[157] See *Das verbütschierte...Buch*, p. CC-v and following. Parts of this are published in Manfred Hoffmann, ed., *Toleranz und Reformation* (Gütersloh, 1979), pp. 73-74.

[158] "hie prüff vnd üb ich meyn glauben/ dort zeuge ich jn." *Das verbütschierte...Buch*, p. BBvi-v.

[159] J. Endriß, *Sebastian Francks Ulmer Kämpfe*, p. 40.

blasphemy and foolishness."[160] Frecht and the preachers were involved shortly thereafter in presenting a new complaint about Franck's errors to the city
council. On July 1, 1538 the council reappointed a committee, including the
school committee members, to look into Franck's case again and to advise the
council on what to do.[161] It is on the basis of Frecht's list of Franck's "im-
proper writings and dealings" that the council, on July 15, decreed that he must
leave the city, with wife and children, by September 29.[162] Once more Franck
composed and gave to the council a plea defending himself and asking that he
not be expelled unheard.

Franck's letter to the council expresses real surprise that he had once
again been expelled.[163] He protests that he does not even know what charges
were brought against him.

> I know indeed that I promised to the council three years ago, I
> would not attempt to publish without the appointed inspector.
> Your honors had understood [it to mean], to be sure, as I, what I
> published here in Ulm.[164]

He admits to publishing in Augsburg, but cannot imagine that is what has broken his promise. He has kept his oath, has published only inoffensive items,
and has avoided history, faith, or religion. He is ready to prove this point.
Franck goes on to defend his *Arch* as a confession of his own faith which he
knows would be praised by all. He has heard of few whom it did not please.
He expresses his confusion over the situation in which the censor in Augsburg
allowed publication whereas Ulm would not.

> That I could let something go that displeased one or two people is
> not possible for me. Then I would have to believe something new

---

[160] *Blarer Briefwechsel*, vol. 1, p. 877. The letter is dated May 14, 1538.

[161] Hegler, *Beiträge*, p. 191. The date given in Hegler is erroneous. The
document reads "Uf Mitwoch nach Anne, A. 1538" which is July 1, not July 15.
Ulm Archive, A 1208/II, p. 802.

[162] Hegler, *Beiträge*, pp. 190-191.

[163] "Uf den 15 juli ist mir, auch mein unschuldigen weib und kindern,...ain
erschrocklich urthel durch die geschwornen ainunger verkündt..." Hegler, *Beiträge*, p. 191.

[164] "Ich waisz fast wol, das ich vor drewen jarn ainem hocherbern rath zu-
gesagt hab, ich wölle nicht on die verordneten besichtiger zu trucken fürnemen.
Das hat freylich E R W verstanden, wie auch ich, was ich hie zu Ulm truck."
Hegler, *Beiträge*, p. 192.

every day, since today this person would speak and inculcate this in me, someone else that.[165]

Franck protests his impartiality, his love for all people of faith, and claims never to speak to anyone of faith, but testifies with his life. In closing he tells of the glory he has brought to Ulm with his new chronicle, how he has so carefully described the history of the city to its honor. Franck poses the question: is he the sort of person that the city would want to expel?[166]

Franck's letter had its effect. The five man commission appointed to investigate the case advised the council to look into the charges first before making a decision so that the cunning and difficult Franck could not claim he was poorly treated and expelled before being heard.[167] Frecht had his eye closely focussed on Franck.[168] On September 23 the school committee handed over a report, written in Frecht's hand, to the council-appointed committee, detailing Franck's many sins.[169]

The case marshalled against Franck is not very impressive. Many complaints are made on the basis of incidents which occurred before the original trial. Also brought forward is the republication of the *Chronica*, which the committee, with some justification, claims is still offensive to authority.[170] Perhaps the most damning charge is that, when his books had been rejected by the censor and he had stated his intention to publish it elsewhere, Franck was warned that this was a dangerous action.[171] The central charge of the report, however, is that Franck published behind the backs of the school committee and the censor. Here very little new is added. The committee mentions the many

---

[165] "Das ich auch ain ding gleich könnd fallen laszen, das etwan ainem oder zwayen miszföllt, ist mir nicht müglich. Dann also mueszt ich alle tag etwas newes glauben, dieweil heut der disz, ain anderer das in mich wurde bilden und reden." Hegler, *Beiträge*, p. 193.

[166] Hegler, *Beiträge*, pp 194-195.

[167] Hegler, *Beiträge*, pp. 195-196.

[168] His letter A. Blarer of August 27, 1538 shows the intensity with which he was focussing on the cases of Schwenckfeld and Franck. *Blarer Briefwechsel*, vol. 2, pp. 1-2.

[169] Hegler, *Beiträge*, pp. 196 and following.

[170] Hegler, *Beiträge*, p. 197.

[171] Hegler, *Beiträge*, p. 198.

books denied publication. It also charges that he appended material of his own to Sebastian Münster and to his psalter,[172] with the result that the Münster volume was forbidden in Straßburg. The report states, "he is supposed to publish a good book here for once, namely a psalter, which he soils then with a foreword."[173]   Also mentioned is a satirical poem about lice, published by Franck with a foreword, which the committee describes as shameful. "Now it is a peculiar thing about Sebastian Franck, " reads the report,

> that he, out of one mouth...can blow warm and cold, can publish a psalter and such an offensive lousy song (*läusig lied*), that everyone should see that this wondrous man directs his publishing and writing only toward profit.[174]

Here, as in his detailed chronicle of every possible offense by Franck, Frecht's exasperation is audible.   The report goes on to attack *Die Guldin Arch* and Franck's claims about his past life: it chronicles all the disapproval he has found among outside theologians and in Straßburg, and even challenges Franck's claim to live a godly life by noting that he lives next to a guest house.[175] "Franck has changed nothing in his other books which were published here and elsewhere, but let everything remain irritating."[176]   Here is their main complaint against Franck; he persists in his public expression of his unorthodox ideas, the rest of the charges being the measure of their frustration at not being able to silence him.

The report of the committee appointed by the council was presented on September 23, but it contained suggestions mostly concerning how the preachers

---

[172] See footnote # 140.

[173] "soll er einmal ein güt büchlin hie trückt haben, namlich ein psalter, den er auch mit ainer vorred besudlet hat." Hegler, *Beiträge*, p. 200.

[174] "Nun es ist dennoch ein seltzam ding von Bastian Franck, das er ausz einem mund, wie man sagt, kalt und warm kan blasen, kan ein psalter trucken und so ein schamper läusig lied, das iederman sehen soll, das diser wunderparlich man nür sien truck und schreiben uf gwinn richt." Hegler, *Beiträge*, pp. 200-201.

[175] Hegler, *Beiträge*, pp. 202-203.

[176] "Also hat auch Franck in ander seynen buchern hie und anderstwo getruckt noch nichts geendert, sonder lasszts alles also ergerlich bleyben..." Hegler, *Beiträge*, p. 204.

might control the traffic in books, including Franck's, within the city.[177] On October 11 the council requested the committee to proceed with the investigation of Franck. It was to get his answers to the school committee's charges, and then to compare and seek to unify the two sides one to another. If this were to be unsuccessful the council would pursue the matter further.[178]

There was no real possibility of a reconciliation between Frecht and Franck. Frecht wrote to Capito on October 31 about the differences between the followers of Franck and Schwenckfeld and himself over the Trinity.[179] The extent of Frecht's objections to Franck is made clear in a report he sent to the council-appointed committee. Frecht was not satisfied that the heterodox nature of Franck's teachings had been sufficiently exposed in the school committee's report, so here he systematically counts off the dangerous teachings found in his works. Frecht starts by reminding the committee of the damage that Franck has done to the commune. Many have written him, Frecht says, wondering why Ulm endures such a person.[180] The various points to which Frecht objects in Franck's writings center on the denigration of all outward means in comparison to the inner Word. This, in Frecht's view, puts him in the company of Müntzer, Hätzer, and Denck.[181] New evidence is adduced from *Die Guldin Arch*.[182] In the face of the obvious danger that Franck represented to good teaching and order, Frecht advised the committee what the godly magistrate was obliged to do:

> The godly want done on earth as in heaven, thus this arrogant, godless word must fly away as a stick in the wind. It is the magistrate's obligation that the *civitas* be a *civitas*, that the city be a

---

[177] Hegler, *Beiträge*, pp. 205-207.

[178] Hegler, *Beiträge*, p. 207.

[179] *Quellen zur Geschichte der Täufer*, vol. 15, *Elsaß: Teil III, Stadt Straßburg 1536-1542* (Gütersloh, 1986), p. 291-292. Who these followers of Franck might be is not clear. Schwenckfeld's following was often noted but there is little mention of any following for Franck. Judging from the letter of November 25 from Frecht to Capito, Schwenckfeld and his sympathizers were the actual protagonists. Frecht, though, frequently lumped Franck and Schwenckfeld together. See *QGT* 15, p. 297.

[180] Hegler, *Beiträge*, p. 208.

[181] Hegler, *Beiträge*, p. 209.

[182] Hegler, *Beiträge*, p. 210.

unity of citizens, although he unfortunately knows well that it will never approach such unity and order; nevertheless he does every-thing within his power, that people live a peaceful and godly exis-tence.[183]

For Frecht there was only one thing to be done.

The first of January, 1539 the council appointees reported the results of their efforts to the council. Little new was added by Franck in his response to the school committee's charges. The opinion of the council committee was that Franck had operated against the desire of the council, that his attitude was directed to the disturbance of the good arts, and that difficulties could arise as a result of his writings.[184] The decision was left to the council. It came on January 4.

> Since the dealings of Sebastian Franck (in which he has gone be-yond the ban of the honorable council, [and] has overstepped his earnest promise in more than one way just too many times) have again come up; it is decided to say to Sebastian Franck that he is to leave the city with wife and children between now and Saint George's day [April 23], and he shall not in any way attempt [to persuade] the honorable council to suffer him here. For the hon-orable council is finally determined not to suffer him further in any way.[185]

This decision was confirmed on January 6.[186]

With this decision Franck had no recourse. The council's decision left no room for protest. For the most part one can only speculate what led to the decisiveness of the council's resolution. It should be noted that the original

---

[183] "der göttlich wil wölle geschehen auf erden wie im himel, so mussen dise gotlose prächtige wort wie der stab vom wind verfliegen. Ein magistrat ist schuldig, das civitas sey civitas, ein stadt sey ainigkeit der burger, ob er laider wol waist, das es nimmer so aynig und eben wiert naher gon; nichts dest minder streckt er all sein vermögen dahin, das man fridlich und gotselig lebe." Hegler, *Beiträge*, p. 212.

[184] Hegler, *Beiträge*, p. 215.

[185] "Als Sebastian Francken handlungen (in den er ains ersamen rats verbot uber gethon sein ernstlich zusagen mer dann in ainer weg noch zu vil malen ubertreten hett) wider ankomen; ist entschlossen, Sebastian Francken zu sagen, dasz er hie zwischen und sanct Jorgen tag schierst ausz der statt mit wib und kindern ziehen, und ain ersamen rat er kainen in kainen weg ine hie zugedulten nit ansuchen soll. Dann ain ersamer rat sy entlich entschlossen, ine verrer nit zu gedulten in kainen weg." Hegler, *Beiträge*, pp. 215-216.

[186] Hegler, *Beiträge*, p. 216.

decision to allow Franck to stay was very tenuous. And Franck had not taken care to make sure he was living by the letter of the decision. Thus Frecht, a persistent opponent and adamantly against Franck's continued presence, was able to mount a case which, with the council no doubt tired of the prolonged proceedings, could only be silenced by expelling Franck. Franck's violations were relatively minor but galling, as the council had risked some prestige in allowing the presence of a person looked at askance by many. Frecht's own efforts against Franck were redoubled this time because his authority and prestige were threatened by Franck's presence. Franck's theology, too, was ultimately not compatible with a city whose official religious creed was gradually being made over in the image of the Wittenberg theology, this for reasons of political expediency as much as conviction. Frecht's appeal to the duty of the magistrate to enforce religious unity shows him to understand well the outlook of the rulers of the Imperial city. Franck's own attempt to show his faith to be congenial to effective rule and the peaceful unity of the city suffered from its lack of coordination to the existing situation. In point of fact the outward forms of the church were not going to be discarded. The council could not produce a church of the spirit. Things had to be ordered outwardly, and the city had to align itself with those other estates which also pursued reform, even if they did not always adhere to the exact same faith. Franck should have known his church of the spirit could not exist in the outer world, as he himself stated so many times. In the end Franck lost even the sympathy of Bernhard Besserer, who in a letter to Philip of Hesse refers to Franck as a knave (*buben*) and compares him unfavorably to Schwenckfeld. Franck was left without his one really influential protector.[187] Ultimately Franck's faith did not find enough sympathy among those who wielded the temporal sword, and among those who wielded the spiritual sword he was anathema.

Franck was faced with the prospect which he had so greatly feared. He had to move his children and wife, and he had to find some place which would accept him and in which he could pursue his trade. A letter dated May 22, 1539, reveals Franck's dilemma.[188] The council had permitted him to stay beyond its original deadline. Franck had traveled by foot to Basel, from whence he wrote the letter, in order to investigate relocation. The letter is written to an acquaintance of Franck's in Bern, and in it he recounts his efforts and problems, and inquires after the situation in Bern. He confides that he has not

---

[187] *Corpus Schwenckfeldianorum*, vol. 6, pp. 540-541.

[188] Printed in *Alemannia* 4 (1877), pp. 27-30.

become rich, and now must leave Ulm. One reason, according to Franck, is the lack of paper in the city for printing. "Secondly, and more importantly," he continues, "that people there are too Lutheran, or I don't know what to call it." He tells of his troubles getting his books published, not daring to publish anything but trivialities. He explains Ulm's paranoia about its community.[189] He desires to be among the Swiss, especially in Bern or Basel. Bern seems too distant, especially with five children, one born only the week before, and two loaded wagons full of possessions. Basel, however, already has a wealth of printers and book dealers. Franck prays that God will lead him to the right place.[190] His letter bespeaks a good deal of weariness at his various burdens; he speaks of the forty years loaded upon him. It also bespeaks Franck's own persistence in the face of all that would discourage him, a persistence which rests in the sincerity and depth of his unconventional faith in God. This persistence is perhaps the most admirable aspect of Franck's character and the source of most of his troubles.

Frecht did not let Franck leave the city without one more thrust at him. On June 23 Frecht sent him a letter, reporting to him Bucer's and Melanchthon's disapproval of his person, and wishing him a better understanding.[191] At the request of the council, Franck answered, as well as translated Frecht's letter into German.[192] The letters show the bitterness that existed between the two. Franck's letter in particular expresses his understandable feeling of personal injury at the hands of Frecht. These complaints against a particular individual are unique among Franck's writings.

Franck eventually left Ulm for Basel, where he had received conditional citizenship for at least a year.[193] His departure from Ulm ended his longest tenure in any one place as an adult, almost six years. He took with him a wife who was in very ill health, and five children, the youngest barely two months old. His difficulties in Straßburg and Ulm could not have encouraged him

---

[189] "Zum anderen das das gröszt ist, dy man etwas zu vil Lutherisch, oder waisz nit, wie ichs soll nennen, bey uns ist." *Alemannia* 4, pp. 28.

[190] *Alemannia* 4, pp. 29-30.

[191] Hegler, *Beiträge*, p. 97-99.

[192] Franck's letter is published in Hegler, *Beiträge*, pp. 99-102. The German translation of Frecht's letter is contained in the Ulm Archive, Tresor.

[193] See Frecht's letter to A. Blarer dated July 13, 1539, *Blarer Briefwechsel*, vol. 2, pp. 29-30.

about the prospects for the future.

Frecht did not stop with the expulsion of Franck. Franck's letter reveals that Frecht had written Basel warning them against Franck.[194] And in 1540 Frecht travelled to Schmalkald where he was able to get a statement, drafted by Melanchthon, condemning both Franck and Schwenckfeld, signed by the theologians gathered there.[195] This was never officially accepted by the Ulm city council,[196] though for Frecht it was his final stroke against the opponents of his authority in the city. Frecht's tenacious pursuit of his two eminent opponents is indicative of the complete commitment to the church to which he had been called to minister. Franck's and Schwenckfeld's use of the vernacular alarmed him, and their success in opposing his will and attracting sympathy among the authorities of the council frustrated him. In the end he, too, paid for his own commitment to a putative heresy. With the fall of Ulm to the Emperor in 1547, Frecht was forced either to renounce the evangelical church or to resist the will of the Emperor. By choosing the latter he incurred the wrath of Charles V, and he was led out of the city in chains to imprisonment, never to be permitted to reside in the city again.[197]

---

[194] Hegler, *Beiträge*, p. 101.

[195] A letter to the Ulm council from the theologians, dated March 25, 1540, announces their action. Ulm Archive, vol. A 1208/II, pp. 953 and following. Also there are copies of the official statement both in Latin and German, Ulm Archive A 1208/II, pp. 957-962, 963-968. The text is published in *Corpus Reformatorum*, vol. 3, pp. 983-986. Only Frecht's initial controversy with Schwenckfeld has been here discussed. He was able to move the council to ask Schwenckfeld to find residence elsewhere, also in 1539, under the threat that if he were allowed to stay, the preachers would resign. See Julius Endriß, *Kaspar Schwenckfelds Ulmer Kämpfe* (Ulm, 1936), and R.E. McLaughlin, *Caspar Schwenckfeld*, pp. 202-204. Schwenckfeld's "expulsion" was much more ambiguous that Franck's, but indicated the turn in mood in Ulm.

[196] See Frecht's letter to Blarer dated January 21, 1542, *Blarer Briefwechsel*, vol. 2, p. 101.

[197] See the contemporary account in Sebastian Fischer's *Chronick*, pp. 265-v, 270. This is edited and published by Karl Veesenmeyer as a volume of *Ulm und Oberschwaben* 5-8 (1896). See also W.-U. Deetjen, "Licentiat Martin Frecht," pp. 308-311.

CHAPTER FIVE: FRANCK IN BASEL

Franck's move to Basel did not turn out to be the disaster he had feared. He did not have to take up the beggar's staff. His children were not cast out into the street. This does not mean the move was not hard. Its most severe consequence was the death of his wife of eleven years, Ottilia. She had been ill prior to the move, having just borne their sixth child, and it is possible the strain of the move proved the final straw. The date of her death is not recorded.[1] Franck did not remain a widower for long. In 1541 he married Margerete Beck in Straßburg, the step-daughter of Balthasar Beck, the printer of Franck's original edition of the *Chronica*.[2]

In all other ways Franck's move to Basel marked an upturn in his fortunes. In addition to citizenship he obtained guild membership.[3] He worked with the printer Nicolaus Brylinger, with whom he put out a number of editions, including a parallel Greek and Latin Bible based on Erasmus' edition.[4] Having learned the pitfalls involved, he did not publish any of his own works, however.[5]

This does not mean Franck gave up composing or having his own works published by others. The most substantial of his published works from this

---

[1] Peuckert records the year of her death as 1540 (p. 474), which has been repeated in the literature on Franck. There is no supporting evidence for Peuckert's conjecture. Franck, in the Ulm supplications and his letter to Bern, mentions the ill health of his wife, whereupon many have assumed her death occurred on the ensuing trip. See Christoph Dejung, *Wahrheit und Häresie*, p. 248, and Teufel, *"Landräumig"*, p. 94.

[2] See Adolf Hauffen, "Fischart-Studien XVI," *Euphorion* 19 (1912), p. 8, and *Johann Fischart*, vol. 2 (Berlin and Leipzig, 1922), p. 150. Hauffen incorrectly identifies Margerete as the daughter of Balthasar Beck. See François Ritter, "Elsassische Buchdrucker..." , p. 105.

[3] Paul Koellner, *Die Safranzunft zu Basel und ihre Handwerke und Gewerbe* (Basel, 1935), p. 424.

[4] *Novum Testamentum/ Graece et Latine* (Basel: Nicolaus Brylinger and Sebastian Franck, 1541).

[5] See the list of works printed by Franck in this period in Kaczerowsky, pp. 138-141.

period was his *Sprichwörter*.[6] This book is very much in the spirit of Franck's other writings. He collects together sayings from a number of different sources, and places in between them his own commentary on the various themes that are raised, much as he did in *Die Guldin Arch* and other places.[7] There is, Franck states,

> to be seen herein what wisdom, art, understanding, religion, and hidden mysteries lie in the old German, Latin, Greek, and Hebrew proverbs.[8]

Franck's belief "that God has written and placed [something] in all people's hearts and mouths,"[9] leads him to search the sayings of the world for God's hidden meaning. He is also led to this work by his pride in his native land and its tongue.[10] "In all nations and tongues the greatest wisdom of all the wise is

---

[6] Sebastian Franck, *Sprichwörter* (Frankfurt a.M.: Christian Egenolff, 1541). Franck put out a number of minor works in the late Ulm and Basel period: *Schriftliche vnd gantz gründtliche außlegung/ des LXIII Psalm* (Tübingen: Ulrich Morhart d.Ä., 1539), and interesting choice of texts, as its contents ("Hear my voice, O God, in my complaint, preserve my life from dread of the enemy...who whet their tongues like swords," etc.) betray Franck's feelings of persecution. On this work see André Séguenny, "L'exégèse spirituelle de Sebastian Franck sur l'exemple du commentaire du Psaume 64," *Histoire de l'exégèse au seizième siècle*, eds. Olivier Fatio and Pierre Fraenkel (Geneva, 1978), pp. 179- 184. In addition Franck wrote his *Handbüchlin* (Frankfurt a.M.: Cyriacus Jacob, 1539), a handbook of what he considered the seven chief points of the Bible, a nice short introduction to his thought, though it adds little new. He also published his edition of Georg Birckemeyer's *Von dem auffrichtigen wandel...der glaubigen* (Frankfurt a.M.: Cyriacus Jacob, 1539-1543?), which Franck enthusiastically recommends in his introduction.

[7] The sources for the *Sprichwörter* are traced in Ulrich Meisser, *Die Sprichwörtersammlung Sebastian Francks von 1541* (Amsterdam, 1974).

[8] "Darinnen zu sehen/ was weißheyt/ kunst/ verstand/ religion/ vnd verborgener gheym in der alten Teutschen/ Latiner/ Griechen vnd Hebraer Sprichwörten steckt." *Sprichwörter*, p. t3-v.

[9] "das Gott in aller menschen hertz vnd mund geschriben vnnd gelegt hat/ wie in der außlegung ettlicher Sprichwörter ersehen würt." *Sprichwörter*, p. t3-v.

[10] See *Sprichwörter*, p. t4.

in such regal sayings and short parables," Franck asserts.[11] There is somewhat more practical and down-to-earth tone to this work, for so many of the themes in these sayings deal with the every-day, but it is surprising how much gets turned to the use of Franck's spiritualizing and favorite polemic. For instance the saying "learned fools are above all fools" leads into the expected tirade against the learned.[12] Opportunities are found to comment on the dual nature of humans, God, the joy of poverty, and other stock subjects. The *Sprichwörter* is one of Franck's most interesting works. It exemplifies his lifelong passion for short sayings and folklore, and was one of his most popular works.[13] Franck felt that with the *Sprichwörter* he had made his contribution to the education of German youth, who he believed could do no better in their education than study parables.[14] Undoubtedly Franck felt that his work, being a collection of wise sayings, was above suspicion, but once again a number of voices were raised denouncing it, though Franck did not live to hear them.[15]

Though the *Sprichwörter* is the last published work of Franck's, he left behind a number of manuscript works from this period, some of which were subsequently published in the Netherlands in the seventeenth century. The largest of these survived only in manuscript form, Franck's Latin translation of his beloved *Theologia Deutsch*. Actually the word translation does not accurately describe what Franck's efforts produced. The definitive commentary on the

---

[11] "Und ist bei allen Nationen vnnd Zungen die gröst weißheyt aller weisen in solich hoffred vnd abgekürtzte Sprichwörter." *Sprichwörter*, p. t4.

[12] "Gelert narren/ sindt über all narren." *Sprichwörter*, p. Z.

[13] Though it should be emphasized that the later editions were re-edited by the various publishers until the original form was substantially changed.

[14] *Sprichwörter*, p. t3-v.

[15] Luther's only real comment on Franck, a complete denunciation of him, was in response to some epigrams on women included in the *Sprichwörter*, pp. G and following. See *Luthers Werke*, 54, pp. 172 and following. This was an introduction to Johann Freder's *Dialogus dem Ehestand zu Ehren* (Wittenberg, 1545), which was written in reaction to the epigrams in Franck's collection. On Freder's work see Scott H. Hendrix, "Christianizing Domestic Relations: Women and Marriage in Johann Freder's *Dialogus dem Ehestand zu Ehren*," *Sixteenth Century Journal* 23 (1992), pp. 251-266, esp. pp. 251-256, which details Freder's mistaken assumptions about Franck's purpose in publishing these epigrams.

work refers to it as a paraphrase.[16] It is perhaps best this work never found a publisher. Franck's strength was not his Latin style, though maybe if he had stuck to the text of the *Theologia Deutsch* with its simplicity of style, he would have been within his abilities.[17] In this work, though, Franck let loose with all his worst habits, his repetitions, unidentified interjections, simplifications, and digressions.[18] Yet his great love for the *Theologia Deutsch* does come through. Perhaps Franck's troubled life had taken its toll on him, to the detriment of his authorial skills. Or perhaps he felt uncomfortable in the foreign territory of Latin, a language he knew well but in which he rarely composed. The result is revealing of Franck's limitations as a humanist scholar as well as his shortcomings as a writer.[19]

Two books published in Holland in the early seventeenth century are Dutch translations of a number of pieces by Franck stemming from the later period of his life.[20] These works are focussed exclusively on Franck's mystical theology, the kingdom of Christ being defined exclusively over and against the kingdom of the world in the largest of the pieces, and show Franck to have retained his mystical view of the world until the end. If anything these works represent a deepening of this vision.

No doubt all these works would have found publication eventually. Franck, however, did not live long enough to see them to the printer. The plague swept Basel in 1542, and it is probable that one of its victims was Sebastian Franck. No account exists of his death, and it was not remarked upon by contemporaries until well after the fact. On October 31, 1542, though, an in-

---

[16] Alfred Hegler, *Sebastian Francks lateinische Paraphrase der Deutschen Theologie und seine holländische erhaltenen Traktate* (Tübingen, 1901).

[17] Hegler, *Sebastian Francks lateinische Paraphrase*, p. 34.

[18] See the sample in Hegler, *Sebastian Francks lateinische Paraphrase*, pp. 39-43.

[19] See Hegler, *Sebastian Francks lateinische Paraphrase*, for a masterly analysis of this work.

[20] *Van het rycke Christi* (Gouda: Jaspar Tournay, 1611), and *Een stichtelijck Tractaet van de werelt* (Gouda: Jaspar Tournay für Andreas Burier, 1618). For a discussion of Franck's works in Dutch see Bruno Becker, "Nederlandsche Vertalingen van Sebastiaan Franck's Geschriften," *Nederlandsch archief voor Kerkgeschiedenis* 21 (1928), pp. 149-160; and Alfred Hegler, *Sebastian Francks lateinische Paraphrase der Deutschen Theologie und seine holländische erhaltenen Traktate.*

ventory of Franck's goods was made, in the wake of the owner's demise.[21] The inventory shows Franck to have been well off at the time of his death. The year before he had purchased a house, which, judging from the list of items, was well furnished. It is obvious from this that Franck's undertakings as a printer and book dealer must have prospered during his time in Basel. Perhaps, too, his wife had added to the household with the marriage. Though by no means rich, Franck did not die in poverty or despair. A list was also made of Franck's books at his death.[22] They reflect very well Franck's eclectic interests—humanism, history, mysticism, even orthodox apologies. The absence of many works of Franck's own as well as other known favorites of his suggests either the attrition caused by his many moves or the existence of a library which escaped the cataloguer's eye. Though Franck's library contains a few surprises, for the most part it is made up of works which were dear to Franck's heart.[23] Franck's final years lacked any of the drama of the rest of his life. The criticism which continued after his death, though, indicates that he would not have remained at peace for long. For one so at odds with his world only death would bring relief from its trials, a fact Franck himself had often confessed.

---

[21] The inventory is published in Christoph Dejung, *Wahrheit und Häresie*, p. 278.

[22] The book list was first published by Albert Bruckener, "Verzeichnis der hinterlassenen Bücher Sebastian Francks," *Zentralblatt für Bibliothekswesen* 54 (1937), pp. 286-289, and also by Christoph Dejung, "Sebastian Franck," *Bibliotheca Dissidentium*, vol. 7 (Baden-Baden, 1986), pp. 99-119, with useful identifications. Se also the article by Dejung, "Sebastian Francks nachgelassene Bibliothek," *Zwingliana* 16 (1984), pp. 315-336.

[23] See Dejung's comments, "...nachgelassene Bibliothek," pp. 334-335.

CHAPTER SIX: CONCLUSION

Sebastian Franck was the product of changing times. The two great movements of the age, Renaissance and Reformation, the reform of letters and religion, deeply affected him. Though he was a better observer than scholar, the revival of classical learning and of patristic writings made its impression on Franck's mind. Not that Franck became a disciple of Platonism or developed a new theological system based on the fathers. Franck was no Ficino or Servetus. What impressed Franck was the variety of views which had been held by humans. To Franck's mind the heathens were often more at one with what he considered true Christianity than the saints and scholars of the church. In the work of Erasmus he found tradition cleared away and ammunition supplied for a critique of doctrine. It was not the humanist critique of the Church which motivated Franck to turn against Rome. He came after the cry against the corruption of Rome had moved beyond humanist satire to out and out revolt. It was the breakup of the church which most deeply impressed him. At first he joined the movement for reform, but his experience as a minister convinced him of the futility of the new message to effect the sort of change he desired. The only reform Franck saw as meaningful would have to happen in the human spirit, which, covered over by sin and worldly pursuits, was turned away from God. Outward reform only served to split the church up even more. When Franck moved to study history he was increasingly convinced of the "turned aboutness" of humans and the world, both in the past and especially in his own time. His solution directed one outside of everyday life and human history, both inwardly into the regenerate portion of the soul still capable of receiving God's Spirit, and outwardly beyond history to that moment in which time will find its redemption as the purpose of creation will be realized in one glorious act of God, just as the soul itself is enlightened in a flash after much tribulation. Only God could effect this change, and only outside time and space. Franck's intellectual life, in which he poured so much emotion and energy, was bent on trying to express the unity and purpose which he was convinced must be perceptible somewhere in human life and history. Appropriating medieval mysticism, he was able to find meaning only in the hidden, inward, spiritual Word which God spoke, both past and present, to those who cleared away the physical barriers of world and self.

To cling to the inward Word did not stop the outward course of the world. Before God's final act one had to negotiate in the devil's kingdom. The tenacity and vehemence of Franck's writings reflect in part the tension of living with his inward vision in the world. For those who pursued reform and rule, especially the clerical reformers in Straßburg and Ulm, Franck's literary attempts to convey his message were seen as a challenge to their own legitimacy. Franck was more successful in fashioning his message for the ears of the city magistrates, to whom he presented an alternative, inward church, more suitable to civic unity and peaceful rule than the outward church. Franck's faith, though, was a faith of dissent, not of rule, and the best he could have achieved was tolerance. He would never be reconciled to those who maintained the newly reformed church. Only tensions between the spiritual and temporal regimes in the city created space for Franck to reside.

The tensions between temporal and spiritual rule in Ulm were a result of competing visions of reform in the church. The pastors desired the discipline of morals and doctrine, which would be carried out by the temporal authorities who would be responsive to the dictates of the guardians of the church. The council also considered order in the church to be important, but were willing to sacrifice specificity in doctrinal matters to civic unity and the maintenance of their own monopoly on coercive force and prerogatives in the area of religion. To a certain degree they saw the very aim of reform to be the reestablishment of the proper relationship between the temporal and spiritual swords. The aims of the pastors threatened to bring back the situation where a priestly order abused its calling by claiming coercive authority properly belonging to the council. The reform of religion had consolidated the councils hold on the worldly rule of the church. Even in areas of doctrine the competing theologies in the early years of the reform allowed the secular authorities in Ulm a good deal of influence in shaping the teaching of the church. This situation did not sit well with the pastors, but their dependence on the council for protection against those forces hostile to the newly reformed church circumscribed the avenues available to them to force the council to action. The tolerance that Franck found in Ulm was a function of these conditions. By the end of the 1530's the political situation in the Empire, which saw the rise of the Schmalkaldic League and the continuing efforts to present a united Protestant front against the Emperor, tended to create greater solidarity between pastorate and council. In such circumstances Franck was a less desirable guest.

Franck's solitary life on the margins of society, and the public nature of his activities created a unique relationship to authority. Unlike Schwenckfeld, whose noble status gave him access to power, Franck had nothing other than his ideas with which to appeal to the sensibilities of those who ruled. The variant calculations of spiritual and temporal magistrates in evaluating heterodoxy are thrown in stark relief by the career of Sebastian Franck. Perhaps more than any other figure, Franck's life demonstrates the tensions between reformers and the secular authorities. Franck lived in the breach which existed between the pastors' vision of reform and orthodoxy, and the councils' understanding of a Christian polity.

Franck's life was a conscious attempt to live outside the various movements of his day. He reached back to a medieval mysticism which made the tribulations of this world one's passage into the next. The monastic life was the contemplative setting in which this faith thrived. Franck's life showed how tenuously this faith survived out in the world. In this sense Franck's faith was something of an anachronism. And yet his intensely inward view, his mysticism of the inner Word which was separated from all historical faiths, would find its resonances in other alienated spirits from the Romantics to those in the modern church whose faith was ravaged by historical criticism, or who were trying to make the church universal in an age of individualism and proliferating beliefs.[1] Franck seemed to fit so poorly into his own day, that one should not be surprised he was more eagerly greeted by people living over three hundred years later. For the historian, though, he is clearly a product of his own time, a man of his age who tried, very imperfectly, to solve in his own mind the tensions of this age, and who despite, or more accurately perhaps because of, his efforts found himself caught up in its turbulence. He was neither a martyr—many suffered far more than he—nor a victim, but one who chose not to participate in what he considered the vain and sinful strivings of people within the world. It is the tension between the inner Word and the outer world in Franck's life that makes him an interesting subject of study, and frustrates the attempt to capture an image of him, whether in a coherent philosophy or a consistent set of activities, except in the depiction of the whole of his life.

---

[1] The most recent example of this is Gerd Schimansky, *Christ ohne Kirche: Rückfrage beim ersten Radikalen der Reformation, Sebastian Franck* (Stuttgart, 1980).

BIBLIOGRAPHY

Manuscript Sources:

Ludwigsburg, Staatsarchiv
    Band 207/208, Bü. 68, 69

Ulm, Stadtarchiv
    Tresor
    A 1208/II
    A 1753
    A 1753/I
    A 1754
    8983/I
    A [9000]
    Georg Veesenmeyerische Briefsammlung
    Ulmer Bürgerbuch

Printed Sources:

"Aus dem 1. Ehebuch der Pfarrei St. Sebald zu Nürnberg." Ed. Karl
    Schornbaum. *Beiträge zur bayerischen Kirchengeschichte* 10 (1904): 82-86.
Beiträge zur Geschichte der Mystik in der Reformationszeit. Ed. Alfred Hegler.
    Archiv für Reformationsgeschichte, Texte und Untersuchungen,
    Ergänzungsband I. Berlin, 1906.
Blaurer, Ambrosius and Thomas. *Briefwechsel der Brüder Ambrosius und Thomas*
    Blaurer. 3 vols. Ed. Traugott Schieß. Freiburg i. Br., 1908-1912.
Bucer, Martin. *Martini Buceri opera omnia*. Series I: *Deutsche Schriften*. Ed.
    Robert Stupperich. Gütersloh and Paris, 1972-
Bünderlin, Johannes. *Ein gemeyne berechnung vber der heyligen schrifft innhalt*.
    Straßburg, [Balthasar Beck], 1529.
_____. *Ausz was vrsach sich Gott in die nyder gelassen und in Christo vermenschet*
    ist. [Straßburg, Balthasar Beck], 1529.
_____. *Ein gemayne einlayttung in den aygentlichen verstand Mosi*. [Straßburg,
    Balthasar Beck], 1529.
_____. *Erklerung durch vergleichung der Biblischen geschrifft*. [Straßburg,
    Balthasar Beck], 1530.
[Cochlaeus, Johannes]. *Syben artickel zu Wormbs von Jacob Kautzen angeschlagen*
    vnnd gepredigt. Without place or publisher, 1527.
_____. *Von ankunfft der Meß vnnd der wandlung brots vnd weins im hochwürdigen*
    Sacrament des Alters. Dresden, without publisher, 1533.
_____. *Was von Kayser Sigismunds Reformation zu halten sei*. Dresden, without
    publisher, 1533.
Corpus Reformatorum. Braunschweig, 1834ff.

Denck, Hans. *Schriften. Quellen zur Geschichte der Täufer, vol. 4.* Quellen und
    Forschungen zur Reformationsgeschichte, vol. 24. Gütersloh, 1955.
Der deutschen Bauernkrieg in zeitgenössischen Quellenzeugnissen. 2 vols. Ed.
    Hermann Barge. Leipzig, without date.
"Dicta Melanthonis." *Zeitschrift für Kirchengeschichte* 4 (1881): 324-333.
Entfelder, Christian. *Von den manigfaltigen im glauben zerspaltungen.*
    [Straßburg?, without publisher, 1530?].
_____. *Von warer Gottsäligkeyt vnd Art der Liebe.* Without place, publisher, or
    date.
_____. *Von Gottes vnnd Christi Jesu unsers Herren erkandtnuß.* Without place,
    publisher, or date.
Epistolae ab ecclesiae helveticae reformatoribus vel ad eos scriptae. Ed. Johann
    Konrad Füssli. Zurich, 1742.
Erasmus, Desiderius. *Ausgewählte Schriften.* 5 vols. Ed. Werner Welzig.
    Darmstadt, 1969.
_____. *Erasmi opera omnia.* Ed. J. Clericus. Leiden, 1703-1706.
_____. *Luther and Erasmus on Free Will and Salvation.* Eds. and trans. E.
    Gordon Rupp and Philip S. Watson. The Library of Christian Classics,
    vol. 17. London, 1969.
_____. *Opus Epistolarum Des. Erasmi Roterdami.* Eds. P.S. Allen, H.M. Allen,
    and H.W. Garrod. Oxford, 1906-1947.
_____. *The Praise of Folly.* Trans. Betty Radice. London, 1971.
Die evangelischen Katechismusversuche vor Luthers Enchiridion. Vol. 3: *Die
    evangelischen Katechismusversuche aus den Jahren 1528/29.* Ed. Ferdinand
    Cohrs. Monumenta Germaniae Pedagogica, vol. 22. Berlin, 1901.
[Simon Fish]. *A supplicacyon for the beggars.* [Antwerp, J. Grapheus, 1528].
_____. [Simon Fish, of Gray's Inn, gentleman]. *A Supplication for the Beggars.*
    Ed. Edward Arbor. The English Scholars Library of Old and Modern
    Classics, vol. 4. Westminster, 1895.
_____. *Supplicatorius libellus pauperum oblatus, contra religiosorum iniurias.*
    Without place publisher or date [ca. 1530].
Sebastian Franck. *Diallage.* Nuremberg, Freidrich Peypus for Lienhard zur Aich,
    1528.
_____. *Diallage.* Without place or publisher, 1556.
_____. *Von dem greüwlichen laster der trunckenhayt.* [Augsburg, Heinrich
    Steiner], 1528.
_____, trans. *Klagbrief.* [Nuremberg, Friedrich Peypus], 1529.
_____. *Chronica vnnd beschreibung der Türckey.* Nuremberg, Friedrich Peypus,
    1530.
_____. *"Chronica und Beschreibung der Türckey" mit einer vorrhed Martini
    Lutheri. Neudruck der Ausgabe Nürnberg 1530.* Intro. Carl Göllner.
    Schriften zur Landeskunde Siebenbürgens, vol. 6. Cologne, 1983.
_____. *Cronica, Abconterfayung vnd entwerffung der Türckey.* Augsburg, Heinrich
    Steiner, 1530.
_____, trans. Philip Beroaldus. *Ein Künstlich höflich Declamation.* Nuremberg,
    Friedrich Peypus, 1531.

_____. *Chronica, Zeytbuch vnd geschychtbibel.* Straßburg, Balthasar Beck, 1531.

_____. *Chronica Zeitbuch vnnd Geschichtbibell.* Ulm, Hans Varnier d. Ä., 1536.

_____. *Weltbuch.* Tübingen, Ulrich Morhart d. Ä., 1534.

_____. *Das Theür vnd Künstlich Büchlin Moriae Encomion.* Ulm, Hans Varnier d. Ä., [1534].

_____. *Das Gott das aining ain vnd höchstes gut...sey.* [Augsburg, Silvan Otmar], 1534.

_____. *Paradoxa ducenta octoginta.* Ulm, Hans Varnier d. Ä., [1534].

_____. *Paradoxa Dvcenta Octoginta.* Pforzheim, Georg Rab, 1558.

_____, intro. [Valentin Krautwald]. *Von der gnaden Gottes.* [Hans Varnier d. Ä., 1535].

_____, conclusion. [Valentin Krautwald]. *Epistola Ministri cuivsdam verbi.* [Ulm, Hans Varnier d. Ä., 1535].

_____, ed.? [Konrad Sam]. *Catechismus, oder Christenlicher Kinder bericht.* Ulm, Hans Varnier d. Ä., 1536/37.

_____, trans. and ed. [Sebastian Münster]. *Sechshundert Dreyzehen Gebot vnd Verpot der Juden.* Ulm, Sebastian Franck, 1537.

_____. *Des Grossen Nothelffers vnnd Weltheiligen Sant Gelts oder S. Pfennings Lobgesang.* Ulm, Sebastian Franck, 1537.

_____. *Wie man Beten vnnd Psallieren soll.* [Ulm, Sebastian Franck], 1537.

_____. *Der ganze Psalter.* [Ulm, Sebastian Franck and Philipp Ulhart in Augsburg], 1537.

_____. *Der New gesang psalter.* [Ulm, Sebastian Franck and Philipp Ulhart in Augsburg], 1538.

_____. *Die Guldin Arch.* Augsburg, Heinrich Steiner, 1538.

_____. *Die Guldin Arch.* Bern, [Benedikt Ulmann], 1569.

_____. Germaniae Chronicon. [Frankfurt a.M., Christian Egenolff], 1538.

_____. *Das verbütschiert mit siben Sigeln verschlossene Buch.* [Augsburg, Heinrich Steiner], 1539.

_____. Handbüchlin. Frankfurt a.M., Cyriacus Jacob, 1539.

[_____]. *Das Kriegbüchlin des frides.* [Augsburg, Heinrich Steiner], 1539.

_____. *Krieg Büchlin des Friedes:...Hie bey auch von dem grewlichen laster der Trunckenheyt.* Frankfurt a.M., Cyriacus Jacob, 1550.

_____. *Schrifftliche vnd gantz gründtliche außlegung des LXIIII. Psalm.* [Tübingen, Ulrich Morhart d. Ä.,], 1539.

_____, ed. Georg Birckeymer. *Von dem auffrichtegen wandel leben vnd gutten gewissen der glaubigen.* Frankfurt a.m., Cyriacus Jacob, [ca. 1539-43].

_____. *Sprichwörter.* Frankfurt a.M., Christian Egenolff, 1541.

_____, publisher. *Novvm Testamentvm.* Basel, Nikolaus Brylinger and Sebastian Franck, 1541.

_____. *Van het Rycke Christi.* Gouda, Jasper Tournay, 1611.

_____. *Een stichtelijck Tractaet van de Werelt.* Gouda, Jasper Tournay for Andries Burier, 1618.

_____. "Zwei Briefe Seb. Franck." Ed. Franz Weinkauff. *Alemannia* 4 (1877): 27-30.

_____. "Beiträge zur brandenburgischen Reformationsgeschichte: VI. Sebastian

Franck, Frühmesser in Büchenbach bei Schwabach." Ed. Karl
    Schornbaum. *Beiträge zur bayerischen Kirchengeschichte* 10 (1904): 40-42.
_____. "Fragment van Francks latijnse brief aan Campanus." Ed. Bruno
    Becker. *Nederlands archief voor kerkgeschiedenis* n.s. 46 (1963-65): 197-205.
Frecht, Martin. " Ein Brief Martin Frechts an Mathäus Nägelin von Straßburg,
    vom 22. Juni 1556." Ed. W. Friedensberg. *Zeitschrift für die Geschichte
    des Oberrheins* 86 [n.s. 47] (1934): 387-392.
Luther, Martin. *D. Martin Luthers Werke.* Weimar, 1883ff.
_____. *D. Martin Luthers Werke. Briefe.* Weimar, 1930-1948.
_____. *D. Martin Luthers Werke. Tischreden.* Weimar, 1912-1921.
_____. *Luther's Works. American Edition.* Philadelphia, 1957ff.
Die Matrikel der Ludwig-Maximillians-Universität Ingolstadt-Landshut-München.
    Ed. Gotz Freiherrn von Pölnitz. Munich, 1937.
Politische Correspondenz der Stadt Straßburg im Zeitalter der Reformation. Ed.
    Otto Winckelmann, et al. 5 vols. Urkunden und Akten der Stadt
    Straßburg, 2. Abtheilung. Straßburg and Heidelberg, 1882-1933.
Quellen zur Geschichte der Täufer. Vol. 4, *Baden und Pfalz.* Ed. Manfred Krebs.
    Quellen und Forschungen zur Reformationsgeschichte, vol. 22. Gütersloh,
    1951.
Quellen zur Geschichte der Täufer. Vol. 7, *Elsaß I. Teil, Stadt Straßburg 1522-
    1532.* Eds. M. Krebs and H.G. Rott. Quellen und Forschungen zur
    Reformationsgeschichte, vol. 26. Gütersloh, 1959.
Quellen zur Geschichte der Täufer. Vol. 8, *Elsaß II. Teil, Stadt Straßburg 1533-
    1536.* Eds. M. Krebs and H.G. Rott. Quellen und Forschungen zur
    Reformationsgeschichte, vol. 27. Gütersloh, 1960.
Quellen zur Geschichte der Täufer. Vol. 15, *Elsaß III. Teil, Stadt Straßburg 1536-
    1542.* Eds. Marc Lienhard, Stephan F. Nelson, and H.G. Rott. Quellen
    und Forschungen zur Reformationsgeschichte, vol 53. Gütersloh, 1986.
Quellen zur Nürnberger Reformationsgeschichte. Ed. Gerhard Pfeiffer.
    Nuremberg, 1968.
*Die Schriften der Münsterischen Täufer und ihrer Gegner. III. Teil, Schriften von
    evangelischer Seite gegen die Täufer.* Ed. Robert Stupperich.
    Veröffentlichungen der historischen Kommission für Westfalen, vol. 32.
    Münster, 1983.
Spiritual and Anabaptist Writers. Eds. George H. Williams and Angel M. Mergel.
    Philadelphia, 1957.
Schwenckfeld, Caspar. *Corpus Schwenckfeldianorum.* Leipzig, 1907-1961.
Tauler, Johannes. *Joannis Tauleri: des heiligen lerers Predig.* Basel, Adam Petri,
    1521.
_____. *Die Predigten Taulers.* Ed. Ferdinand Vetter. Deutsche Texte des
    Mittelalters, vol. 11. Berlin, 1910.
Theologia Deutsch. Ed. Hermann Mandel. Quellenschriften zur Geschichte des
    Protestantismus, vol. 7. Leipzig, 1908.

Secondary Literature

Abray, Lorna Jane. *The People's Reformation.* Ithaca, N.Y., 1985.

Adam, Johann. *Evangelische Kirchengeschichte der Stadt Straßburg bis zur französischen Revolution.* Straßburg, 1922.

Anrich, Gustav. "Die Ulmer Kirchenordnung von 1531." *Blätter für württembergische Kirchengeschichte* 35 (1931): 95-107.

Austin, Gregory A. *Alcohol in Western Society from Antiquity to 1800.* Santa Barbara, 1985.

Barbers, Meinulf. *Toleranz bei Sebastian Franck.* Untersuchungen zur allgemeiner Religionsgeschichte, vol. 4. Bonn, 1964.

Baron, Hans. "Religion and Politics in the German Imperial Cities during the Reformation." *English Historical Review* 52 (1937): 405-427, 614-633.

Bauch, G. *Die Anfänge des Humanismus in Ingolstadt.* Ingolstadt, 1901.

Bauer, Günther. *Anfänge täuferischer Gemeindebildungen in Franken.* Einzelarbeiten aus der Kirchengeschichte Bayern, vol. 43. Nuremberg, 1966.

Bizer, Ernst. *Studien zur Geschichte des Abendmahlsstreits im 16. Jahrhundert.* Second edition, Darmstadt, 1962.

Blanke, Fritz. "Reformation und Alkoholismus." *Zwingliana* 9 (1949): 75-89.

Blaschke, Lotte. "Der Toleranzgedanke bei Sebastian Franck." *Blätter für deutsche Philosophie* 2 (1928/29): 40-56.

Bolte, Johannes. "Zwei satirische Gedichte von Sebastian Franck." *Sitzungsberichte der preussischen Akademie der Wissenschaften 1925. Philosoph- historischen Klasse.* Berlin, 1925: 89-114.

Bossert, Gustav. "Martin Frecht." *Realenzyklopädie für protestantische Theologie und Kirche.* vol. 6. Leipzig, 1899: 242-244.

Brady, Thomas A., Jr. *Ruling Class, Regime and Reformation at Straßburg, 1520-1555.* Studies in Medieval and Reformation Thought, vol. 22. Leiden, 1978.

Brecht, Martin. "Die gemeinsame Politik der Reichsstädte und die Reformation." *Zeitschrift der Savignystiftung für Rechtsgeschichte. Kanonistische Abteilung* 94 (1977): 180-263.

———, and Hermann Ehmer. *Südwestdeutsche Reformationsgeschichte.* Stuttgart, 1984.

———. "Ulm und die deutsche Reformation." *Ulm und Oberschwaben* 42/43 (1978): 96-119.

Bruckener, Albert. "Verzeichnis der hinterlassenen Bücher Sebastian Francks." *Zentralblatt für Bibliothekwesen* 54 (1937): 286-289.

Capesius, Bernhard. "Sebastian Francks Verdeutschung des *Tractatus de ritu et moribus Turcorum.*" *Deutsche Forschung im Südosten* 3 (1944): 61-88.

Chrisman, Miriam. *Lay Culture, Learned Culture.* New Haven, 1982.

———. *Strasbourg and the Reform.* New Haven, 1967.

Clasen, Claus-Peter. *The Anabaptists in South and Central Germany, Switzerland and Austria.* Ann Arbor, 1978.

———. "Executions of Anabaptists, 1527-1618." *Mennonite Quarterly Review* 47 (1973): 115-153.

Clebsch, William. *England's Earliest Protestants, 1520-1535.* Yale Publications in Religion, vol. 11. New Haven, 1964.

Colie, Rosalie. *Paradoxia Epidemica.* Princeton, 1966.

Deetjen, Werner-Ulrich. "Licentiat Martin Frecht, Professor und Prädikant (1499-1556)." *Die Einführung der Reformation in Ulm.* Eds. Hans Eugen Specker and Gebhard Weig. Forschungen zur Geschichte der Stadt Ulm: Reihe Dokumentation, vol. 2. Ulm, 1981: 269-321.

_____. "Martin Frecht." *Theologische Realenzyklopädie,* vol. 11. Berlin and New York, 1983: 482-484.

Dejung, Christoph. "Sebastian Franck." *Bibliotheca Dissidentium,* vol. 7. Baden-Baden, 1986: 39-119.

_____. "Sebastian Francks nachgelassene Bibliothek." *Zwingliana* 16 (1984): 315-336.

_____. *Wahrheit und Häresie: Eine Untersuchung zur Geschichtsphilosophie bei Sebastian Franck.* Zurich, 1979.

Deppermann, Klaus. *Melchior Hoffmann.* Göttingen, 1979.

Deppermann, Klaus. "Sebastian Francks Straßburger Aufenthalt." *Mennonitische Geschichtsblätter* 46 (1989): 145-160.

Endriß, Julius. *Kaspar Schwenckfelds Ulmer Kämpfe.* Ulm, 1936.

_____. *Sebastian Francks Ulmer Kämpfe.* Ulm, 1935.

_____. *Die Ulmer Abstimmungslisten vom November 1530.* Ulm, 1931.

_____. *Die Ulmer Reformationsjahr 1531 in seinen entscheidenen Vorgängen.* Ulm, 1931.

Furcha, E.J. "The Paradoxon as Hermaneutical Principle: The Case of Sebastian Franck." *Spirit within Structure.* Ed. E.J. Furcha. Allison Park, 1983.

Gäbler, Ulrich. "Johannes Bünderlin." *Bibliotheca Dissidentium,* vol. 3. Ed. André Séguenny. Baden-Baden, 1982: 9-42.

Gerrish, Brian. "'To the Unknown God'." *The Old Protestantism and the New.* Chicago, 1982: 131-149, 334-345.

_____. "*De libero arbitrio* (1524): Erasmus on Piety, Theology, and Lutheran Dogma." *Essays on the Works of Erasmus.* Ed. Richard L. DeMolen. New Haven, 1978: 187-209.

Göllner, Carl. "Die Auflagen des *Tractatus de ritu et moribus Turcorum.*" *Deutsche Forschung im Südosten* 3 (1944): 129-151.

Goldammer, Kurt. "Friedensidee und Toleranzgedanke bei Paracelsus und den Spiritualisten. 1. Teil: Paracelsus." *Archiv für Reformationsgeschichte* 46 (1955): 20-46. "2. Teil: Franck und Weigel." *Archiv für Reformationsgeschichte* 47 (1956): 180-211.

Goldbach, Günter. "Hans Denck und Thomas Müntzer-ein Vergleich ihrer wesentlichen theologischen Auffassungen." Dissertation, Hamburg, 1969.

Greiner, Hans. "Ulm und Umgebung im Bauernkrieg." *Ulm und Oberschwaben* 16 (1909): 1-68.

Greyerz, Kaspar von. "Stadt und Reformation: Stand und Aufgaben der Forschung." *Archiv für Reformationsgeschichte* 76 (1985): 6-63.

Guggisberg, Hans, ed. *Religiöse Toleranz: Dokumente zur Geschichte einer Förderung.* Neuzeit im Aufbau: Darstellung und Dokumentation, vol. 4.

Stuttgart, 1984.

Haller, Johannes. "Die Ulmer Katechismusliteratur vom 16. bis 18. Jahrhundert." *Blätter für württembergische Kirchengeschichte* 9 (1905): 42-70, 124-142.

Hauffen, Adolf. *Johann Fischart*. 2 vols. Berlin and Leipzig, 1922.

_____. "Fischart-Studien XIV." *Euphorion* 19 (1912): 8.

_____. "Sebastian Franck als Verfasser freichristlicher Reimdichtungen." *Zeitschrift für deutsche Philologie* 45 (1913): 389-426.

_____. "Die Trinklitteratur in Deutschland bis zum Ausgang des sechszehnten Jahrhunderts." *Vierteljahrschrift für Literaturgeschichte* 2 (1889): 481-515.

Hautz, Johann Friedrich. *Geschichte der Universität Heidelberg*. 2 vols. Mannheim, 1862.

Hegler, Alfred. *Geist und Schrift bei Sebastian Franck*. Freiburg i. Br., 1892.

_____. "Sebastian Franck." *Realenenzyklopädie für protestantische Theologie und Kirche*. Leipzig, 1899.

_____. *Sebastian Francks lateinische Paraphrase der Deutschen Theologie und seine holländische erhaltenen Traktate*. Tübingen, 1901.

Hess, Günter. *Deutsch- lateinische Narrenzunft: Studien zum Verhältnis von Volkssprache und Latinität in der satirischen Literature des 16. Jahrhunderts*. Munich, 1971.

_____. "Kommentarstruktur und Leser. Das *Lob der Torheit* des Erasmus von Rotterdam, kommentiert von Gerardus Listrius und Sebastian Franck." *Der Kommentar in der Renaissance*. Eds. August Buck and Otto Herding. Kommission für Humanismusforschung, Mitteilung I. Boppard, 1975: 147-165.

Hillerbrand, Hans. *A Fellowship of Discontent*. New York, 1967.

Hofer, Paul. "Die Reformation im Ulmer Landgebiet." Dissertation, Tübingen, 1977.

Hoffmann, Manfred, ed. *Toleranz und Reformation*. Gütersloh, 1979.

Jäger, Herbert. *Reichsstadt und schwäbischer Kreis*. Göppinger akedemische Beiträge, vol. 95. Göppingen, 1975.

Jellinek, E.M. "Classics in Alchohol Literature." *Quarterly Journal of Studies on Alchohol* 2 (1941): 391-395.

Kaczerowsky, Klaus. *Sebastian Franck: Bibliographie*. Wiesbaden, 1976.

Keim, Carl Theodore. *Die Reformation der Reichsstadt Ulm*. Stuttgart, 1851.

Kintner, Philip L. "Studies in the Historical Writings of Sebastian Franck (1499-1542)." Dissertation, Yale University, 1958.

Kittelson, James. *Wolfgang Capito*. Studies in Medieval and Reformation Thought, vol. 17. Leiden, 1975.

Köhler, Walther. "Zur Frage nach dem Herausgeber des Ulmer Katechismus von 1536." *Blätter für württembergische Kirchengeschichte* 10 (1906): 188.

_____. "Das Täufertum in der neueren kirchenhistorischen Forschung: 4. Teil: Die Spiritualisten." *Archiv für Reformationsgeschichte* 41 (1948): 164-186.

Koellner, Paul. *Die Safranzunft zu Basel und ihre Handwerke und Gewerbe*. Basel, 1935.

Könneker, Barbara. *Wesen und Wandlung der Narrenidee im Zeitalter des*

Humanismus. Wiesbaden, 1966.

Kohls, Ernst-Wilhelm. "Ein Abschnitt aus Martin Bucers Entwurf für die Ulmer Kirchenordnung vom Jahr 1531." *Blätter für württembergische Kirchengeschichte* 60/61 (1960/61): 177-213.

_____. "Martin Bucers Anteil und Anliegen bei der Abfassung der Ulmer Kirchenordnung im Jahre 1531." *Zeitschrift für evangelisches Kirchenrecht* 15 (1970): 333-360.

Kolde, Theodore. "Hans Denck und die gottlosen Maler von Nürnberg." *Beiträge zur bayerischen Kirchengeschichte* 8 (1902): 1-32.

_____. "Zum Prozeß des Johannes Dencks und die drei gottlosen Maler von Nürnberg." *Kirchengeschichtliche Studien, Hermann Reuter...gewidmet.* Leipzig, 1888.

Kommoß, Rudolf. *Sebastian Franck und Erasmus von Rotterdam.* Germanische Studien, vol. 153. Berlin, 1934.

Kroon, Marijn de. *Studien zu Martin Bucers Obrigkeitsverständnis.* Gütersloh, 1984.

Littell, Franklin H. *Landgraf Philipp und die Toleranz.* Bad Nauheim, 1957.

Lübke, Konrad. "Die Verfassung der freien Reichsstadt Ulm am Ende des Alten Reiches." Dissertation, Tübingen, 1955.

McLaughlin, R. Emmet. *Caspar Schwenckfeld, Reluctant Radical.* New Haven, 1986.

_____. "Schwenckfeld and the Strasbourg Radicals." *Mennonite Quarterly Review* 59 (1985): 268-278.

Meisser, Ulrich. *Die Sprichwörtersammlung Sebastian Francks.* Amsterdamer Publikationen zur Sprache und Literatur, vol. 14. Amsterdam, 1974.

Moeller, Bernd. *Reichsstadt und Reformation.* Schriften des Vereins für Reformationsgeschichte, vol. 180. Gütersloh, 1962.

Mühlen, Karl-Heinz zur. *Nos extra Nos: Luthers Theologie zwischen Mystik und Scholastik.* Beiträge zur historischen Theologie, vol. 46. Tübingen, 1972.

_____. "Die Heidelberger Disputation Martin Luthers vom 26. April 1518. Programm und Wirkung." *Semper Apertus: Sechshundert Jahre Ruprecht-Karls-Universität Heidelberg Vol. 1, Mittelalter und frühe Neuzeit: 1386-1803.* Ed. Wilhelm Doerr. Berlin, 1985: 188-212.

Müller, Gerhard. "Sebastian Francks *Kriegsbüchlein des Friedens* und der Friedensgedanke im Reformationszeitalter." Dissertation, Münster, 1954.

Nauert, Charles. G., Jr. *Agrippa and the Crisis of Renaissance Thought.* Illinois Studies in the Social Sciences, vol. 55. Urbana, Ill., 1965.

Naujoks, Eberhard. *Obrigkeitsgedanke, Zunftverfassung und Reformation.* Veröffentlichungen der Kommission für geschichtliche Landeskunde in Baden-Württemberg. Reihe B, Forschungen, vol. 3. Stuttgart, 1958.

_____. "Ulms Sozialpolitik im 16. Jahrhundert." *Ulm und Oberschwaben* 33 (1953): 88-98.

Nicoladoni, Alexander. *Johannes Bünderlin von Linz.* Berlin, 1893.

Oberman, Heiko. *The Harvest of Medieval Theology.* Cambridge, Mass., 1963.

Oncken, Hermann. *Historisch- politische Aufsätze und Reden.* 2 vols. Berlin, 1914.

Ozment, Steven. *Homo Spiritualis*. New Haven, 1969.

_____. *Mysticism and Dissent*. New Haven, 1973.

Packull, Werner O. *Mysticism and the Early South German-Austrian Anabaptist Movement, 1525-1531*. Studies in Anabaptist and Mennonite History, vol. 19. Scottsdale, Pa., 1977.

Peuckert, Will-Erich. *Sebastian Franck. Ein deutscher Sucher*. Munich, 1943.

Pollet, Jacques V., O.P. *Martin Bucer: Etudes sur la Correspondence*. 2 vols. Paris, 1962.

Prenzel, Willi. *Kritische Untersuchung und Würdigung von Sebastian Francks "Chronicon Germaniae"*. Marburg i. H., 1908.

Rabus, Karl. "Der Ulmer Bürgermeister bis 1548." Dissertation, Tübingen, 1952.

Räber, Kuno. *Studien zur Geschichtsbibel Sebastian Franck*. Basel, 1952.

Ritter, Francois. "Elsässische Buchdrucker im Dienste der Strassburger Sektenbewegungen zur Zeit der Reformation." *Gutenberg Jahrbuch* (1962): 225-233; (1963): 97-108.

Rublack, Hans-Christoph. "Forschungsbericht Stadt und Reformation." *Stadt und Kirche im 16. Jahrhundert*. Ed. Bernd Moeller. Gütersloh, 1978: 9-26.

Scheible, Heinz. "Die Universität Heidelberg und Luthers Disputation." *Zeitschrift für die Geschichte des Oberrheins* 131 (1983): 309-329.

Schimansky, Gerd. *Christ ohne Kirche: Rückfrage beim ersten Radikalen der Reformation, Sebastian Franck*. Stuttgart, 1980.

Schmid, H.D. *Täufertum und Obrigkeit in Nürnberg*. Nürnberger Werkstücke zur Stadt- und Landesgeschichte, vol. 10. Nuremberg, 1972.

Schmidt, Georg. *Die Städtetag in der Reichsverfassung. Eine Untersuchung zur korporativen Politik der Freien- und Reichstädte in den ersten Hälfte des 16. Jahrhunderts*. Veröffentlichungen des Instituts für Europäische Geschichte, Mainz, vol. 113. Wiesbaden, 1984.

Schmidt, Heinrich R. *Reichsstädte, Reich und Reformation*. Veröffentlichungen des Instituts für Europäische Geschichte, Mainz, vol. 122. Stuttgart, 1986.

Schottenloher, K. *Philipp Ulhart*. Historische Forschungen und Quellen, vol. 4. Munich, 1921.

Schulze, W. "Die Überlistung des Teufels." *Archiv für Reformationsgeschichte* 46 (1955): 106-107.

Screech, M.A. *Ecstasy and the Praise of Folly*. London, 1980.

Séguenny, André. "Christian Entfelder." *Bibliotheca Dissidentium*, vol. 1. Ed. André Séguenny. Baden-Baden, 1980: 37-48.

_____. "L'exegese spirituelle de Sebastien Franck sur l'exemple du Commentaire de Psaume 64." *Histoire de l'exegese au seizième siècle*. Eds. Olivier Fatio and Pierre Fraenkel. Geneva, 1978: 179-184.

_____. "Johannes Campanus." *Bibliotheca Dissidentium*, vol. 1. Ed. André Séguenny. Baden-Baden, 1980: 13-35.

_____. "A l'origine de la philosophie et de la théologie spirituelles en Allemagne au seizième siècle: Christian Entfelder." *Revue d'histoire et de Philosophie religieuses* 57 (1977): 167-182.

_____. "Sebastian Franck." *Theologische Realenzyklopädie*, vol. 11. Berlin and

New York, 1983: 307-312.

Seifert, Arno. *Statuten und Verfassungsgeschichte der Universität Ingolstadt (1472-1586)*. Berlin, 1971.

Spitz, Lewis W. "Luther's Ecclesiology and his Concept of the Prince as *Notbischof.*" *Church History* 22 (1953): 113-141.

_____. *The Protestant Reformation 1517-1559*. New York, 1985.

_____. *The Religious Renaissance of the German Humanists*. Cambridge, Mass., 1963.

Steck, Hermann. "Die Reichsstadt Ulm und der Augsburger Reichstag im Jahre 1530." Dissertation, Tübingen, 1927.

Strauss, Gerald. *Historian in an Age of Crisis: The Life and Works of Johannes Aventinus, 1477-1534*. Cambridge, Mass., 1963.

_____. *Nuremberg in the Sixteenth Century*. Revised edition, Bloomington, Ind., 1976.

Teufel, Eberhard. "Die *Deutsche Theologie* und Sebastian Franck im Lichte der neueren Forschung. II. Teil: Sebastian Franck." *Theologische Rundschau* 12 (1940): 99-129.

_____. *"Landräumig": Sebastian Franck, ein Wanderer am Donau, Neckar und Rhein*. Neustadt a. d. Aisch, 1954.

_____. "Luther und Luthertum in Urteil Sebastian Francks." *Festgabe von Fachgenossen und Freunden Karl Müllers zum siebzigsten Geburtstag dargebraucht*. Ed. Otto Scheel. Tübingen, 1922: 132-144.

Trostel, Eugen. *Das Kirchengut im Ulmer Territorium*. Forschungen zur Geschichte der Stadt Ulm, vol. 15. Ulm, 1976.

Veesenmeyer, G. *Collectaneen von Melanchthons Verhältnissen, in welcher er mit Ulmern stand*. Ulm, 1797.

Veesenmeyer, Kar., ed. "Sebastian Fischers Chronick besonders von Ulmischen Sachen." *Ulm und Oberschwaben* 5-8 (1896): 1-272.

Walther, Heinrich. "Bernhard Besserer und die Politik der Reichsstadt Ulm während der Reformationszeit." *Ulm und Oberschwaben* 27 (1930): 1-69.

Weigelt, Horst. "Sebastian Franck und Caspar Schwenckfeld in ihren Beziehungen zueinander." *Zeitschrift für bayerische Kirchengeschichte* 39 (1970): 3-19.

_____. *Sebastian Franck und die lutherische Reformation*. Gütersloh, 1972.

_____. "Valentin Krautwald: der führende Theologe des frühen Schwenckfeldertums: Biographische und kirchen historische Aspekte." *Les Dissidents du seizième siècle entre l'Humanisme et le Catholisme*. Ed. Marc Lienhard. Bibliotheca Dissidentium, scripta et studia, vol. 1. Baden-Baden, 1983: 175-190.

Weinkauff, Franz. "Sebastian Franck von Donauwerd." *Alemannia* 5 (1877): 131-147; 6 (1878): 49-86; 7 (1879): 1-66.

Weis, F.L. *The Life, Teachings, and Works of Hans Denck, 1495-1527*. Strasbourg, 1924.

Williams, George H. *The Radical Reformation*. Philadelphia, 1962.

Wolfart, Karl. "Zur Biographie des M. Bonificius Wolfhart." *Beiträge zur bayerischen Kirchengeschichte* 7 (1901): 167-180.

Zambelli, Paola. "Magic and Radical Reformation in Agrippa von Nettesheim." *Journal of the Warburg and Courtauld Institutes* 39 (1976): 69-103.

Zelzer, Maria. *Geschichte der Stadt Donauwörth.* Vol. 1. Donauwörth, 1958.

Zschelletzschky, Herbert. *Die "drei gottlosen Maler" von Nürnberg.* Leipzig, 1975.

Renaissance and Baroque
Studies and Texts

This series deals with various aspects of the European Renaissance and Baroque. Studies on the history, literature, philosophy and the visual arts of these periods are welcome. The series will also consider translations of important works, especially from Latin into English. These translations should, however, include a substantial introduction and notes. Books in the series will include original monographs as well as revised or reconceived dissertations. The series editor is:

Eckhard Bernstein
Department of Modern Languages
and Literatures
College of the Holy Cross
Worcester, MA 01610